Docker Deep

Zero to Docker in a single book

2020 Edition

Nigel Poulton @nigelpoulton

About this edition

This edition was published in May 2020.

In producing this edition, I've gone through every page and every example to make sure everything is up-to-date with the latest versions of Docker and the latest trends in the cloud-native ecosystem.

Important updates include:

- The Compose specification (announced April 2020).

- Using TLS to secure client-daemon communications added to chapter 5.

- Simplified Installing Docker chapter. Too much space was wasted on this topic in previous editions.

Finally, I was able to reduce the cost of the paperback edition by shortening the book from ~400 pages to ~250 pages. I achieved this by reducing the font size to a more professional size that I already use in The Kubernetes Book (previous editions used a very large font). I also removed duplicate content and chapters that related to Docker Enterprise Edition which is no longer a strategic focus. The resulting book is shorter, sharper, and easier to navigate and consume!

Enjoy the book!

Education is about inspiring and creating opportunities. I hope this book, and my video training courses, inspire you and create lots of opportunities!

A huge thanks to my wife and daughters for putting up with me. It can't be easy living with a geek who wants to mess about with Docker and Kubernetes every hour of the day. I'm also grateful to my younger brother who manages the operational aspects of everything I do --- he also proof-read the manuscript, so we share the blame for any typos ;-).

Thank you, as well, to everyone who watches my training videos at pluralsight.com, acloud.guru, and udemy.com. I love connecting with you and appreciate all the feedback you give --- keep it coming, it's what inspired me to write this book.

Finally, I love to connect. You can reach me at nigelpoulton.com, Twitter, LinkedIn, YouTube, and many other places where I spend too much time talking about tech.

@nigelpoulton

About the author

Nigel is a techoholic who spends his life creating books, training videos, and online hands-on training. He's the author of best-selling books on Docker and Kubernetes, as well as the most popular online training videos on the same topics (pluralsight.com. acloud.guru, and udemy.com). He's also a Docker Captain. Prior to all of this, Nigel held various senior infrastructure roles at large enterprises (mainly banks).

When he's not playing with technology, he's dreaming about it. When he's not dreaming about it, he's reading and watching scifi. He wishes he lived in the future so he could explore space-time, the universe, and tons of other mind-blowing stuff. He likes cars, football, food, and bees (yes, that's the fuzzy insect and not a typo). He has a fabulous wife and three fabulous children.

Feel free to connect via:

- Twitter (@nigelpoulton)

- LinkedIn (https://www.linkedin.com/in/nigelpoulton/)

- nigelpoulton.com

- YouTube: Nigel Poulton - KubeTrainer

Contents

0: About the book

This is a book about Docker, no prior knowledge required. In fact, the motto of the book is **Zero to Docker in a single book**.

So, if you're involved in the development and operations of cloud-native microservices apps and need to learn Docker, or if you want to be involved in that stuff, this book is dedicated to you.

In fact, Book Authority (featured on CNN, Forbes) rated this as the best Docker book of all time!

Best Docker book of all time - winner

Why should I read this book or care about Docker?

Docker is here and there's no point hiding. In fact, if you want the best jobs working on the best technologies, you need to know Docker and containers.

What if I'm not a developer

If you think Docker is just for developers, prepare to have your world turned upside-down.

Most applications, even the funky cloud-native microservices ones, need high-performance production-grade infrastructure to run on. If you think traditional developers are going to take care of that, think again. To cut a long story short, if you want to thrive in the modern cloud-first world, you need to know Docker. But don't stress, this book will give you all the skills you need.

Should I buy the book if I've already watched your video training courses?

The choice is yours, but I normally recommend people watch my videos **and** read my books. And no, it's not to make me rich. Learning via different mediums is a proven way to learn fast. So, I recommend you read my books, watch my videos, and get as much hands-on experience as possible.

Also, if you like my video courses[1] you'll probably like the book. If you don't like my video courses you probably won't like the book.

If you haven't watched my video courses, you should! They're fast-paced, lots of fun, and get *rave reviews*.

How the book is organized

I've divided the book into two sections:

1. The big picture stuff
2. The technical stuff

The big picture stuff section covers things like:

- What is Docker
- Why do we have containers
- What do things like "cloud-native" and "microservices" mean...

It's the kind of stuff that you need to know if you want a good rounded knowledge of Docker and containers.

The technical stuff section is where you'll find everything you need to start working with Docker. It gets into the detail of *images*, *containers*, and the increasingly important topic of *orchestration*. It even cover's the stuff that enterprises love — TLS, image signing, high-availability, backups, and more.

Each chapter covers theory and includes plenty of commands and examples.

Most of the chapters in the *technical stuff* section are divided into three parts:

- The TLDR
- The Deep Dive
- The Commands

The TLDR gives you two or three paragraphs that you can use to explain the topic at the coffee machine. They're also a great way to remind yourself what something is about.

The Deep Dive explains how things work and gives examples.

The Commands lists all the relevant commands in an easy to read list with brief reminders of what each one does. I think you'll love that format.

---

[1]https://app.pluralsight.com/library/search?q=nigel+poulton

Editions of the book

Docker and the cloud-native ecosystem is developing at a warp speed. As a result, I'm committed to updating the book every year!**

If that sounds a bit excessive, **welcome to the new normal**.

We no-longer live in a world where a 1-year old book on a technology like Docker is valuable. That makes my life as an author really hard, but I'm not going to argue with the truth.

Don't worry though, your investment in this book is safe.

If you buy the paperback copy from **Amazon.com**, you get the Kindle version for a couple of bucks through the Kindle MatchBook scheme. This is an Amazon service that's only available on Amazon.com and is a bit buggy. If you bought the paperback and can't see how to get your Kindle version through MatchBook, you need to contact Kindle support — I can't help you with this :-(

The Kindle and Leanpub versions get all updates free of charge!

That's the best I can currently do!

Having problems getting the latest updates on your Kindle?

It's come to my attention that Kindle doesn't always download the latest version of the book. To fix this:

Go to http://amzn.to/2l53jdg

Under `Quick Solutions` (on the left) select `Digital Purchases`. Search for your purchase of Docker Deep Dive kindle edition and select `Content and Devices`. Your purchase should show up in the list with a button that says "Update Available". Click that button. Delete your old version on your Kindle and download the new one.

If this doesn't work, contact Kindle support and they'll resolve the issue for you. https://kdp.amazon.com/en_-US/self-publishing/contact-us/.

The paperback edition

I'm a huge fan of ink and paper. As a result, this book is available as a high-quality, full-color, paperback edition via Amazon. None of this black-and-white nonsense. I think you'll love it.

Leave a review

Last but not least... be a legend and write a quick review on Amazon. You can even do this if you bought the book on Leanpub.

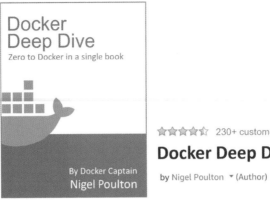

That's everything. Let's get rocking with Docker!

Part 1: The big picture stuff

1: Containers from 30,000 feet

Containers are definitely a *thing*.

In this chapter we'll get into things like; why we have containers, what they do for us, and where we can use them.

The bad old days

Applications are at the heart of businesses. If applications break, businesses break. Sometimes they even go bust. These statements get truer every day!

Most applications run on servers. In the past we could only run one application per server. The open-systems world of Windows and Linux just didn't have the technologies to safely and securely run multiple applications on the same server.

As a result, the story went something like this... Every time the business needed a new application, the IT department would buy a new server. Most of the time nobody knew the performance requirements of the new application, forcing the IT department to make guesses when choosing the model and size of the server to buy.

As a result, IT did the only thing it could do — it bought big fast servers that cost a lot of money. After all, the last thing anyone wanted, including the business, was under-powered servers unable to execute transactions and potentially losing customers and revenue. So, IT bought big. This resulted in over-powered servers operating as low as 5-10% of their potential capacity. **A tragic waste of company capital and environmental resources!**

Hello VMware!

Amid all of this, VMware, Inc. gave the world a gift — the virtual machine (VM). And almost overnight, the world changed into a much better place. We finally had a technology that allowed us to safely and securely run multiple business applications on a single server. Cue wild celebrations!

This was a game changer. IT departments no longer needed to procure a brand-new oversized server every time the business needed a new application. More often than not, they could run new apps on existing servers that were sitting around with spare capacity.

All of a sudden, we could squeeze massive amounts of value out of existing corporate assets, resulting in a lot more bang for the company's buck ($).

VMwarts

But... and there's always a *but!* As great as VMs are, they're far from perfect!

The fact that every VM requires its own dedicated operating system (OS) is a major flaw. Every OS consumes CPU, RAM and other resources that could otherwise be used to power more applications. Every OS needs patching and monitoring. And in some cases, every OS requires a license. All of this results in wasted time and resources.

The VM model has other challenges too. VMs are slow to boot, and portability isn't great — migrating and moving VM workloads between hypervisors and cloud platforms is harder than it needs to be.

Hello Containers!

For a long time, the big web-scale players, like Google, have been using container technologies to address the shortcomings of the VM model.

In the container model, the container is roughly analogous to the VM. A major difference is that containers do not require their own full-blown OS. In fact, all containers on a single host share the host's OS. This frees up huge amounts of system resources such as CPU, RAM, and storage. It also reduces potential licensing costs and reduces the overhead of OS patching and other maintenance. Net result: savings on the time, resource, and capital fronts.

Containers are also fast to start and ultra-portable. Moving container workloads from your laptop, to the cloud, and then to VMs or bare metal in your data center is a breeze.

Linux containers

Modern containers started in the Linux world and are the product of an immense amount of work from a wide variety of people over a long period of time. Just as one example, Google LLC has contributed many container-related technologies to the Linux kernel. Without these, and other contributions, we wouldn't have modern containers today.

Some of the major technologies that enabled the massive growth of containers in recent years include; **kernel namespaces**, **control groups**, **union filesystems**, and of course **Docker**. To re-emphasize what was said earlier — the modern container ecosystem is deeply indebted to the many individuals and organizations that laid the strong foundations that we currently build on. Thank you!

Despite all of this, containers remained complex and outside of the reach of most organizations. It wasn't until Docker came along that containers were effectively democratized and accessible to the masses.

> **Note:** There are many operating system virtualization technologies similar to containers that pre-date Docker and modern containers. Some even date back to System/360 on the Mainframe. BSD Jails and Solaris Zones are some other well-known examples of Unix-type container technologies. However, in this book we are restricting our conversation to *modern containers* made popular by Docker.

Hello Docker!

We'll talk about Docker in a bit more detail in the next chapter. But for now, it's enough to say that Docker was the magic that made Linux containers usable for mere mortals. Put another way, Docker, Inc. made containers simple!

Windows containers

Over the past few years, Microsoft Corp. has worked extremely hard to bring Docker and container technologies to the Windows platform.

At the time of writing, Windows containers are available on the Windows desktop and Windows Server platforms (certain versions of Windows 10 and later, and Windows Server 2016 and later). In achieving this, Microsoft has worked closely with Docker, Inc. and the open-source community.

The core Windows kernel technologies required to implement containers are collectively referred to as *Windows Containers*. The user-space tooling to work with these *Windows Containers* can be Docker. This makes the Docker experience on Windows almost exactly the same as Docker on Linux. This way developers and sysadmins familiar with the Docker toolset from the Linux platform can feel at home using Windows containers.

This revision of the book includes a mix of Linux and Windows examples.

Windows containers vs Linux containers

It's vital to understand that a running container shares the kernel of the host machine it is running on. This means that a containerized Windows app will not run on a Linux-based Docker host, and vice-versa — Windows containers require a Windows host, and Linux containers require a Linux host. Only... it's not always that simple.

It is possible to run Linux containers on Windows machines. For example, Docker Desktop running on Windows has two modes — "Windows containers" and "Linux containers". Depending on your version of Docker Desktop, Linux container run either inside a lightweight Hyper-V VM or using the Windows Subsystem for Linux (WSL). The WSL option is newer and the strategic option for the future as it doesn't require a Hyper-V VM and offers better performance and compatibility.

What about Mac containers?

There is currently no such thing as Mac containers.

However, you can run Linux containers on your Mac using *Docker Desktop*. This works by seamlessly running your containers inside of a lightweight Linux VM on your Mac. It's extremely popular with developers, who can easily develop and test Linux containers on their Mac.

What about Kubernetes

Kubernetes is an open-source project out of Google that has quickly emerged as the de facto orchestrator of containerized apps. That's just a fancy way of saying *Kubernetes is the most popular tool for deploying and managing containerized apps*.

> **Note:** A containerized app is an application running as a container.

At the time of writing, Kubernetes uses Docker as its default container runtime — the low-level technology that pulls images and starts and stops containers. However, Kubernetes has a pluggable container runtime interface (CRI) that makes it easy to swap-out Docker for a different container runtime. In the future, Docker might be replaced by `containerd` as the default container runtime in Kubernetes. More on `containerd` later in the book, but for now it's enough to know that containerd is the small specialized part of Docker that does the low-level tasks of starting and stopping containers.

The important thing to know about Kubernetes, at this stage, is that it's a higher-level platform than Docker, and it currently uses Docker for its low-level container-related operations.

I have the following resources to help you learn Kubernetes:

- The Kubernetes Book
- Getting Started with Kubernetes video course (pluralsight.com)
- Kubernetes 101 video course (udemy.com)

Getting Started with Kubernetes is available at pluralsight.com and Kubernetes 101 is available at udemy.com.

Chapter Summary

We used to live in a world where every time the business wanted a new application we had to buy a brand-new server. VMware came along and enabled us to drive more value out of new and existing company IT assets. As good as VMware and the VM model is, it's not perfect. Following the success of VMware and hypervisors came a newer more efficient and lightweight virtualization technology called containers. But containers were initially hard to implement and were only found in the data centers of web giants that had Linux kernel engineers on staff. Along came Docker, Inc. and suddenly containers were available to the masses.

Speaking of Docker... let's go find who, why, and what Docker is!

2: Docker

No book or conversation about containers is complete without talking about Docker. But when we say "Docker", we can be referring to either of the following:

1. Docker, Inc. the company
2. Docker the technology

Docker - The TLDR

Docker is software that runs on Linux and Windows. It creates, manages, and can even orchestrate containers. The software is currently built from various tools from the *Moby* open-source project. Docker, Inc. is the company that created the technology and continues to create technologies and solutions that make it easier to get the code on your laptop running in the cloud.

That's the quick version. Let's dive a bit deeper.

Docker, Inc.

Docker, Inc. is a San Francisco based technology company founded by French-born American developer and entrepreneur Solomon Hykes. Solomon is no longer at the company.

(old logo)

(new logo)

Figure 2.1 Docker, Inc. logo.

The company started out as a platform as a service (PaaS provider called *dotCloud*. Behind the scenes, the dotCloud platform was built on Linux containers. To help create and manage these containers, they built an in-house tool that they eventually nick-named "Docker". And that's how the Docker technology was born!

It's also interesting to know that the word "Docker" comes from a British expression meaning **dock** worker — somebody who loads and unloads cargo from ships.

In 2013 they got rid of the struggling PaaS side of the business, rebranded the company as "Docker, Inc.", and focussed on bringing Docker and containers to the world. They were immensely successfully in bringing containers into mainstream IT, but so far they've struggled to make a profitable business.

At the time of writing, Docker, Inc. is focussing on their Docker Desktop and Docker Hub products to streamline the process of getting from source code on a laptop, all the way to a running application in the cloud.

Throughout this book we'll use the term "Docker, Inc." when referring to Docker the company. All other uses of the term "Docker" will refer to the technology.

The Docker technology

When most people talk about Docker, they're referring to the technology that runs containers. However, there are at least three things to be aware of when referring to Docker as a technology:

1. The runtime
2. The daemon (a.k.a. engine)
3. The orchestrator

Figure 2.2 shows the three layers and will be a useful reference as we explain each component. We'll get deeper into each later in the book.

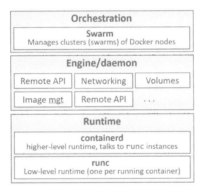

Figure 2.2 Docker architecture.

The runtime operates at the lowest level and is responsible for starting and stopping containers (this includes building all of the OS constructs such as namespaces and cgroups). Docker implements a tiered runtime architecture with high-level and low-level runtimes that work together.

The low-level runtime is called runc and is the reference implementation of Open Containers Initiative (OCI) runtime-spec. Its job is to interface with the underlying OS and start and stop containers. Every running container on a Docker node has a runc instance managing it.

The higher-level runtime is called containerd. containerd does a lot more than runc. It manages the entire lifecycle of a container, including pulling images, creating network interfaces, and managing lower-level runc instances. containerd is pronounced "container-dee' and is a graduated CNCF project used by Docker and Kubernetes as a container runtime.

A typical Docker installation has a single containerd process (`docker-containerd`) controlling the runc (`docker-runc`) instances associated with each running container.

The Docker daemon (`dockerd`) sits above `containerd` and performs higher-level tasks such as; exposing the Docker remote API, managing images, managing volumes, managing networks, and more...

A major job of the Docker daemon is to provide an easy-to-use standard interface that abstracts the lower levels.

Docker also has native support for managing clusters of nodes running Docker. These clusters are called swarms and the native technology is called Docker Swarm. Docker Swarm is easy-to-use and many companies are using it in real-world production. However, most people are choosing to use Kubernetes instead of Docker Swarm.

The Open Container Initiative (OCI)

Earlier in the chapter we mentioned the Open Containers Initiative — OCI[2].

The OCI is a governance council responsible for standardizing the low-level fundamental components of container infrastructure. In particular it focusses on *image format* and *container runtime* (don't worry if you're not comfortable with these terms yet, we'll cover them in the book).

It's also true that no discussion of the OCI is complete without mentioning a bit of history. And as with all accounts of history, the version you get depends on who's doing the talking. So, this is container history according to Nigel :-D

From day one, use of Docker grew like crazy. More and more people used it in more and more ways for more and more things. So, it was inevitable that some parties would get frustrated. This is normal and healthy.

The TLDR of this *history according to Nigel* is that a company called CoreOS (acquired by Red Hat which was then acquired by IBM) didn't like the way Docker did certain things. So, they created an open standard called **appc**[3] that defined things like image format and container runtime. They also created an implementation of the spec called **rkt** (pronounced "rocket").

This put the container ecosystem in an awkward position with two competing standards.

Getting back to the story, this threatened to fracture the ecosystem and present users and customers with a dilemma. While competition is usually a good thing, *competing standards* is usually not. They cause confusion and slowdown user adoption. Not good for anybody.

With this in mind, everybody did their best to act like adults and came together to form the OCI — a lightweight agile council to govern container standards.

At the time of writing, the OCI has published two specifications (standards) -

- The image-spec[4]
- The runtime-spec[5]

An analogy that's often used when referring to these two standards is *rail tracks*. These two standards are like agreeing on standard sizes and properties of rail tracks, leaving everyone else free to build better trains,

---

[2]https://www.opencontainers.org
[3]https://github.com/appc/spec/
[4]https://github.com/opencontainers/image-spec
[5]https://github.com/opencontainers/runtime-spec

better carriages, better signalling systems, better stations... all safe in the knowledge that they'll work on the standardized tracks. Nobody wants two competing standards for rail track sizes!

It's fair to say that the two OCI specifications have had a major impact on the architecture and design of the core Docker product. As of Docker 1.11, the Docker Engine architecture conforms to the OCI runtime spec.

The OCI is organized under the auspices of the Linux Foundation.

Chapter summary

In this chapter, we learned about Docker, Inc. the company, and the Docker technology.

Docker, Inc. is a technology company out of San Francisco with an ambition to change the way we do software. They were arguably the *first-movers* and instigators of the modern container revolution.

The Docker technology focuses on running and managing application containers. It runs on Linux and Windows, can be installed almost anywhere, and is currently the most popular container runtime used by Kubernetes.

The Open Container Initiative (OCI) was instrumental in standardizing the container runtime format and container image format.

3: Installing Docker

There are lots of ways and places to install Docker. There's Windows, Mac, and Linux. You can install in the cloud, on premises, and on your laptop. And there are manual installs, scripted installs, wizard-based installs... There literally are loads of ways and places to install Docker.

But don't let that scare you. They're all really easy, and a simple search for "how to install docker on <insert your choice here>" will reveal up-to-date instructions that are easy to follow. As a result, we won't waste too much space here. We'll cover the following.

- Docker Desktop installs on
    - Windows 10
    - Mac
- Server installs on
    - Linux
    - Windows Server 2019
- Play with Docker

Docker Desktop

Docker Desktop is a packaged product from Docker, Inc. It runs on 64-bit versions of Windows 10 and Mac, and it's easy to download and install.

Once the installation is complete, you have a single-engine Docker environment that is great for development purposes. It includes Docker Compose and you can choose to enable a single-node Kubernetes cluster.

Early versions of Docker Desktop experienced some feature-lag while the product was developed with a *stability first, features second* approach. However, the product is now mature and a key technology in Docker, Inc's focus on making it easier to get from the source code on your laptop to running applications in the cloud.

Docker Desktop on Windows 10 can run native Windows containers as well as Linux containers. Docker Desktop on Mac can only run Linux containers.

Windows pre-reqs

Docker Desktop on Windows requires all of the following:

- 64-bit version of Windows 10 Pro/Enterprise/Education (does not work with Home edition)
- Hardware virtualization support must be enabled in your system's BIOS
- The *Hyper-V* and *Containers* features must be enabled in Windows

The installer can enable the Hyper-V and Containers features, but it's your responsibility to enable hardware virtualization in your BIOS (be very careful changing anything in your system's BIOS).

Installing Docker Desktop on Windows 10

Perform a google search for "install Docker Desktop". This will take you to the relevant download page where you can download the installer and follow the instructions. It's that simple!

At the time of writing, you can choose between the stable channel and the edge channel. The names are self-explanatory, with the edge channel providing earlier access bleeding-edge features.

Once the installation is complete you may have to manually start Docker Desktop from the Windows Start menu. It can take a minute for it to start, and you can watch the start progress via the animated whale icon on the Windows task bar at the bottom of the screen.

Once it's up and running you can open a PowerShell prompt and type some simple docker commands.

```
$ docker version
Client: Docker Engine - Community
 Version:           19.03.8
 API version:       1.40
 Go version:        go1.12.17
 Git commit:        afacb8b
 Built:             Wed Mar 11 01:23:10 2020
 OS/Arch:           windows/amd64
 Experimental:      true
Server: Docker Engine - Community
 Engine:
  Version:          19.03.8
  API version:      1.40 (minimum version 1.12)
  Go version:       go1.12.17
  Git commit:       afacb8b
  Built:            Wed Mar 11 01:29:16 2020
  OS/Arch:          linux/amd64
  Experimental:     true
<Snip>
```

Notice the output is showing OS/Arch: linux/amd64 for the **Server** component. This is because a default installation assumes you'll be working with Linux containers. It does this by running the Docker daemon inside of a lightweight Linux Hyper-V VM.

Switching to Windows containers is as simple as right-clicking the Docker whale icon in the Windows notifications tray and selecting Switch to Windows containers.... You can achieve the same thing from the command line with the following command (located in the \Program Files\Docker\Docker directory):

```
C:\Program Files\Docker\Docker> .\dockercli -SwitchDaemon
```

Be aware that any existing Linux containers will keep running in the background, but you won't be able to see or manage them until you switch back to Linux containers mode.

You'll be prompted to enable the Windows Containers feature if it isn't already enabled.

Run another docker version command and look for the windows/amd64 line in the Server section of the output.

```
C:\> docker version
Client:
 <Snip>

Server:
 Engine:
  Version:      19.03.8
  API version:  1.40 (minimum version 1.24)
  Go version:   go1.12.17
  Git commit:   afacb8b
  Built:        Wed Mar 11 01:37:20 2020
  OS/Arch:      windows/amd64
  Experimental: true
```

You can now run and manage Windows containers (containers running Windows applications).

Congratulations. You now have a working installation of Docker on your Windows 10 machine.

Installing Docker Desktop on Mac

Docker Desktop for Mac is like Docker Desktop on Windows 10 — a packaged product from Docker, Inc with a simple installer that gets you a single-engine installation of Docker that's ideal for local development needs. You can also enable a single-node Kubernetes cluster.

We'll look at a simple installation in a second, but before doing that it's worth noting that *Docker Desktop* on Mac doesn't give you the Docker Engine running natively on the Mac OS Darwin kernel. Behind the scenes, the Docker daemon is running inside a lightweight Linux VM that seamlessly exposes the daemon and API to your Mac environment. This means you can open a terminal on your Mac and use the regular Docker commands.

Although this works seamlessly on your Mac, don't forget that it's Docker on Linux under the hood — so it's only going work with Linux-based Docker containers. This is good though, as it's where most of the container action is.

Figure 3.1 shows the high-level architecture for Docker Desktop on Mac.

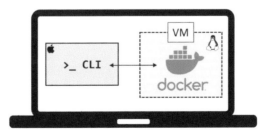

Figure 3.1

The simplest way to install Docker Desktop on your Mac is perform a google search for "install Docker Desktop". Follow the links to the download page where you can download the installer and follow the instructions. It's that simple.

As with Docker Desktop on Windows 10, you can choose the stable channel or the edge channel — the edge channel providing earlier access bleeding-edge features.

Download the installer and follow the step-by-step instructions.

Once the installation is complete you may have to manually start Docker Desktop from the MacOS Launchpad. It can take a minute for it to start, and you can watch the animated Docker whale icon in the status bar at the top of your screen. Once Docker Desktop is started, the whale will stop being animated. You can click the whale icon to manage Docker Desktop.

Open a terminal window and run some regular Docker commands. Try the following.

```
$ docker version
Client: Docker Engine - Community
 Version:           19.03.8
 API version:       1.40
 Go version:        go1.12.17
 Git commit:        afacb8b
 Built:             Wed Mar 11 01:21:11 2020
 OS/Arch:           darwin/amd64
 Experimental:      true

Server: Docker Engine - Community
 Engine:
  Version:          19.03.8
  API version:      1.40 (minimum version 1.12)
  Go version:       go1.12.17
  Git commit:       afacb8b
  Built:            Wed Mar 11 01:29:16 2020
  OS/Arch:          linux/amd64
  Experimental:     true
```

Notice that the OS/Arch: for the **Server** component is showing as linux/amd64. This is because the daemon is running inside of the Linux VM we mentioned earlier. The **Client** component is a native Mac application and runs directly on the Mac OS Darwin kernel (OS/Arch: darwin/amd64).

You can now use Docker on your Mac.

Installing Docker on Linux

There are lots of ways to install Docker on Linux and most of them are easy. The hardest part is usually deciding which Linux distro to use.

The internet has lots of guides for installing and working with Docker on many distributions of Linux. In this section we'll look at one of the ways to install on Ubuntu Linux 20.04 LTS. The procedure assumes you've already installed Linux and are logged on.

1. Update the apt package index.

```
$ sudo apt-get update
Get:1 http://eu-west-1.ec2.archive.ubuntu.com/ubuntu focal InRelease [265 kB]
...
```

2. Install Docker from the official repo.

```
$ sudo apt-get install docker.io
Reading package lists... Done
Building dependency tree
...
```

Docker is now installed and you can test by running some commands.

```
$ sudo docker --version
Docker version 19.03.8, build afacb8b7f0

$ sudo docker info
Server:
 Containers: 0
  Running: 0
  Paused: 0
  Stopped: 0
  ...
```

Installing Docker on Windows Server 2019

Most of the public cloud platforms offer off-the-shelf copies of Windows Server 2019 with Docker pre-installed. Simply choose one of these – such as Microsoft Windows Server 2019 Base with Containers - `ami-0b809eef92577a4f1` on AWS – and you're good to go.

Installing Docker on other versions of Windows Server 2019 is incredibly easy.

The following procedure assumes you've installed Windows Server 2019 and are logged on with administrator privileges.

1. Install the Docker Provider

   Run this command from a PowerShell terminal.

```
PS C:\> Install-Module DockerMsftProvider –Force
NuGet provider is required to continue
PowerShellGet requires NuGet provider version
<Snip>
Do you want PowerShellGet to install and import the NuGet provider now?
[Y] Yes  [N] No  [S] Suspend  [?] Help (default is "Y"): y
```

2. Install Docker

```
PS C:\> Install-Package Docker -ProviderName DockerMsftProvider -Force
WARNING: A restart is required to enable the containers feature. Please restart.
Name       Version    Source       Summary
----       -------    ------       -------
Docker     19.03.5    DockerDefault    Contains Docker EE for use with Windows Server.
```

3. Restart your machine

Congratulations, Docker is now installed and configured to automatically start when the system boots.

Run some commands to verify Docker is working.

```
PS C:\> docker version
Client: Docker Engine - Enterprise
 Version:           19.03.5
 API version:       1.40
 Go version:        go1.12.12
 Git commit:        2ee0c57608
 Built:             11/13/2019 08:00:16
 OS/Arch:           windows/amd64
 Experimental:      false
Server: Docker Engine - Enterprise
 Engine:
  Version:          19.03.5
  API version:      1.40 (minimum version 1.24)
  Go version:       go1.12.12
  Git commit:       2ee0c57608
  Built:            11/13/2019 07:58:51
  OS/Arch:          windows/amd64
  Experimental:     false
```

Docker is now installed and you are ready to start using Windows containers.

Play with Docker

Play with Docker (PWD) provides a free-to-use fully functional Docker playground that lasts for 4 hours. You can add multiple nodes and even cluster them in a swarm.

Sometimes performance can be slow, but for a free-to-use service it is excellent!

Visit https://labs.play-with-docker.com/

Chapter Summary

You can run Docker almost anywhere and most of the installation methods are simple.

Docker Desktop provides you a single-engine Docker environment on your Mac or Windows 10 laptop. It's simple to install, is intended for development activities and even allows you to spin-up a single-node Kubernetes cluster.

Docker can be installed on Windows Server and Linux, with most operating systems having packages that are simple to install.

Play with Docker is a free 4-hour Docker playground on the internet.

4: The big picture

The aim of this chapter is to paint a quick big-picture of what Docker is all about before we dive in deeper in later chapters.

We'll break this chapter into two:

- The Ops perspective
- The Dev perspective

In the Ops Perspective section, we'll download an image, start a new container, log in to the new container, run a command inside of it, and then destroy it.

In the Dev Perspective section, we'll focus more on the app. We'll clone some app-code from GitHub, inspect a Dockerfile, containerize the app, run it as a container.

These two sections will give you a good idea of what Docker is all about and how the major components fit together. **It's recommended that you read both sections to get the *dev* and the *ops* perspectives**. DevOps anyone?

Don't worry if some of the stuff we do here is totally new to you. We're not trying to make you an expert in this chapter. This is about giving you a *feel of things* — setting you up so that when we get into the details in later chapters, you have an idea of how the pieces fit together.

If you want to follow along, all you need is a single Docker host with an internet connection. I recommend Docker Desktop for your Mac or Windows PC. However, the examples will work anywhere that you have Docker installed. We'll be showing examples using Linux containers and Windows containers.

If you can't install software and don't have access to a public cloud, another great way to get Docker is Play With Docker (PWD). This is a web-based Docker playground that you can use for free. Just point your web browser to https://labs.play-with-docker.com/ and you're ready to go (you'll need a Docker Hub or GitHub account to be able to login).

As we progress through the chapter, we may use the terms "Docker host" and "Docker node" interchangeably. Both refer to the system that you are running Docker on.

The Ops Perspective

When you install Docker, you get two major components:

- the Docker client
- the Docker daemon (sometimes called the "Docker engine")

The daemon implements the runtime, API and everything else required to run Docker.

In a default Linux installation, the client talks to the daemon via a local IPC/Unix socket at `/var/run/docker.sock`. On Windows this happens via a named pipe at `npipe:////./pipe/docker_engine`. Once installed, you can use the `docker version` command to test that the client and daemon (server) are running and talking to each other.

```
> docker version
Client: Docker Engine - Community
 Version:        19.03.8
 API version:    1.40
 Go version:     go1.12.17
 Git commit:     afacb8b
 Built: Wed Mar 11 01:23:10 2020
 OS/Arch:        linux/amd64
 Experimental:   false

Server:
 Engine:
  Version:        19.03.8
  API version:    1.40 (minimum version 1.12)
  Go version:     go1.12.17
  Git commit:     afacb8b
  Built:          Wed Mar 11 01:29:16 2020
  OS/Arch:        linux/amd64
  Experimental:   false
 containerd:
  Version:        v1.2.13
  ...
```

If you get a response back from the `Client` **and** `Server`, you're good to go.

If you are using Linux and get an error response from the Server component, make sure that Docker is up and running. Also, try the command again with `sudo` in front of it: `sudo docker version`. If it works with `sudo` you will need to add your user account to the local `docker` group, or prefix the remainder of the commands in the book with `sudo`.

Images

It's useful to think of a Docker image as an object that contains an OS filesystem, an application, and all application dependencies. If you work in operations, it's like a virtual machine template. A virtual machine template is essentially a stopped virtual machine. In the Docker world, an image is effectively a stopped container. If you're a developer, you can think of an image as a *class*.

Run the `docker image ls` command on your Docker host.

```
$ docker image ls
REPOSITORY      TAG        IMAGE ID       CREATED        SIZE
```

If you are working from a freshly installed Docker host, or Play With Docker, you will have no images and it will look like the previous output.

Getting images onto your Docker host is called "pulling". If you are following along with Linux, pull the `ubuntu:latest` image. If you are following along on Windows, pull the `mcr.microsoft.com/powershell:lts-nanoserver-1903` image.

```
$ docker image pull ubuntu:latest
latest: Pulling from library/ubuntu
50aff78429b1: Pull complete
f6d82e297bce: Pull complete
275abb2c8a6f: Pull complete
9f15a39356d6: Pull complete
fc0342a94c89: Pull complete
Digest: sha256:fbaf303...c0ea5d1212
Status: Downloaded newer image for ubuntu:latest
```

Windows images can be large and take a long time to pull.

Run the `docker image ls` command again to see the image you just pulled.

```
$ docker images
REPOSITORY     TAG       IMAGE ID        CREATED         SIZE
ubuntu         latest    1d622ef86b13    16 hours ago    73.9MB
```

We'll get into the details of where the image is stored and what's inside of it in later chapters. For now, it's enough to know that an image contains enough of an operating system (OS), as well as all the code and dependencies to run whatever application it's designed for. The `ubuntu` image that we've pulled has a stripped-down version of the Ubuntu Linux filesystem, including a few of the common Ubuntu utilities. The `mcr.microsoft.com/powershell:lts-nanoserver-1903` image contains a Windows Server Core OS plus PowerShell.

If you pull an application container such as `nginx` or `mcr.microsoft.com/windows/servercore/iis`, you will get an image that contains some OS, as well as the code to run either `NGINX` or `IIS`.

It's also worth noting that each image gets its own unique ID. When referencing images, you can refer to them using either `ID`s or names. If you're working with image ID's, it's usually enough to type the first few characters of the ID — as long as it's unique, Docker will know which image you mean.

Containers

Now that we have an image pulled locally, we can use the `docker container run` command to launch a container from it.

For Linux:

```
$ docker container run -it ubuntu:latest /bin/bash
root@6dc20d508db0:/#
```

For Windows:

```
> docker container run -it mcr.microsoft.com/powershell:lts-nanoserver-1903 pwsh.exe

PowerShell 7.0.0
Copyright (C) Microsoft Corporation. All rights reserved.
PS C:\>
```

Look closely at the output from the previous commands. You should notice that the shell prompt has changed in each instance. This is because the -it flags switch your shell into the terminal of the container — you are literally inside of the new container!

Let's examine that docker container run command.

docker container run tells the Docker daemon to start a new container. The -it flags tell Docker to make the container interactive and to attach the current shell to the container's terminal (we'll get more specific about this in the chapter on containers). Next, the command tells Docker that we want the container to be based on the ubuntu:latest image (or the mcr.microsoft.com/powershell:lts-nanoserver-1903 image if you're following along with Windows). Finally, we tell Docker which process we want to run inside of the container. For the Linux example we're running a Bash shell, for the Windows container we're running PowerShell.

Run a ps command from inside of the container to list all running processes.

Linux example:

```
root@6dc20d508db0:/# ps -elf
F S UID    PID  PPID  NI ADDR SZ WCHAN  STIME TTY        TIME CMD
4 S root     1     0   0 -  4560 -      13:38 pts/0   00:00:00 /bin/bash
0 R root     9     1   0 -  8606 -      13:38 pts/0   00:00:00 ps -elf
```

Windows example:

```
PS C:\> ps
```

NPM(K)	PM(M)	WS(M)	CPU(s)	Id	SI	ProcessName
5	0.90	3.78	0.00	1068	1	CExecSvc
6	0.97	4.12	0.03	1184	1	conhost
6	0.87	2.16	0.00	972	1	csrss
0	0.06	0.01	0.00	0	0	Idle
18	4.38	12.32	0.00	272	1	lsass
54	34.82	65.09	1.27	1212	1	pwsh
9	1.61	4.99	0.00	1020	1	services
4	0.49	1.18	0.00	948	0	smss
14	1.98	6.61	0.00	628	1	svchost
12	2.95	10.02	0.00	752	1	svchost
8	1.83	6.02	0.00	788	1	svchost
7	1.42	4.70	0.00	1040	1	svchost
16	6.12	11.41	0.00	1120	1	svchost
24	3.73	10.38	0.00	1168	1	svchost
15	9.60	18.96	0.00	1376	1	svchost
0	0.16	0.14	0.00	4	0	System
8	1.16	4.12	0.00	1004	1	wininit

The Linux container only has two processes:

- PID 1. This is the `/bin/bash` process that we told the container to run with the `docker container run` command.
- PID 9. This is the `ps -elf` command/process that we ran to list the running processes.

The presence of the `ps -elf` process in the Linux output can be a bit misleading as it is a short-lived process that dies as soon as the `ps` command completes. This means the only long-running process inside of the container is the `/bin/bash` process.

The Windows container has a lot more going on. This is an artefact of the way the Windows Operating System works. However, even though the Windows container has a lot more processes than the Linux container, it is still a lot less than a regular Windows **Server**.

Press `Ctrl-PQ` to exit the container without terminating it. This will land your shell back at the terminal of your Docker host. You can verify this by looking at your shell prompt.

Now that you are back at the shell prompt of your Docker host, run the `ps` command again.

Notice how many more processes are running on your Docker host compared to the container you just ran. Windows containers run far fewer processes than Windows hosts, and Linux containers run far less than Linux hosts.

In a previous step, you pressed `Ctrl-PQ` to exit from the container. Doing this from inside of a container will exit you from the container without killing it. You can see all running containers on your system using the `docker container ls` command.

```
$ docker container ls
CONTAINER ID   IMAGE           COMMAND        CREATED   STATUS      NAMES
6dc20d508db0   ubuntu:latest   "/bin/bash"    7 mins    Up 7 min    vigilant_borg
```

The output above shows a single running container. This is the container that you created earlier. The presence of the container in this output proves that it's still running. You can also see that it was created 7 minutes ago and has been running for 7 minutes.

Attaching to running containers

You can attach your shell to the terminal of a running container with the `docker container exec` command. As the container from the previous steps is still running, let's make a new connection to it.

Linux example:

This example references a container called "vigilant_borg". The name of your container will be different, so remember to substitute "vigilant_borg" with the name or ID of the container running on your Docker host.

```
$ docker container exec -it vigilant_borg bash
root@6dc20d508db0:/#
```

Windows example:

This example references a container called "pensive_hamilton". The name of your container will be different, so remember to substitute "pensive_hamilton" with the name or ID of the container running on your Docker host.

```
> docker container exec -it pensive_hamilton pwsh.exe

PowerShell 7.0.0
Copyright (C) Microsoft Corporation. All rights reserved.
PS C:\>
```

Notice that your shell prompt has changed again. You are logged into the container again.

The format of the `docker container exec` command is: `docker container exec <options> <container-name or container-id> <command/app>`. In our examples, we used the `-it` options to attach our shell to the container's shell. We referenced the container by name, and told it to run the bash shell (PowerShell in the Windows example). We could easily have referenced the container by its hex ID.

Exit the container again by pressing `Ctrl-PQ`.

Your shell prompt should be back to your Docker host.

Run the `docker container ls` command again to verify that your container is still running.

```
$ docker container ls
CONTAINER ID   IMAGE           COMMAND       CREATED   STATUS     NAMES
6dc20d508db0   ubuntu:latest   "/bin/bash"   9 mins    Up 9 min   vigilant_borg
```

Stop the container and kill it using the `docker container stop` and `docker container rm` commands. Remember to substitute the names/IDs of your own containers.

```
$ docker container stop vigilant_borg
vigilant_borg

$ docker container rm vigilant_borg
vigilant_borg
```

Verify that the container was successfully deleted by running the `docker container ls` command with the `-a` flag. Adding `-a` tells Docker to list all containers, even those in the stopped state.

```
$ docker container ls -a
CONTAINER ID    IMAGE     COMMAND     CREATED     STATUS     PORTS     NAMES
```

You've just pulled a Docker image, started a container from it, attached to it, executed a command inside it, stopped it, and deleted it.

The Dev Perspective

Containers are all about the apps.

In this section, we'll clone an app from a Git repo, inspect its Dockerfile, containerize it, and run it as a container.

The Linux app can be cloned from: https://github.com/nigelpoulton/psweb.git

The Windows app can be cloned from: https://github.com/nigelpoulton/win-web.git

The rest of this section will focus on the Linux NGINX example. However, both examples are containerizing simple web apps, so the process is the same. Where there are differences in the Windows example we will highlight them to help you follow along.

Run all of the following commands from a terminal on your Docker host.

Clone the repo locally. This will pull the application code to your local Docker host ready for you to containerize it.

Be sure to substitute the following repo with the Windows repo if you are following along with the Windows example.

```
$ git clone https://github.com/nigelpoulton/psweb.git
Cloning into 'psweb'...
remote: Counting objects: 15, done.
remote: Compressing objects: 100% (11/11), done.
remote: Total 15 (delta 2), reused 15 (delta 2), pack-reused 0
Unpacking objects: 100% (15/15), done.
Checking connectivity... done.
```

Change directory into the cloned repo's directory and list its contents.

```
$ cd psweb
$ ls -l
total 40
-rw-r--r--@ 1 ubuntu ubuntu  338 24 Apr 19:29 Dockerfile
-rw-r--r--@ 1 ubuntu ubuntu  396 24 Apr 19:32 README.md
-rw-r--r--@ 1 ubuntu ubuntu  341 24 Apr 19:29 app.js
-rw-r--r--  1 ubuntu ubuntu  216 24 Apr 19:29 circle.yml
-rw-r--r--@ 1 ubuntu ubuntu  377 24 Apr 19:36 package.json
drwxr-xr-x  4 ubuntu ubuntu  128 24 Apr 19:29 test
drwxr-xr-x  3 ubuntu ubuntu   96 24 Apr 19:29 views
```

The Linux example is a simple nodejs web app. The Windows example is an IIS server running some static HTML.

Both Git repos contain a file called `Dockerfile`. This is a plain-text document that tells Docker how to build an app and dependencies into a Docker image.

List the contents of the Dockerfile.

```
$ cat Dockerfile

FROM alpine
LABEL maintainer="nigelpoulton@hotmail.com"
RUN apk add --update nodejs nodejs-npm
COPY . /src
WORKDIR /src
RUN  npm install
EXPOSE 8080
ENTRYPOINT ["node", "./app.js"]
```

The contents of the Dockerfile in the Windows example are different. However, this isn't important at this stage. For now, it's enough to understand that each line represents an instruction that Docker uses to build an image.

At this point we have pulled some application code from a remote Git repo. We also have a Dockerfile containing instructions on how to build the app into a Docker image.

Use the `docker image build` command to create a new image using the instructions in the Dockerfile. This example creates a new Docker image called `test:latest`.

The command is the same for the Linux and Windows examples, and be sure to run it from within the directory containing the app code and Dockerfile.

```
$ docker image build -t test:latest .

Sending build context to Docker daemon  74.75kB
Step 1/8 : FROM alpine
latest: Pulling from library/alpine
88286f41530e: Pull complete
Digest: sha256:f006ecbb824...0c103f4820a417d
Status: Downloaded newer image for alpine:latest
 ---> 76da55c8019d
<Snip>
Successfully built f154cb3ddbd4
Successfully tagged test:latest
```

> **Note:** It may take a long time for the build to finish in the Windows example. This is because of the image being pulled is several gigabytes in size.

Once the build is complete, check to make sure that the new `test:latest` image exists on your host.

```
$ docker image ls
REPO    TAG      IMAGE ID       CREATED        SIZE
test    latest   f154cb3ddbd4   1 minute ago   81.5MB
...
```

You have a newly-built Docker image with the app and dependencies inside.

Run a container from the image and test the app.

Linux example:

```
$ docker container run -d \
  --name web1 \
  --publish 8080:8080 \
  test:latest
```

Open a web browser and navigate to the DNS name or IP address of the Docker host that you are running the container from, and point it to port 8080. You will see the following web page.

If you are following along with Docker for Windows or Docker for Mac, you will be able to use `localhost:8080` or `127.0.0.1:8080`. If you're following along on Play With Docker, you will be able to click the `8080` hyperlink above the terminal screen.

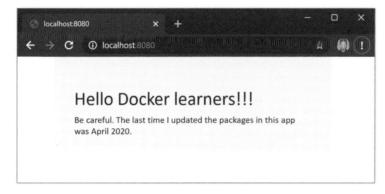

Figure 4.1

Windows example:

```
> docker container run -d \
  --name web1 \
  --publish 8080:80 \
  test:latest
```

Open a web browser and navigate to the DNS name or IP address of the Docker host that you are running the container from, and point it to port 8080. You will see the following web page.

The same rules apply if you're following along with Docker Desktop or Play With Docker.

Figure 4.2

Well done. You've taken some application code from a remote Git repo and built it into a Docker image. You then ran a container from it. We call this "containerizing an app".

Chapter Summary

In the Ops section of the chapter you downloaded a Docker image, launched a container from it, logged into the container, executed a command inside of it, and then stopped and deleted the container.

In the Dev section, you containerized a simple application by pulling some source code from GitHub and building it into an image using instructions in a Dockerfile. You then ran the containerized app.

This *big picture* view should help you with the up-coming chapters where we will dig deeper into images and containers.

Part 2: The technical stuff

5: The Docker Engine

In this chapter, we'll take a quick look under the hood of the Docker Engine.

You can use Docker without understanding any of the things we'll cover in this chapter. So, feel free to skip it. However, to be a real master of anything, you need to understand what's going on under the hood. So, to be a *real* Docker master, you need to know the stuff in this chapter.

This will be a theory-based chapter with no hands-on exercises.

As this chapter is part of the **technical section** of the book, we're going to employ the three-tiered approach where we split the chapter into three sections:

- **The TLDR**: Two or three quick paragraphs that you can read while standing in line for a coffee
- **The deep dive**: The really long bit where we get into the detail
- **The commands**: A quick recap of the commands we learned

Let's go and learn about the Docker Engine!

Docker Engine - The TLDR

The *Docker engine* is the core software that runs and manages containers. We often refer to it simply as *Docker*. If you know a thing or two about VMware, it might be useful to think of it as being like ESXi.

The Docker engine is modular in design and built from many small specialised tools. Where possible, these are based on open standards such as those maintained by the Open Container Initiative (OCI).

In many ways, the Docker Engine is like a car engine — both are modular and created by connecting many small specialized parts:

- A car engine is made from many specialized parts that work together to make a car drive — intake manifolds, throttle body, cylinders, spark plugs, exhaust manifolds etc.
- The Docker Engine is made from many specialized tools that work together to create and run containers — APIs, execution driver, runtimes, shims etc.

At the time of writing, the major components that make up the Docker engine are; the *Docker daemon*, *containerd*, *runc*, and various plugins such as networking and storage. Together, these create and run containers.

Figure 5.1 shows a high-level view.

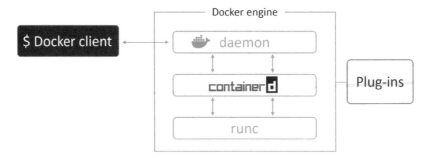

Figure 5.1

Throughout the book we'll refer to `runc` and `containerd` with lower-case "r" and "c". This means sentences starting with either `runc` or `containerd` will not start with a capital letter. This is intentional and not a mistake.

Docker Engine - The Deep Dive

When Docker was first released, the Docker engine had two major components:

- The Docker daemon (hereafter referred to as just "the daemon")
- LXC

The Docker daemon was a monolithic binary. It contained all of the code for the Docker client, the Docker API, the container runtime, image builds, and **much** more.

LXC provided the daemon with access to the fundamental building-blocks of containers that existed in the Linux kernel. Things like *namespaces* and *control groups (cgroups)*.

Figure 5.2. shows how the daemon, LXC, and the OS, interacted in older versions of Docker.

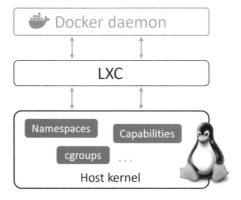

Figure 5.2 Original Docker architecture

Getting rid of LXC

The reliance on LXC was an issue from the start.

First up, LXC is Linux-specific. This was a problem for a project that had aspirations of being multi-platform.

Second up, being reliant on an external tool for something so core to the project was a huge risk that could hinder development.

As a result, Docker. Inc. developed their own tool called *libcontainer* as a replacement for LXC. The goal of *libcontainer* was to be a platform-agnostic tool that provided Docker with access to the fundamental container building-blocks that exist in the host kernel.

Libcontainer replaced LXC as the default *execution driver* in Docker 0.9.

Getting rid of the monolithic Docker daemon

Over time, the monolithic nature of the Docker daemon became more and more problematic:

1. It's hard to innovate on
2. It got slower
3. It wasn't what the ecosystem wanted

Docker, Inc. was aware of these challenges and began a huge effort to break apart the monolithic daemon and modularize it. The aim of this work was to break out as much of the functionality as possible from the daemon, and re-implement it in smaller specialized tools. These specialized tools can be swapped out, as well as easily re-used by third parties to build other tools. This plan follows the tried-and-tested Unix philosophy of building small specialized tools that can be pieced together into larger tools.

This work of breaking apart and re-factoring the Docker engine has seen **all of the *container execution* and container *runtime* code entirely removed from the daemon and refactored into small, specialized tools**.

Figure 5.3 shows a high-level view of the current Docker engine architecture with brief descriptions.

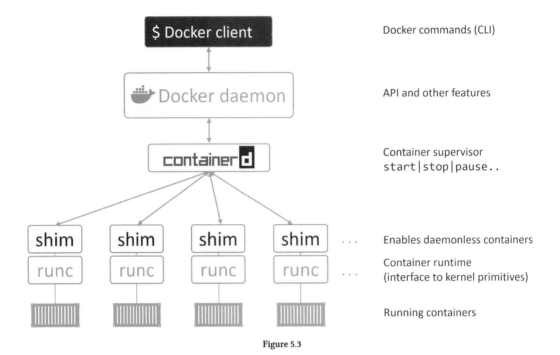

Docker commands (CLI)

API and other features

Container supervisor
start|stop|pause..

Enables daemonless containers

Container runtime
(interface to kernel primitives)

Running containers

Figure 5.3

The influence of the Open Container Initiative (OCI)

While Docker, Inc. was breaking the daemon apart and refactoring code, the OCI[6] was in the process of defining two container-related specifications (a.k.a. standards):

1. Image spec[7]
2. Container runtime spec[8]

Both specifications were released as version 1.0 in July 2017 and we shouldn't see too much change, as stability is the name of the game here. The latest image spec is v1.0.1 released in November 2017. The latest runtime spec is v1.0.2 released March 2020.

Docker, Inc. was heavily involved in creating these specifications and contributed a lot of code.

As of Docker 1.11 (early 2016), the Docker engine implements the OCI specifications as closely as possible. For example, the Docker daemon no longer contains any container runtime code — all container runtime code is implemented in a separate OCI-compliant layer. By default, Docker uses *runc* for this. runc is the *reference implementation* of the OCI container-runtime-spec. This is the runc container runtime layer in Figure 5.3.

As well as this, the *containerd* component of the Docker Engine makes sure Docker images are presented to *runc* as valid OCI bundles.

---

[6]https://www.opencontainers.org/
[7]https://github.com/opencontainers/image-spec
[8]https://github.com/opencontainers/runtime-spec

runc

As previously mentioned, *runc* is the reference implementation of the OCI container-runtime-spec. Docker, Inc. was heavily involved in defining the spec and developing runc.

If you strip everything else away, runc is a small, lightweight CLI wrapper for libcontainer (remember that libcontainer originally replaced LXC as the interface layer with the host OS in the early Docker architecture).

runc has a single purpose in life — create containers. And it's damn good at it. And fast! But as it's a CLI wrapper, it's effectively a standalone container runtime tool. This means you can download and build the binary, and you'll have everything you need to build and play with runc (OCI) containers. But it's bare bones and very low-level, meaning you'll have none of the richness that you get with the full-blown Docker engine.

We sometimes call the layer that runc operates at, "the OCI layer". See Figure 5.3.

You can see runc release information at:

- https://github.com/opencontainers/runc/releases

containerd

As part of the effort to strip functionality out of the Docker daemon, all of the container execution logic was ripped out and refactored into a new tool called containerd (pronounced container-dee). Its sole purpose in life was to manage container lifecycle operations — `start | stop | pause | rm...`

containerd is available as a daemon for Linux and Windows, and Docker has been using it on Linux since the 1.11 release. In the Docker engine stack, containerd sits between the daemon and runc at the OCI layer.

As previously stated, containerd was originally intended to be small, lightweight, and designed for a single task in life — container lifecycle operations. However, over time it has branched out and taken on more functionality. Things like image pulls, volumes and networks.

One of the reasons for adding more functionality is to make it easier to use in other projects. For example, in projects like Kubernetes, it was beneficial for containerd to do additional things like push and pull images. For these reasons, containerd now does a lot more than simple container lifecycle management. However, all the extra functionality is modular and optional, meaning you can pick and choose which bits you want. So, it's possible to include containerd in projects such as Kubernetes, but only to take the pieces your project needs.

containerd was developed by Docker, Inc. and donated to the Cloud Native Computing Foundation (CNCF). At the time of writing, containerd is a fully graduated CNCF project, meaning it's stable and considered ready for production. You can see the latest releases here:

- https://github.com/containerd/containerd/releases

Starting a new container (example)

Now that we have a view of the big picture, and some of the history, let's walk through the process of creating a new container.

The most common way of starting containers is using the Docker CLI. The following `docker container run` command will start a simple new container based on the `alpine:latest` image.

```
$ docker container run --name ctr1 -it alpine:latest sh
```

When you type commands like this into the Docker CLI, the Docker client converts them into the appropriate API payload and POSTs them to the API endpoint exposed by the Docker daemon.

The API is implemented in the daemon and can be exposed over a local socket or the network. On Linux the socket is /var/run/docker.sock and on Windows it's \pipe\docker_engine.

Once the daemon receives the command to create a new container, it makes a call to containerd. Remember that the daemon no-longer contains any code to create containers!

The daemon communicates with containerd via a CRUD-style API over gRPC[9].

Despite its name, *containerd* cannot actually create containers. It uses *runc* to do that. It converts the required Docker image into an OCI bundle and tells runc to use this to create a new container.

runc interfaces with the OS kernel to pull together all of the constructs necessary to create a container (namespaces, cgroups etc.). The container process is started as a child-process of runc, and as soon as it is started runc will exit.

Voila! The container is now started.

The process is summarized in Figure 5.4.

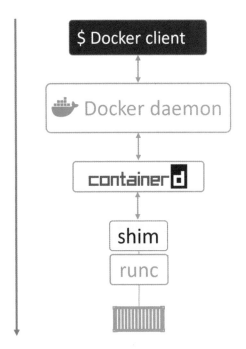

Figure 5.4

──────────────────────
[9]https://grpc.io/

One huge benefit of this model

Having all of the logic and code to start and manage containers removed from the daemon means that the entire container runtime is decoupled from the Docker daemon. We sometimes call this "daemonless containers", and it makes it possible to perform maintenance and upgrades on the Docker daemon without impacting running containers!

In the old model, where all of container runtime logic was implemented in the daemon, starting and stopping the daemon would kill all running containers on the host. This was a huge problem in production environments — especially when you consider how frequently new versions of Docker are released! Every daemon upgrade would kill all containers on that host — not good!

Fortunately, this is no longer a problem.

What's this shim all about?

Some of the diagrams in the chapter have shown a shim component.

The shim is integral to the implementation of daemonless containers (what we just mentioned about decoupling running containers from the daemon for things like daemon upgrades).

We mentioned earlier that *containerd* uses runc to create new containers. In fact, it forks a new instance of runc for every container it creates. However, once each container is created, the parent runc process exits. This means we can run hundreds of containers without having to run hundreds of runc instances.

Once a container's parent runc process exits, the associated containerd-shim process becomes the container's parent. Some of the responsibilities the shim performs as a container's parent include:

- Keeping any STDIN and STDOUT streams open so that when the daemon is restarted, the container doesn't terminate due to pipes being closed etc.
- Reports the container's exit status back to the daemon.

How it's implemented on Linux

On a Linux system, the components we've discussed are implemented as separate binaries as follows:

- `dockerd` (the Docker daemon)
- `docker-containerd` (containerd)
- `docker-containerd-shim` (shim)
- `docker-runc` (runc)

You can see all of these on a Linux system by running a `ps` command on the Docker host. Obviously, some of them will only be present when the system has running containers.

What's the point of the daemon

With all of the execution and runtime code stripped out of the daemon you might be asking the question: "what is left in the daemon?".

Obviously, the answer to this question will change over time as more and more functionality is stripped out and modularized. However, at the time of writing, some of the major functionality that still exists in the daemon includes; image management, image builds, the REST API, authentication, security, core networking, and orchestration.

Securing client and daemon communication

Let's finish the chapter by looking at how to secure the daemon over the network.

Docker implements a client-server model.

- The client component implements the CLI
- The server (daemon) component implements the functionality, including the public-facing REST API

The client is called `docker` (`docker.exe` on Windows) and the daemon is called `dockerd` (`dockerd.exe` on Windows). A default installation puts them on the same host and configures them to communicate over a local IPC socket:

- `/var/run/docker.sock` on Linux
- `//./pipe/docker_engine` on Windows

It's also possible to configure them to communicate over the network. By default, network communication occur over an unsecured HTTP socket on port `2375/tcp`.

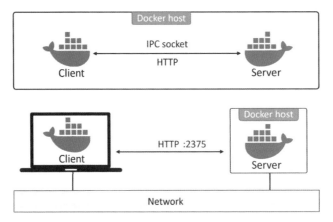

Figure 5.5

An insecure configuration like this might be suitable for labs, but it's unacceptable for anything else.

TLS to the rescue!

Docker lets you force the client and daemon to only accept network connections that are secured with TLS. This is recommended for production environments, even if all traffic is traversing trusted internal networks.

You can secure both the client and the daemon. Securing the client forces the client to only connect to Docker daemons with certificates signed by a trusted Certificate Authority (CA). Securing the daemon forces the daemon to only accept connections from clients presenting certificates from a trusted CA. A combination of both modes offers the most security.

We'll use a simple lab environment to walk through the process of configuring Docker for **daemon mode** and **client mode** TLS.

Lab setup

We'll use the lab setup shown in Figure 5.6 for the remainder of the examples. Your lab will look different, but it's vital that the client and daemon can resolve each other by name.

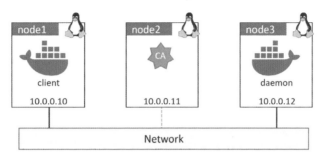

Figure 5.6 Sample lab setup

The high-level process will be as follows:

1. **Configure a CA and certificates**
2. Create a CA
3. Create and sign keys for the Daemon
4. Create and sign keys for the Client
5. Distribute keys
6. **Configure Docker to use TLS**
7. Configure daemon mode
8. Configure client mode

Create a CA (self-signed certs)

You only need to complete this step if you are following along in a lab and don't already have a CA. Also, the CA we're building here is to help demonstrate how to configure Docker, we're **not** attempting to build something production-grade.

Run the following commands from the CA node in the lab.

1. Create a new private key for the CA.

    You'll set a passphrase as part of the operation. Don't forget it!

```
$ openssl genrsa -aes256 -out ca-key.pem 4096

Generating RSA private key, 4096 bit long modulus
.............................................++
..++
e is 65537 (0x10001)
Enter pass phrase for ca-key.pem:
Verifying - Enter pass phrase for ca-key.pem:
```

You'll have a new file in your current directory called `ca-key.pem`. This is the CA's private key.

2. Use the CA's private key to generate a public key (certificate).

   You'll need to enter the passphrase from the previous step. Hopefully you haven't forgotten it ;-)

   ```
   $ openssl req -new -x509 -days 730 -key ca-key.pem -sha256 -out ca.pem
   ```

   This has added a second file to your working directory called `ca.pem`. This is the CA's public key, a.k.a. "certificate".

You now have two files in your current directory: `ca-key.pem` and `ca.pem`. These are the CA's key-pair and form the *identity* of the CA. At this point, the CA is ready to use.

Create a key-pair for the daemon

In this step, we'll generate a new key-pair for the Docker daemon on `node3`. It's a four-step process:

1. Create the private key
2. Create the signing request
3. Add IP addresses and make it valid for *server authorization*
4. Generate the certificate

Let's do it.

Run these commands from the CA (node2).

1. Create the private key for the daemon.

   ```
   $ openssl genrsa -out daemon-key.pem 4096
   <Snip>
   ```

   This has created a new file in your working directory called `daemon-key.pem`. This is the private key for the daemon node.

2. Create a certificate signing request (CSR) for the CA to create and sign a certificate for the daemon. Be sure to use the correct DNS name for your daemon node. The example uses `node3`.

```
$ openssl req -subj "/CN=node3" \
  -sha256 -new -key daemon-key.pem -out daemon.csr
```

You now have a fourth file in your working directory. This one is the CSR and it is called `daemon.csr`.

3. Add required attributes to the certificate.

This step creates a file that tells the CA to add a couple of extended attributes to the daemon's certificate when it signs it. These add the daemon's DNS name and IP address, as well as configure the certificate to be valid for *server authentication*.

Create a new file called `extfile.cnf` with the following values. The example uses the DNS name and IP of the daemon node in the lab from Figure 5.6. The values in your environment might be different.

```
subjectAltName = DNS:node3,IP:10.0.0.12
extendedKeyUsage = serverAuth
```

4. Generate the certificate.

This step uses the CSR file, CA keys, and the `extfile.cnf` file to sign and configure the daemon's certificate. It will output the daemon's public key (certificate) as a new file called `daemon-cert.pem`

```
$ openssl x509 -req -days 730 -sha256 \
  -in daemon.csr -CA ca.pem -CAkey ca-key.pem \
  -CAcreateserial -out daemon-cert.pem -extfile extfile.cnf
```

At this point, you have a working CA, as well as a key-pair for `node3` that can be used to secure the Docker daemon.

Delete the CSR and `extfile.cnf` before moving on.

```
$ rm daemon.csr extfile.cnf
```

Create a key-pair for the client

The next steps will repeat what we just did for the `node3`, but this time we'll do it for `node1` which will run the Docker client.

Run all commands from the CA (`node2`).

1. Create a private key for `node1`.

This will generate a new file in your working directory called `client-key.pem`.

```
$ openssl genrsa -out client-key.pem 4096
```

2. Create a CSR. Be sure to use the correct DNS name of the node that will be your secure Docker client. The example uses `node1`.

```
$ openssl req -subj '/CN=node1' -new -key client-key.pem -out client.csr
```

This will create a new file in your current directory called `client.csr`.

3. Create a file called `extfile.cnf` and populate it with the following value. This will make the certificate valid for client authentication.

```
extendedKeyUsage = clientAuth
```

4. Create the certificate for node1 using the CSR, the CA's public and private keys, and the `extfile.cnf` file. This will create the client's signed public key as a new file in your current directory called `client-cert.pem`.

```
$ openssl x509 -req -days 730 -sha256 \
  -in client.csr -CA ca.pem -CAkey ca-key.pem \
  -CAcreateserial -out client-cert.pem -extfile extfile.cnf
```

Delete the CSR and `extfile.cnf` files, as these are no longer needed.

```
$ rm client.csr extfile.cnf
```

At this point you should have the following 7 files in your working directory:

```
ca-key.pem          << CA private key
ca.pem              << CA public key (cert)
ca.srl              << Tracks serial numbers
client-cert.pem     << client public key (Cert)
client-key.pem      << client private key
daemon-cert.pem     << daemon public key (cert)
daemon-key.pem      << daemon private key
```

Before moving on, you should remove write permission from the private keys and make them only readable to you and other accounts that are members of your group.

```
$ chmod 0400 ca-key.pem client-key.pem daemon-key.pem
```

You should also remove write access to the public key certificates.

```
$ chmod -v 0444 ca.pem client-cert.pem daemon-cert.pem
```

Distribute keys

Now that you've got all of the required keys and certificates, you need to distribute them to the client and daemon nodes as follows:

- `ca.pem`, `daemon-cert.pem`, and `daemon-key.pem` from the CA to the node3 (the daemon node).
- `ca.pem`, `client-cert.pem`, and `client-key.pem` from the CA to node1 (the client node).

There are various ways to copy files between nodes and these can vary between systems. The important thing to know is that Docker requires the copied files to have the following names and locations:

- daemon-cert.pem -> ~/.docker/cert.pem

- daemon-key.pem –> ~/.docker/key.pem
- client-cert.pem –> ~/.docker/cert.pem
- client-key.pem –> ~/.docker/key.pem

You may have to create the ~/.docker hidden directory on the daemon and client nodes. You may also have to change permissions on the .docker directory to enable the copy — chmod 777 .docker will work, but is not secure.

If you've been following, the lab now looks like Figure 5.7

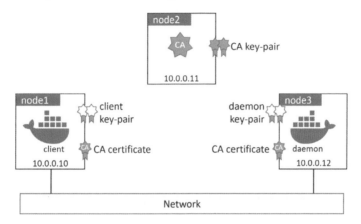

Figure 5.7 Updated lab with keys

The presence of the CA's public key (ca.pem) on the client and daemon nodes is what tells them to trust the certificates signed by the CA.

With the certificates in place, it's time to configure Docker so that the client and daemon use TLS.

Configure Docker for TLS

As previously mentioned, Docker has two TLS modes:

- daemon mode
- client mode

Daemon mode forces the daemon only to allow connections from clients with a valid certificate. Client mode tells the client only to connect with daemons that have a valid certificate.

We'll configure the daemon process on node1 for *daemon mode*, and test it. After that, we'll configure the client process on node2 for *client mode*, and test that.

Configuring the Docker daemon for TLS

Securing the daemon is as simple as setting a few daemon flags in the daemon.json configuration file:

- `tlsverify` enables TLS verification
- `tlscacert` tells the daemon which CA to trust
- `tlscert` tells Docker where the daemon's certificate is located
- `tlskey` tells Docker where the daemon's private key is located
- `hosts` tells Docker which sockets to bind the daemon on

We'll configure these in the platform-independent `daemon.json` configuration file. This is found in `/etc/docker/` on Linux, and `C:\ProgramData\Docker\config\` on Windows.

Perform all of the following operations on the node that will run your secure Docker daemon (`node3` in the example lab).

Edit the `daemon.json` file and add the following lines. It assumes a user called `ubuntu`, yours may be different.

```
{
    "hosts": ["tcp://node3:2376"],
    "tls": true,
    "tlsverify": true,
    "tlscacert": "/home/ubuntu/.docker/ca.pem",
    "tlscert": "/home/ubuntu/.docker/cert.pem",
    "tlskey": "/home/ubuntu/.docker/key.pem"
}
```

Warning! Linux systems running `systemd` don't allow you to use the "hosts" option in `daemon.json`. Instead, you have to specify it in a systemd override file. You may be able to do this with the `sudo systemctl edit docker` command. This will open a new file called `/etc/systemd/system/docker.service.d/override.conf` in an editor. Add the following three lines and save the file.

```
[Service]
ExecStart=
ExecStart=/usr/bin/dockerd -H tcp://node3:2376
```

Now that the TLS and host options are set, you need to restart Docker.

Once Docker has restarted, you can check that the new `hosts` value is in effect by inspecting the output of a `ps` command.

```
$ ps -elf | grep dockerd
4 S root  ... /usr/bin/dockerd -H tcp://node3:2376
```

The presence of "`-H tcp://node3:2376`" in the command output is evidence the daemon is listening on the network. Port `2376` is the standard port for Docker using TLS. `2375` is the default unsecured port.

At this point, running a command such as `docker version` from `node1` won't work. This is because the **daemon** is configured to listen on the network, but the **Docker client** is still trying use the local IPC socket. Try the command again, but this time adding the `-H tcp://node3:2376` flag.

```
$ docker -H tcp://node3:2376 version
Client:
 Version:       19.03.8
 API version:   1.40
 <Snip>
Get http://daemon:2376/v1.35/version: net/http: HTTP/1.x transport connection broken:
malformed HTTP response "\x15\x03\x01\x00\x02\x02".
* Are you trying to connect to a TLS-enabled daemon without TLS?
```

The command looks better, but it's still not working. This is because the daemon is rejecting all connections from unauthenticated clients.

Congratulations. The Docker daemon is configured to listen on the network and is rejecting connections from unauthenticated clients.

Let's configure the Docker client on `node1` to use TLS.

Configuring the Docker client for TLS

In this section, you'll configure the Docker client on `node1` for two things:

- To connect to a remote daemon over the network
- To sign all `docker` commands

Run all of the following from the node that will run your secure Docker client (`node1` in the example lab).

Export the following environment variable to configure the client to connect to the remote daemon over the network. The client must be able to connect to the daemon by name for this to work.

```
export DOCKER_HOST=tcp://node3:2376
```

Try the following command.

```
$ docker version
Client:
 Version:       19.03.8
 <Snip>
Get http://daemon:2376/v1.35/version: net/http: HTTP/1.x transport connection broken:
malformed HTTP response "\x15\x03\x01\x00\x02\x02".
* Are you trying to connect to a TLS-enabled daemon without TLS?
```

The Docker client is now sending commands to the remote daemon across the network without you having to explicitly specify the `-H tcp://node3:2376` flag. However, you still need to configure the client to sign commands.

Export one more environment variable to tell the Docker client to sign all commands with its certificate.

```
export DOCKER_TLS_VERIFY=1
```

Run the `docker version` command again.

```
$ docker version
Client:
 Version:       19.03.8
<Snip>
Server:
 Engine:
  Version:       19.03.8
  API version:   1.40 (minimum version 1.12)
  Go version:    go1.12.17
  Git commit:    afacb8b
  Built:         Wed Mar 11 01:29:16 2020
  OS/Arch:       linux/amd64
  Experimental:  true
```

Congratulations. The client is successfully talking to the remote daemon over a secure network connection. The final configuration of the lab is shown in Figure 5.8

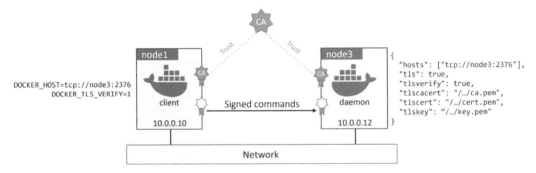

Figure 5.8

A couple of final points before we do a quick recap.

1. This last example works because you copied the clients TLS keys to the folder that Docker expects them to be in. This is a hidden folder in your user's home directory called .docker. You also gave the keys the default filenames that Docker expects (ca.pem, cert.pem, and key.pem). You can specify a different folder by exporting DOCKER_CERT_PATH.

2. You will probably want to make the environment variables (DOCKER_HOST and DOCKER_TLS_VERIFY) more permanent fixtures of your environment.

Chapter summary

The Docker engine is modular in design and based heavily on open-standards from the OCI.

The *Docker daemon* implements the Docker API which is currently a rich, versioned, HTTP API that has developed alongside the rest of the Docker project.

Container execution is handled by *containerd*. containerd was written by Docker, Inc. and contributed to the CNCF. You can think of it as a container supervisor that handles container lifecycle operations. It is small and lightweight and can be used by other projects and third-party tools. For example, it's becoming the most common container runtime in Kubernetes.

containerd needs to talk to an OCI-compliant container runtime to actually create containers. By default, Docker uses *runc* as its default container runtime. runc is the de facto implementation of the OCI runtime-spec and expects to start containers from OCI-compliant bundles. containerd talks to runc and ensures Docker images are presented to runc as OCI-compliant bundles.

runc can be used as a standalone CLI tool to create containers. It's based on code from libcontainer, and can also be used by other projects and third-party tools.

There is still a lot of functionality implemented in the Docker daemon. More of this may be broken out over time. Functionality currently still inside of the Docker daemon includes, but is not limited to; the Docker API, image management, authentication, security features and core networking.

6: Images

In this chapter we'll dive deep into Docker images. The aim of the game is to give you a **solid understanding** of what Docker images are, how to perform basic operations, and how they work under-the-hood.

We'll see how to build new images with our own applications inside of them in a later chapter.

We'll split this chapter into the usual three parts:

- The TLDR
- The deep dive
- The commands

Docker images - The TLDR

A Docker image is a unit of packaging that contains everything required for an application to run. This includes; application code, application dependencies, and OS constructs. If you have an application's Docker image, the only other thing you need to run that application is a computer running Docker.

If you're a former VM admin, you can think of Docker images as similar to VM templates. A VM template is like a stopped VM — a Docker image is like a stopped container. If you're a developer you can think of them as similar to *classes*.

You get Docker images by *pulling* them from an image registry. The most common registry is Docker Hub[10], but others exist. The *pull* operation downloads the image to your local Docker host where Docker can use it to start one or more containers.

Images are made up of multiple *layers* that are stacked on top of each other and represented as a single object. Inside of the image is a cut-down operating system (OS) and all of the files and dependencies required to run an application. Because containers are intended to be fast and lightweight, images tend to be small (Microsoft images tend to be huge).

Congrats! You now have half a clue what a Docker image is :-D Now it's time to blow your mind!

Docker images - The deep dive

We've mentioned a couple of times already that **images** are like stopped containers (or **classes** if you're a developer). In fact, you can stop a container and create a new image from it. With this in mind, images are considered *build-time* constructs, whereas containers are *run-time* constructs.

---

[10]https://hub.docker.com

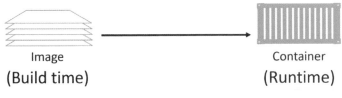

Image   Container
(Build time)   **(Runtime)**

Figure 6.1

Images and containers

Figure 6.1 shows high-level view of the relationship between images and containers. We use the `docker container run` and `docker service create` commands to start one or more containers from a single image. Once you've started a container from an image, the two constructs become dependent on each other and you cannot delete the image until the last container using it has been stopped and destroyed. Attempting to delete an image without stopping and destroying all containers using it will result in an error.

Images are usually small

The whole purpose of a container is to run a single application or service. This means it only needs the code and dependencies of the app/service it is running — it does not need anything else. This results in small images stripped of all non-essential parts.

For example, Docker images do not ship with 6 different shells for you to choose from. In fact, many application images ship without a shell – if the application doesn't need a shell to run it doesn't need to be included in the image. General purpose images such as busybox and Ubuntu ship with a shell, but when you package your business applications for production, you will probably package them without a shell.

Image also don't contain a kernel — all containers running on a Docker host share access to the host's kernel. For these reasons, we sometimes say images contain *just enough operating system* (usually just OS-related files and filesystem objects).

> **Note:** Hyper-V containers run a single container inside of a dedicated lightweight VM. The container leverages the kernel of the OS running inside the VM.

The official *Alpine Linux* Docker image is about 5MB in size and is an extreme example of how small Docker images can be. That's not a typo! It really is about 5 megabytes! Some images are even smaller, however, a more typical example might be something like the official Ubuntu Docker image which is currently about 40MB. These are clearly stripped of most non-essential parts!

Windows-based images tend to be a lot bigger than Linux-based images because of the way that the Windows OS works. It's not uncommon for Windows images to be several gigabytes and take a long time to pull.

Pulling images

A cleanly installed Docker host has no images in its local repository.

The local image repository on a Linux-based Docker host is usually located at `/var/lib/docker/<storage-driver>`. On Windows-based Docker hosts this is `C:\ProgramData\docker\windowsfilter`. If you're using Docker on your Mac or PC with Docker Desktop, everything runs inside of a VM.

You can use the following command to check if your Docker host has any images in its local repository.

```
$ docker image ls
REPOSITORY   TAG       IMAGE ID      CREATED       SIZE
```

The process of getting images onto a Docker host is called *pulling*. So, if you want the latest Busybox image on your Docker host, you'd have to *pull* it. Use the following commands to *pull* some images and then check their sizes.

> If you are following along on Linux and haven't added your user account to the local `docker` Unix group, you may need to add `sudo` to the beginning of all the following commands.

Linux example:

```
$ docker image pull redis:latest
latest: Pulling from library/ubuntu
latest: Pulling from library/redis
54fec2fa59d0: Already exists
9c94e11103d9: Pull complete
04ab1bfc453f: Pull complete
5f71e6b94d83: Pull complete
2729a8234dd5: Pull complete
2683d7f17745: Pull complete
Digest: sha256:157a9...ad7d28c0f9f
Status: Downloaded newer image for redis:latest
docker.io/library/redis:latest

$ docker image pull alpine:latest
latest: Pulling from library/alpine
cbdbe7a5bc2a: Pull complete
Digest: sha256:9a839e63dad54c3a6d1834e29692c8492d93f90c59c978c1ed79109ea4fb9a54
Status: Downloaded newer image for alpine:latest
docker.io/library/alpine:latest

$ docker image ls
REPOSITORY    TAG       IMAGE ID      CREATED         SIZE
alpine        latest    f70734b6a266  40 hours ago    5.61MB
redis         latest    a4d3716dbb72  45 hours ago    98.3MB
```

Windows example:

```
> docker image pull mcr.microsoft.com/powershell:latest
latest: Pulling from powershell
5b663e3b9104: Pull complete
9018627900ee: Pull complete
133ab280ee0f: Pull complete
084853899645: Pull complete
399a2a3857ed: Pull complete
6c1c6d29a559: Pull complete
d1495ba41b1c: Pull complete
190bd9d6eb96: Pull complete
7c239384fec8: Pull complete
21aee845547a: Pull complete
f951bda9026b: Pull complete
Digest: sha256:fbc9555...123f3bd7
Status: Downloaded newer image for mcr.microsoft.com/powershell:latest
mcr.microsoft.com/powershell:latest

> docker image ls
REPOSITORY                          TAG      IMAGE ID       CREATED      SIZE
mcr.microsoft.com/powershell        latest   73175ce91dff   2 days ago   495MB
mcr.microsoft.com/.../iis           latest   6e5c6561c432   3 days ago   5.05GB
```

As you can see, the images just pulled are now present in the Docker host's local repository. You can also see that the Windows images are a lot larger and comprise many more layers.

Image naming

As part of each command, we had to specify which image to pull. Let's take a minute to look at image naming. To do that we need a bit of background on how images are stored.

Image registries

We store images in centralised places called *image registries*. This makes it easy to share and access them.

The most common registry is Docker Hub (https://hub.docker.com). Other registries exist, including 3rd party registries and secure on-premises registries. However, the Docker client is opinionated and defaults to using Docker Hub. We'll be using Docker Hub for the rest of the book.

The output of the following command is snipped, but you can see that Docker is configured to use https://index.docker.io/v1/ as its default registry when pushing and pulling images (this actually redirects to v2).

```
$ docker info
Server:
 Containers: 22
 ...
 containerd version: 7ad184331fa3e55e52b890ea95e65ba581ae3429
 runc version: dc9208a3303feef5b3839f4323d9beb36df0a9dd
 Docker Root Dir: /var/lib/docker
 ...
 Registry: https://index.docker.io/v1/
 ...
```

Image registries contain one or more *image repositories*. In turn, image repositories contain one or more images. That might be a bit confusing, so Figure 6.2 shows a picture of an image registry with 3 repositories, and each repository has one or more images.

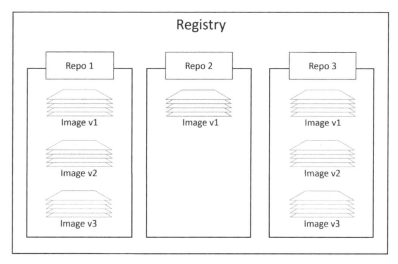

Figure 6.2

Official and unofficial repositories

Docker Hub has the concept of *official repositories* and *unofficial repositories*.

As the name suggests, *official repositories* are the home to images that have been vetted and curated by Docker, Inc. This means they should contain up-to-date, high-quality code, that is secure, well-documented, and in-line with best practices.

Unofficial repositories can be like the wild-west — you should not assume they are safe, well-documented or built according to best practices. That's not saying everything in *unofficial repositories* is bad. There's some excellent stuff in *unofficial repositories*. You just need to be very careful before trusting code from them. To be honest, you should always be careful when trusting software from the internet — even images from *official repositories*.

Most of the popular applications and base operating systems have their own *official repositories* on Docker Hub. They're easy to spot because they live at the top level of the Docker Hub namespace. The following list contains a few of the *official repositories*, and shows their URLs that exist at the top-level of the Docker Hub namespace:

- **nginx**: https://hub.docker.com/_/nginx/
- **busybox**: https://hub.docker.com/_/busybox/
- **redis**: https://hub.docker.com/_/redis/
- **mongo**: https://hub.docker.com/_/mongo/

On the other hand, my own personal images live in the wild west of *unofficial repositories* and should **not** be trusted. Here are some examples of images in my repositories:

- nigelpoulton/tu-demo — https://hub.docker.com/r/nigelpoulton/tu-demo/
- nigelpoulton/pluralsight-docker-ci — https://hub.docker.com/r/nigelpoulton/pluralsight-docker-ci/

Not only are images in my repositories **not** vetted, **not** kept up-to-date, **not** secure, and **not** well documented... they also don't live at the top-level of the Docker Hub namespace. My repositories all live within the `nigelpoulton` second-level namespace.

You'll probably notice that the Microsoft images we've used do not exist at the top-level of the Docker Hub namespace. At the time of writing, they exist under the official `mcr.microsoft.com` second-level namespace. This is due to legal reasons requiring them to be hosted outside of Docker Hub. However, they are integrated into the Docker Hub namespace to make the experience of pulling them as seamless as possible.

After all of that, we can finally look at how we address images on the Docker command line.

Image naming and tagging

Addressing images from official repositories is as simple as providing the repository name and tag separated by a colon (:). The format for `docker image pull`, when working with an image from an official repository is:

```
$ docker image pull <repository>:<tag>
```

In the Linux examples from earlier, we pulled an Alpine and a Redis image with the following two commands:

```
$ docker image pull alpine:latest and docker image pull redis:latest
```

These two commands pull the images tagged as "latest" from the top-level "alpine" and "redis" repositories.

The following examples show how to pull various different images from *official repositories*:

```
$ docker image pull mongo:4.2.6
//This will pull the image tagged as `4.2.6` from the official `mongo` repository.

$ docker image pull busybox:latest
//This will pull the image tagged as `latest` from the official `busybox` repository.

$ docker image pull alpine
//This will pull the image tagged as `latest` from the official `alpine` repository.
```

A couple of points about those commands.

First, if you **do not** specify an image tag after the repository name, Docker will assume you are referring to the image tagged as `latest`. If the repository doesn't have an image tagged as `latest` the command will fail.

Second, the latest tag doesn't have any magical powers. Just because an image is tagged as latest does not guarantee it is the most recent image in a repository. For example, the most recent image in the alpine repository is usually tagged as edge. Moral of the story — take care when using the latest tag.

Pulling images from an *unofficial repository* is essentially the same — you just need to prepend the repository name with a Docker Hub username or organization name. The following example shows how to pull the v2 image from the tu-demo repository owned by a not-to-be-trusted person whose Docker Hub account name is nigelpoulton.

```
$ docker image pull nigelpoulton/tu-demo:v2
//This will pull the image tagged as `v2`
//from the `tu-demo` repository within the `nigelpoulton` namespace
```

In our earlier Windows example, we pulled the PowerShell image with the following command:

```
> docker image pull mcr.microsoft.com/powershell:latest
```

This pulls the image tagged as latest from the mcr.microsoft.com/powershell repository.

If you want to pull images from 3rd party registries (not Docker Hub), you need to prepend the repository name with the DNS name of the registry. For example, the following command pulls the 3.1.5 image from the google-containers/git-sync repo on the Google Container Registry (gcr.io).

```
$ docker image pull gcr.io/google-containers/git-sync:v3.1.5
v3.1.5: Pulling from google-containers/git-sync
597de8ba0c30: Pull complete
b263d8e943d1: Pull complete
a20ed723abc0: Pull complete
49535c7e3a51: Pull complete
4a20d0825f07: Pull complete
Digest: sha256:f38673f25b8...b5f8f63c4da7cc6
Status: Downloaded newer image for gcr.io/google-containers/git-sync:v3.1.5
gcr.io/google-containers/git-sync:v3.1.5
```

Notice how the pull experience is exactly the same from Docker Hub and the Google Container Registry.

Images with multiple tags

One final word about image tags... A single image can have as many tags as you want. This is because tags are arbitrary alpha-numeric values that are stored as metadata alongside the image. Let's look at an example.

Pull all of the images in a repository by adding the -a flag to the docker image pull command. Then run docker image ls to look at the images pulled.

It's probably not a good idea to pull all images from an mcr.microsoft.com repository because Microsoft images can be so large. Also, if the repository you are pulling contains images for multiple architectures and platforms, such as Linux **and** Windows, the command is likely to fail. We recommend you use the command and repository in the following example.

```
$ docker image pull -a nigelpoulton/tu-demo
latest: Pulling from nigelpoulton/tu-demo
aad63a933944: Pull complete
f229563217f5: Pull complete
<Snip>>
Digest: sha256:c9f8e18822...6cbb9a74cf
v1: Pulling from nigelpoulton/tu-demo
aad63a933944: Already exists
f229563217f5: Already exists
<Snip>
fc669453c5af: Pull complete
Digest: sha256:674cb03444...f8598e4d2a
v2: Pulling from nigelpoulton/tu-demo
Digest: sha256:c9f8e18822...6cbb9a74cf
Status: Downloaded newer image for nigelpoulton/tu-demo
docker.io/nigelpoulton/tu-demo

$ docker image ls
REPOSITORY              TAG        IMAGE ID       CREATED       SIZE
nigelpoulton/tu-demo    latest     d5e1e48cf932   2 weeks ago   104MB
nigelpoulton/tu-demo    v2         d5e1e48cf932   2 weeks ago   104MB
nigelpoulton/tu-demo    v1         6852022de69d   2 weeks ago   104MB
```

A couple of things about what just happened:

First. The command pulled three images from the `nigelpoulton/tu-demo` repository: `latest`, `v1`, and `v2`.

Second. Look closely at the `IMAGE ID` column in the output of the `docker image ls` command. You'll see that two of the IDs match. This is because two of the tags refer to the same image. Put another way... one of the images has two tags. If you look closely, you'll see that the `v2` and `latest` tags have the same `IMAGE ID`. This means they're two tags of the **same image**.

This is a perfect example of the warning issued earlier about the `latest` tag. In this example, the `latest` tag refers to the same image as the `v2` tag. This means it's pointing to the older of the two images! Moral of the story, `latest` is an arbitrary tag and is not guaranteed to point to the newest image in a repository!

Filtering the output of `docker image ls`

Docker provides the `--filter` flag to filter the list of images returned by `docker image ls`.

The following example will only return dangling images.

```
$ docker image ls --filter dangling=true
REPOSITORY      TAG        IMAGE ID       CREATED       SIZE
<none>          <none>     4fd34165afe0   7 days ago    14.5MB
```

A dangling image is an image that is no longer tagged, and appears in listings as `<none>:<none>`. A common way they occur is when building a new image giving it a tag that already exists. When this happens, Docker will build the new image, notice that an existing image already has the same tag, remove the tag from the existing image and give it to the new image.

Consider this example, you build a new application image based on `alpine:3.4` and tag it as `dodge:challenger`. Then you update the image to use `alpine:3.5` instead of `alpine:3.4`. When you build the new image, the operation will create a new image tagged as `dodge:challenger` and remove the tags from the old image. The old image will become a dangling image.

You can delete all dangling images on a system with the `docker image prune` command. If you add the `-a` flag, Docker will also remove all unused images (those not in use by any containers).

Docker currently supports the following filters:

- `dangling`: Accepts `true` or `false`, and returns only dangling images (true), or non-dangling images (false).
- `before`: Requires an image name or ID as argument, and returns all images created before it.
- `since`: Same as above, but returns images created after the specified image.
- `label`: Filters images based on the presence of a label or label and value. The `docker image ls` command does not display labels in its output.

For all other filtering you can use `reference`.

Here's an example using `reference` to display only images tagged as "latest".

```
$ docker image ls --filter=reference="*:latest"
REPOSITORY    TAG      IMAGE ID       CREATED       SIZE
alpine        latest   f70734b6a266   3 days ago    5.61MB
redis         latest   a4d3716dbb72   3 days ago    98.3MB
busybox       latest   be5888e67be6   12 days ago   1.22MB
```

You can also use the `--format` flag to format output using Go templates. For example, the following command will only return the size property of images on a Docker host.

```
$ docker image ls --format "{{.Size}}"
5.61MB
98.3MB
1.22MB
```

Use the following command to return all images, but only display repo, tag and size.

```
$ docker image ls --format "{{.Repository}}: {{.Tag}}: {{.Size}}"
alpine:   latest: 5.61MB
redis:    latest: 98.3MB
busybox: latest: 1.22MB
```

If you need more powerful filtering, you can always use the tools provided by your OS and shell such as `grep` and `awk`.

Searching Docker Hub from the CLI

The `docker search` command lets you search Docker Hub from the CLI. This has limited value as you can only pattern-match against strings in the "NAME" field. However, you can filter output based on any of the returned columns.

In its simplest form, it searches for all repos containing a certain string in the "NAME" field. For example, the following command searches for all repos with "nigelpoulton" in the "NAME" field.

```
$ docker search nigelpoulton
NAME                          DESCRIPTION               STARS    AUTOMATED
nigelpoulton/pluralsight..    Web app used in...        22       [OK]
nigelpoulton/tu-demo                                    12
nigelpoulton/k8sbook          Kubernetes Book web app   2
nigelpoulton/workshop101      Kubernetes 101 Workshop   0
<Snip>
```

The "NAME" field is the repository name. This includes the Docker ID, or organization name, for unofficial repositories. For example, the following command will list all repositories that include the string "alpine" in the name.

```
$ docker search alpine
NAME                  DESCRIPTION        STARS    OFFICIAL    AUTOMATED
alpine                A minimal Docker.. 6386     [OK]
mhart/alpine-node     Minimal Node.js..  465
anapsix/alpine-java   Oracle Java 8...   442                  [OK]
<Snip>
```

Notice how some of the repositories returned are official and some are unofficial. You can use `--filter` `"is-official=true"` so that only official repos are displayed.

```
$ docker search alpine --filter "is-official=true"
NAME                  DESCRIPTION        STARS    OFFICIAL    AUTOMATED
alpine                A minimal Docker.. 6386     [OK]
```

You can do the same again, but this time only show repos with automated builds.

```
$ docker search alpine --filter "is-automated=true"
NAME                    DESCRIPTION              OFFICIAL    AUTOMATED
anapsix/alpine-java     Oracle Java 8 (and 7)..              [OK]
frolvlad/alpine-glibc   Alpine Docker image..                [OK]
alpine/git              A simple git container..             [OK]

<Snip>
```

\

One last thing about `docker search`. By default, Docker will only display 25 lines of results. However, you can use the `--limit` flag to increase that to a maximum of 100.

Images and layers

A Docker image is just a bunch of loosely-connected read-only layers, with each layer comprising one or more files. This is shown in Figure 6.3.

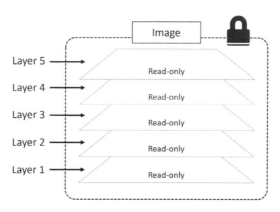

Figure 6.3

Docker takes care of stacking these layers and representing them as a single unified object.

There are a few ways to see and inspect the layers that make up an image. In fact, we saw one earlier when pulling images. The following example looks closer at an image pull operation.

```
$ docker image pull ubuntu:latest
latest: Pulling from library/ubuntu
952132ac251a: Pull complete
82659f8f1b76: Pull complete
c19118ca682d: Pull complete
8296858250fe: Pull complete
24e0251a0e2c: Pull complete
Digest: sha256:f4691c96e6bbaa99d...28ae95a60369c506dd6e6f6ab
Status: Downloaded newer image for ubuntu:latest
docker.io/ubuntu:latest
```

Each line in the output above that ends with "Pull complete" represents a layer in the image that was pulled. As we can see, this image has 5 layers. Figure 6.4 shows this in picture form with layer IDs.

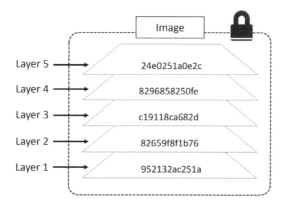

Figure 6.4

Another way to see the layers of an image is to inspect the image with the `docker image inspect` command. The following example inspects the same `ubuntu:latest` image.

```
$ docker image inspect ubuntu:latest
[
    {
        "Id": "sha256:bd3d4369ae.......fa2645f5699037d7d8c6b415a10",
        "RepoTags": [
            "ubuntu:latest"

        <Snip>

        "RootFS": {
            "Type": "layers",
            "Layers": [
                "sha256:c8a75145fc...894129005e461a43875a094b93412",
                "sha256:c6f2b330b6...7214ed6aac305dd03f70b95cdc610",
                "sha256:055757a193...3a9565d78962c7f368d5ac5984998",
                "sha256:4837348061...12695f548406ea77feb5074e195e3",
                "sha256:0cad5e07ba...4bae4cfc66b376265e16c32a0aae9"
            ]
        }
    }
]
```

The trimmed output shows 5 layers again. Only this time they're shown using their SHA256 hashes.

The `docker image inspect` command is a great way to see the details of an image.

The `docker history` command is another way of inspecting an image and seeing layer data. However, it shows the build history of an image and is **not** a strict list of layers in the final image. For example, some Dockerfile instructions ("ENV", "EXPOSE", "CMD", and "ENTRYPOINT") add metadata to the image and do not result in permanent layers being created.

All Docker images start with a base layer, and as changes are made and new content is added, new layers are added on top.

Consider the following oversimplified example of building a simple Python application. You might have a corporate policy that all applications are based on the official Ubuntu 20:04 image. This would be your image's *base layer*. If you then add the Python package, this will be added as a second layer on top of the base layer. If you later add source code files, these will be added as additional layers. Your final image would have three layers as shown in Figure 6.5 (remember this is an over-simplified example for demonstration purposes).

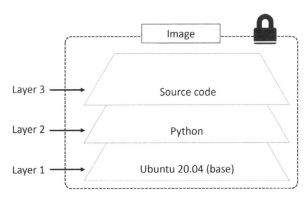

Figure 6.5

It's important to understand that as additional layers are added, the *image* is always the combination of all layers stacked in the order they were added. Take a simple example of two layers as shown in Figure 6.6. Each *layer* has 3 files, but the overall *image* has 6 files as it is the combination of both layers.

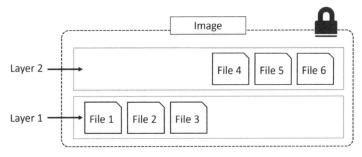

Figure 6.6

> **Note:** We've shown the image layers in Figure 6.6 in a slightly different way to previous figures. This is just to make showing the files easier.

In the slightly more complex example of the three-layer image in Figure 6.7, the overall image only presents 6 files in the unified view. This is because File 7 in the top layer is an updated version of File 5 directly below (inline). In this situation, the file in the higher layer obscures the file directly below it. This allows updated versions of files to be added as new layers to the image.

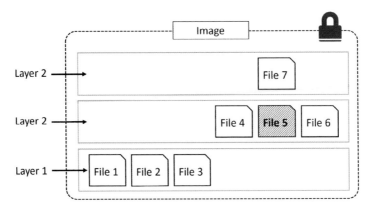

Figure 6.7

Docker employs a storage driver that is responsible for stacking layers and presenting them as a single unified filesystem/image. Examples of storage drivers on Linux include AUFS, overlay2, devicemapper, btrfs and zfs. As their names suggest, each one is based on a Linux filesystem or block-device technology, and each has its own unique performance characteristics. The only driver supported by Docker on Windows is windowsfilter, which implements layering and CoW on top of NTFS.

No matter which storage driver is used, the user experience is the same.

Figure 6.8 shows the same 3-layer image as it will appear to the system. I.e. all three layers stacked and merged, giving a single unified view.

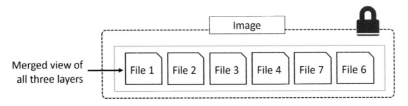

Figure 6.8

Sharing image layers

Multiple images can, and do, share layers. This leads to efficiencies in space and performance.

Let's take a second look at the docker image pull command with the -a flag that we ran previously to pull all tagged images in the nigelpoulton/tu-demo repository.

```
$ docker image pull -a nigelpoulton/tu-demo
latest: Pulling from nigelpoulton/tu-demo
aad63a933944: Pull complete
f229563217f5: Pull complete
<Snip>>
Digest: sha256:c9f8e18822...6cbb9a74cf

v1: Pulling from nigelpoulton/tu-demo
aad63a933944: Already exists
f229563217f5: Already exists
<Snip>
fc669453c5af: Pull complete
Digest: sha256:674cb03444...f8598e4d2a

v2: Pulling from nigelpoulton/tu-demo
Digest: sha256:c9f8e18822...6cbb9a74cf
Status: Downloaded newer image for nigelpoulton/tu-demo
docker.io/nigelpoulton/tu-demo

$ docker image ls
REPOSITORY            TAG       IMAGE ID       CREATED       SIZE
nigelpoulton/tu-demo  latest    d5e1e48cf932   2 weeks ago   104MB
nigelpoulton/tu-demo  v2        d5e1e48cf932   2 weeks ago   104MB
nigelpoulton/tu-demo  v1        6852022de69d   2 weeks ago   104MB
```

Notice the lines ending in `Already exists`.

These lines tell us that Docker is smart enough to recognize when it's being asked to pull an image layer that it already has a local copy of. In this example, Docker pulled the image tagged as `latest` first. Then, when it pulled the `v1` and `v2` images, it noticed that it already had some of the layers that make up those images. This happens because the three images in this repository are almost identical, and therefore share many layers. In fact, the only difference between `v1` and `v2` is the top layer.

As mentioned previously, Docker on Linux supports many storage drivers. Each is free to implement image layering, layer sharing, and copy-on-write (CoW) behaviour in its own way. However, the overall result and user experience is essentially the same. Although Windows only supports a single storage driver, that driver provides the same experience as Linux.

Pulling images by digest

So far, we've shown you how to pull images using their name (tag). This is by far the most common method, but it has a problem — tags are mutable! This means it's possible to accidentally tag an image with the wrong tag (name). Sometimes, it's even possible to tag an image with the same tag as an existing, but different, image. This can cause problems!

As an example, imagine you've got an image called `golftrack:1.5` and it has a known bug. You pull the image, apply a fix, and push the updated image back to its repository using the **same tag**.

Take a moment to consider what happened there... You have an image called `golftrack:1.5` that has a bug. That image is being used by containers in your production environment. You create a new version of the image that includes a fix. Then comes the mistake... you build and push the fixed image back to its repository with the **same**

tag as the vulnerable image!. This overwrites the original image and leaves you without a great way of knowing which of your production containers are using the vulnerable image and which are using the fixed image — they both have the same tag!

This is where *image digests* come to the rescue.

Docker 1.10 introduced a content addressable storage model. As part of this model, all images get a cryptographic *content hash*. For the purposes of this discussion, we'll refer to this hash as the *digest*. As the digest is a hash of the contents of the image, it's impossible to change the contents of the image without creating a new unique digest. Put another way, you cannot change the content of an image and keep the old digest. This means digests are immutable and provide a solution to the problem we just talked about.

Every time you pull an image, the `docker image pull` command includes the image's digest as part of the information returned. You can also view the digests of images in your Docker host's local repository by adding the `--digests` flag to the `docker image ls` command. These are both shown in the following example.

```
$ docker image pull alpine
Using default tag: latest
latest: Pulling from library/alpine
cbdbe7a5bc2a: Pull complete
Digest: sha256:9a839e63da...9ea4fb9a54
Status: Downloaded newer image for alpine:latest
docker.io/library/alpine:latest

$ docker image ls --digests alpine
REPOSITORY    TAG      DIGEST                            IMAGE ID        CREATED      SIZE
alpine        latest   sha256:9a839e63da...9ea4fb9a54    f70734b6a266    2 days ago   5.61MB
```

The snipped output above shows the digest for the `alpine` image as -

`sha256:9a839e63da...9ea4fb9a54`

Now that we know the digest of the image, we can use it when pulling the image again. This will ensure that we get **exactly the image we expect!**

At the time of writing, there is no native Docker command that will retrieve the digest of an image from a remote registry such as Docker Hub. This means the only way to determine the digest of an image is to pull it by tag and then make a note of its digest. This may change in the future.

The following example deletes the `alpine:latest` image from your Docker host and then shows how to pull it again using its digest instead of its tag. The actual digest is truncated in the book so that it fits on one line. Substitute this for the real digest of the version you pulled on your own system.

```
$ docker image rm alpine:latest
Untagged: alpine:latest
Untagged: alpine@sha256:c0537...7c0a7726c88e2bb7584dc96
Deleted: sha256:02674b9cb179d...abff0c2bf5ceca5bad72cd9
Deleted: sha256:e154057080f40...3823bab1be5b86926c6f860

$ docker image pull alpine@sha256:9a839e63da...9ea4fb9a54
sha256:9a839e63da...9ea4fb9a54: Pulling from library/alpine
cbdbe7a5bc2a: Pull complete
Digest: sha256:9a839e63da...9ea4fb9a54
Status: Downloaded newer image for alpine@sha256:9a839e63da...9ea4fb9a54
docker.io/library/alpine@sha256:9a839e63da...9ea4fb9a54
```

A little bit more about image hashes (digests)

Since Docker version 1.10, an image is a very loose collection of independent layers.

In some ways, the *image* itself is just a configuration file that lists the layers and some metadata.

The *layers* are where the data lives (files and code etc.). Each layer is fully independent, and has no concept of being part of an overall bigger image.

Each *image* is identified by a crypto ID that is a hash of the config file. Each *layer* is identified by a crypto ID that is a hash of the layer content. we call these "content hashes".

This means that changing the contents of the image, or any of its layers, will cause the associated crypto hashes to change. As a result, images and layers are immutable, and we can easily identify any changes made to either.

So far, things are pretty simple. But they're about to get a bit more complicated.

When we push and pull images, we compress their layers to save network bandwidth as well as storage space in the image registry. This is great, but compressed content looks different to uncompressed content. As a result, content hashes no longer match after `push` or `pull` operations.

This presents various problems. For example, Docker Hub verifies every pushed layer to make sure it wasn't tampered with en route. To do this, it runs a hash against the layer content and checks it against the hash that was sent. As the layer was compressed (changed) the hash verification will fail.

To get around this, each layer also gets something called a *distribution hash*. This is a hash of the compressed version of the layer and is included with every layer pushed or pulled to a registry. This can then be used to verify that the layer arrived without being tampered with.

As well as providing a cryptographically verifiable way to verify image and layer integrity, it also avoids ID collisions that could occur if image and layer IDs were randomly generated.

Multi-architecture images

One of the best things about Docker is its simplicity. However, as technologies grow, things get more complex. This happened for Docker when it started supporting multiple different platforms and architectures such as Windows and Linux, on variations of ARM, x64, PowerPC, and s390x. All of a sudden, popular images had versions for different platforms and architectures. As developers and operators, we had to make sure we were pulling the correct version for the platform and architecture we were using. This broke the smooth Docker experience.

Note: We're using the term "architecture" to refer to CPU architecture such as x64 and ARM. We use the term "platform" to refer to either the OS (Linux or Windows) or the combination of OS and architecture.

Multi-architecture images to the rescue!

Fortunately, Docker and Docker Hub have a slick way of supporting multi-arch images. This means a single image, such as `golang:latest`, can have an image for Linux on x64, Linux on PowerPC, Windows x64, Linux on different versions of ARM, and more. To be clear, we're talking about a single image tag supporting multiple platforms and architectures. We'll see it in action in a second, but it means you can run a simple `docker image pull goloang:latest` from any platform or architecture and Docker will pull the correct image for your platform and architecture.

To make this happen, the Registry API supports two important constructs:

- **manifest lists**
- **manifests**

The **manifest list** is exactly what it sounds like: a list of architectures supported by a particular image tag. Each supported architecture then has its own *manifest* detailing the layers that make it up.

Figure 6.9 uses the official `golang` image as an example. On the left is the **manifest list** with entries for each architecture the image supports. The arrows show that each entry in the **manifest list** points to a **manifest** containing image config and layer data.

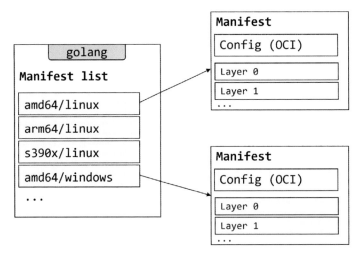

Figure 6.9

Let's look at the theory before seeing it in action.

Assume you are running Docker on a Raspberry Pi (Linux running on ARM architecture). When you pull an image, your Docker client makes the relevant calls to the Docker Registry API exposed by Docker Hub. If a **manifest list** exists for the image, it will be parsed to see if an entry exists for Linux on ARM. If an ARM entry exists, the **manifest** for that image is retrieved and parsed for the crypto ID's of the layers that make up the image. Each layer is then pulled from Docker Hub.

The following examples show how this works by starting a new container from the official `golang` image and running the `go version` command inside the container. The output of the `go version` command shows the version of Go as well as the platform and CPU architecture of the container/host. The thing to note, is that both examples use the exact same `docker container run` command. We do not have to tell Docker that we need the Linux x64 or Windows x64 versions of the image. We just run normal commands and let Docker take care of getting the right image for the platform and architecture we are running!

Linux on x64 example:

```
$ docker container run --rm golang go version
<Snip>
go version go1.14.2 linux/amd64
```

Windows on x64 example:

```
> docker container run --rm golang go version
<Snip>
go version go1.14.2 windows/amd64
```

The Windows Golang image is currently over 5GB in size and may take a long time to download.

The 'docker manifest' command lets you inspect the manifest list of any image on Docker Hub. The following example inspects the manifest list on Docker Hub for the `golang` image. You can see that Linux and Windows are supported on various CPU architectures. You can run the same command without the `grep` filter to see the full JSON manifest list.

```
$ docker manifest inspect golang | grep 'architecture\|os'
            "architecture": "amd64",
            "os": "linux"
            "architecture": "arm",
            "os": "linux",
            "architecture": "arm64",
            "os": "linux",
            "architecture": "386",
            "os": "linux"
            "architecture": "ppc64le",
            "os": "linux"
            "architecture": "s390x",
            "os": "linux"
            "architecture": "amd64",
            "os": "windows",
            "os.version": "10.0.14393.3630"
            "architecture": "amd64",
            "os": "windows",
            "os.version": "10.0.17763.1158"
```

All official images have manifest lists.

You can create your own builds for different platforms and architectures with docker buildx and then use docker manifest create to create your own manifest lists.

The following command builds an image for ARMv7 called myimage:arm-v7 from the contents of the current directory. It's based on code in the code in https://github.com/nigelpoulton/psweb.

```
$ docker buildx build --platform linux/arm/v7 -t myimage:arm-v7 .
[+] Building 44.4s (10/10) FINISHED                                          \

 => [internal] load build definition from Dockerfile          0.1s
 => => transferring dockerfile: 424B                          0.0s
 <Snip>
 => exporting to image                                        3.2s
 => => exporting layers                                       3.2s
 => => writing image sha256:61cc82bdaa...                     0.0s
 => => naming to docker.io/library/myimage:arm-v7             0.0s
```

The beauty of the command is that you don't have to run it from an ARMv7 Docker node. In fact, the example shown was ran on Linux on x64 hardware.

At the time of writing, buildx is an experimental feature and requires experimental=true setting in your ~/.docker/config.json file as follows.

```
{
  "experimental": true
}
```

Deleting Images

When you no longer need an image on your Docker host, you can delete it with the docker image rm command. rm is short for remove.

Deleting an image will remove the image and all of its layers from your Docker host. This means it will no longer show up in docker image ls commands and all directories on the Docker host containing the layer data will be deleted. However, if an image layer is shared by more than one image, that layer will not be deleted until all images that reference it have been deleted.

Delete the images pulled in the previous steps with the docker image rm command. The following example deletes an image by its ID, this might be different on your system.

```
$ docker image rm 02674b9cb179
Untagged: alpine@sha256:c0537ff6a5218...c0a7726c88e2bb7584dc96
Deleted: sha256:02674b9cb179d57...31ba0abff0c2bf5ceca5bad72cd9
Deleted: sha256:e154057080f4063...2a0d13823bab1be5b86926c6f860
```

You can list multiple images on the same command by separating them with whitespace like the following.

```
$ docker image rm f70734b6a266 a4d3716dbb72
```

If the image you are trying to delete is in use by a running container you will not be able to delete it. Stop and delete any containers before trying the delete operation again.

A handy shortcut for **deleting all images** on a Docker host is to run the `docker image rm` command and pass it a list of all image IDs on the system by calling `docker image ls` with the `-q` flag. This is shown next.

If you are following along on a Windows system, this will only work in a PowerShell terminal. It will not work on a CMD prompt.

```
$ docker image rm $(docker image ls -q) -f
```

To understand how this works, download a couple of images and then run `docker image ls -q`.

```
$ docker image pull alpine
Using default tag: latest
latest: Pulling from library/alpine
e110a4a17941: Pull complete
Digest: sha256:3dcdb92d7432d5...3626d99b889d0626de158f73a
Status: Downloaded newer image for alpine:latest

$ docker image pull ubuntu
Using default tag: latest
latest: Pulling from library/ubuntu
952132ac251a: Pull complete
82659f8f1b76: Pull complete
c19118ca682d: Pull complete
8296858250fe: Pull complete
24e0251a0e2c: Pull complete
Digest: sha256:f4691c96e6bba...128ae95a60369c506dd6e6f6ab
Status: Downloaded newer image for ubuntu:latest

$ docker image ls -q
bd3d4369aebc
4e38e38c8ce0
```

See how `docker image ls -q` returns a list containing just the image IDs of all images pulled locally on the system. Passing this list to `docker image rm` will delete all images on the system as shown next.

```
$ docker image rm $(docker image ls -q) -f
Untagged: ubuntu:latest
Untagged: ubuntu@sha256:f4691c9...2128ae95a60369c506dd6e6f6ab
Deleted: sha256:bd3d4369aebc494...fa2645f5699037d7d8c6b415a10
Deleted: sha256:cd10a3b73e247dd...c3a71fcf5b6c2bb28d4f2e5360b
Deleted: sha256:4d4de39110cd250...28bfe816393d0f2e0dae82c363a
Deleted: sha256:6a89826eba8d895...cb0d7dba1ef62409f037c6e608b
Deleted: sha256:33efada9158c32d...195aa12859239d35e7fe9566056
Deleted: sha256:c8a75145fcc4e1a...4129005e461a43875a094b93412
Untagged: alpine:latest
Untagged: alpine@sha256:3dcdb92...313626d99b889d0626de158f73a
Deleted: sha256:4e38e38c8ce0b8d...6225e13b0bfe8cfa2321aec4bba
```

```
Deleted: sha256:4fe15f8d0ae69e1...eeeeebb265cd2e328e15c6a869f

$ docker image ls
REPOSITORY      TAG      IMAGE ID      CREATED      SIZE
```

Let's remind ourselves of the major commands we use to work with Docker images.

Images - The commands

- `docker image pull` is the command to download images. We pull images from repositories inside of remote registries. By default, images will be pulled from repositories on Docker Hub. This command will pull the image tagged as `latest` from the `alpine` repository on Docker Hub: `docker image pull alpine:latest`.
- `docker image ls` lists all of the images stored in your Docker host's local image cache. To see the SHA256 digests of images add the `--digests` flag.
- `docker image inspect` is a thing of beauty! It gives you all of the glorious details of an image — layer data and metadata.
- `docker manifest inspect` allows you to inspect the manifest list of any image stored on Docker Hub. This will show the manifest list for the `redis` image: `docker manifest inspect redis`.
- `docker buildx` is a Docker CLI plugin that extends the Docker CLI to support multi-arch builds.
- `docker image rm` is the command to delete images. This command shows how to delete the `alpine:latest` image — `docker image rm alpine:latest`. You cannot delete an image that is associated with a container in the running (Up) or stopped (Exited) states.

Chapter summary

In this chapter, we learned about Docker images. We learned that they contain everything needed to run an application. This includes; just enough OS, source code files, and dependencies. In some ways, images are like virtual machine templates and are used to start containers. Under the hood they are made up of one or more read-only layers, that when stacked together, make up the overall image.

We used the `docker image pull` command to pull some images into our Docker host's local registry.

We covered image naming, official and unofficial repos, layering, sharing, and crypto IDs.

We looked at how Docker supports multi-architecture and multi-platform images, and we finished off by looking at some of the most common commands used to work with images.

In the next chapter we'll take a similar tour of containers — the runtime sibling of images.

7: Containers

Now that we know a bit about images, it's time to get into containers. As this is a book about Docker, we'll be talking specifically about Docker containers. However, Docker implements the image and container specs published by the Open Container Initiative (OCI) at https://www.opencontainers.org. This means a lot of what you learn here will apply to other container runtimes that are OCI compliant. Also, the things you'll learn will help you if you need to learn and use Kubernetes.

We'll split this chapter into the usual three parts:

- The TLDR
- The deep dive
- The commands

Docker containers - The TLDR

A container is the runtime instance of an image. In the same way that you can start a virtual machine (VM) from a virtual machine template, you start one or more containers from a single image. The big difference between a VM and a container is that containers are faster and more lightweight — instead of running a full-blown OS like a VM, containers share the OS/kernel with the host they're running on. It's also common for containers to be based on minimalist images that only include software and dependencies required by the application.

Figure 7.1 shows a single Docker image being used to start multiple Docker containers.

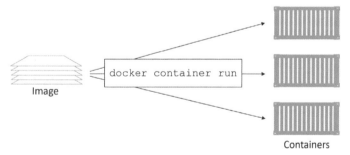

Figure 7.1

The simplest way to start a container is with the `docker container run` command. The command can take a lot of arguments, but in its most basic form you tell it an image to use and a app to run: `docker container run <image> <app>`. The following command will start an Ubuntu Linux container running the Bash shell as its app.

```
$ docker container run -it ubuntu /bin/bash
```

You can use the following command to start a Windows container running the PowerShell app.

```
> docker container run -it mcr.microsoft.com/powershell:nanoserver pwsh.exe
```

In each of the examples, the -it flags will connect your current terminal window to the container's shell.

Containers run until the app they are executing exits. In the previous examples, the Linux container will exit when the Bash shell exits, and the Windows container will exit when the PowerShell process terminates.

A simple way to demonstrate this is to start a new container and tell it to run the sleep command for 10 seconds. The container will start, seize your terminal for 10 seconds, then exit. The following is a simple way to demonstrate this on a Linux Docker host.

```
$ docker container run -it alpine:latest sleep 10
```

You can do the same with a Windows container with the following command.

```
> docker container run microsoft/powershell:nanoserver pwsh -c "Start-Sleep -s 10"
```

You can manually stop a running container with the docker container stop command. You can then restart it with docker container start. To get rid of a container forever, you have to explicitly delete it with docker container rm.

That's the elevator pitch! Now let's get into the detail...

Docker containers - The deep dive

The first things we'll cover here are the fundamental differences between a container and a VM. It's mainly theory at this point, but it's important stuff.

> **Heads-up:** As the author, I'm going to say this before we go any further. A lot of us are passionate about the things we do and the skills we have. You remember *big Unix* people resisting the rise of Linux. You might also remember people resisting VMware in the early days. In both cases **resistance was futile**. In this section I'm going to highlight what I consider some of the advantages the container model has over the VM model. But I'm guessing a lot of you will be VM experts with a lot invested in the VM ecosystem. I'm also guessing that one or two of you might want to fight me over some of the things I say. So let me be clear... I'm a big guy and I'd beat you down in hand-to-hand combat :-D Just kidding. However, I'm not trying to destroy your empire or call your baby ugly. Containers and VMs will run side-by-side for many years to come.

Here we go.

Containers vs VMs

Containers and VMs both need a host to run on. This can be anything from your laptop, a bare metal server in your data center, all the way up to an instance in the public cloud. In fact, many cloud services now offer the ability to run containers on ephemeral serverless back-ends. Don't worry if that sounds like techno-babble, it just means that the back-end is so highly virtualized that the concept of a host or node no longer has any meaning — your container simply runs, and you don't need to care about the *how* or *where*.

Anyway… let's assume a requirement where your business has a single physical server that needs to run 4 business applications.

In the VM model, the physical server is powered on and the hypervisor boots (we're skipping the BIOS and bootloader code etc.). Once booted, the hypervisor lays claim to all physical resources on the system such as CPU, RAM, storage, and NICs. It then carves these hardware resources into virtual versions that look smell and feel exactly like the real thing. It then packages them into a software construct called a virtual machine (VM). We take those VMs and install an operating system and application on each one.

Assuming the scenario of a single physical server that needs to run 4 business applications, we'd create 4 VMs, install 4 operating systems, and then install the 4 applications. When it's all done it looks a bit like Figure 7.2.

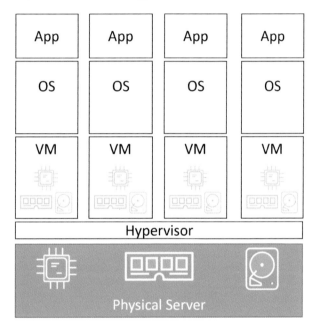

Figure 7.2

Things are a bit different in the container model.

The server is powered on and the OS boots. In the Docker world this can be Linux, or a modern version of Windows that supports the container primitives in its kernel. Similar to the VM model, the OS claims all hardware resources. On top of the OS, we install a container engine such as Docker. The container engine then takes **OS resources** such as the *process tree*, the *filesystem*, and the *network stack*, and carves them into isolated constructs called *containers*. Each container looks smells and feels just like a real OS. Inside of each *container* we run an application.

If we assume the same scenario of a single physical server needing to run 4 business applications, we'd carve the OS into 4 containers and run a single application inside each. This is shown in Figure 7.3.

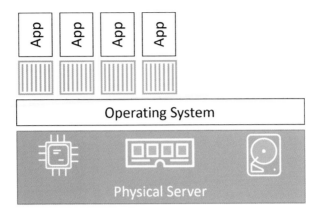

Figure 7.3

At a high level, hypervisors perform **hardware virtualization** — they carve up physical hardware resources into virtual versions called VMs. On the other hand, containers perform **OS virtualization** — they carve OS resources into virtual versions called containers.

The VM tax

Let's build on what we just covered and drill into one of the problems with the hypervisor model.

We started out with a single physical server and the requirement to run 4 business applications. In both models we installed either an OS or a hypervisor (a specialised OS that is highly tuned for VMs). So far, the models are almost identical. But this is where the similarities stop.

The VM model carves **low-level hardware resources** into VMs. Each VM is a software construct containing virtual CPUs, virtual RAM, virtual disks etc. As such, every VM needs its own OS to claim, initialize, and manage all of those virtual resources. And sadly, every OS comes with its own set of baggage and overheads. For example, every OS consumes a slice of CPU, a slice of RAM, a slice of storage etc. Some need their own licenses, as well as people and infrastructure to patch and upgrade them. Each OS also presents a sizable attack surface. We often refer to all of this as the *OS tax*, or *VM tax* — every OS you install consumes resources!

The container model has a single OS/kernel running on the host. It's possible to run tens or hundreds of containers on a single host with every container sharing that single OS/kernel. That means a single OS consuming CPU, RAM, and storage. A single OS that needs licensing. A single OS that needs updating and patching. And a single OS kernel presenting an attack surface. All in all, a single OS tax bill!

That might not seem a lot in our example of a single server running 4 business applications. But when you start talking about hundreds or thousands of apps, it becomes a game-changer.

Another thing to consider is application start times. As a container isn't a full-blown OS, it starts **much faster** than a VM. Remember, there's no kernel inside of a container that needs locating, decompressing, and initializing — not to mention all of the hardware enumerating and initializing associated with a normal kernel bootstrap. None of that is needed when starting a container. The single shared kernel, running on the host machine, is already started. Net result, containers can start in less than a second. The only thing that has an impact on container start time is the time it takes to start the application it's running.

This all amounts to the container model being leaner and more efficient than the VM model. You can pack more applications onto less resources, start them faster, and pay less in licensing and admin costs, as well as present less of an attack surface to the dark side. What's not to like!?

Well, one thing that's not so great about the container model is security. Out of the box, containers are less secure and provide less workload isolation than VMs. Technologies exist to secure containers and lock them down, but at the time of writing, some of them are prohibitively complex.

With the theory out of the way, let's play around with some containers.

Running containers

To follow along with these examples, you'll need a working Docker host. If you don't already have it, I recommend installing Docker Desktop on your Mac or PC (just google "Docker Desktop" and follow the simple next, next, next installation).

We'll show examples for Linux and Windows containers. However, if you're running Docker Desktop on Windows 10, you can follow along with the Linux examples by running Docker Desktop in `Linux containers` mode.

Checking that Docker is running

The first thing I always do when I log on to a Docker host is check that Docker is running.

```
$ docker version
Client: Docker Engine - Community
 Version:          19.03.8
 API version:      1.40
 OS/Arch:          darwin/amd64
 Experimental:     true

Server: Docker Engine - Community
 Engine:
  Version:          19.03.8
  API version:      1.40 (minimum version 1.12)
  OS/Arch:          linux/amd64
  Experimental:     true
  <Snip>
```

As long as you get a response back in the `Client` and `Server` you should be good to go. If you get an error code in the `Server` section, there's a good chance that the Docker daemon (server) isn't running, or that your user account doesn't have permission to access it.

If you're on a Linux machine and your user account doesn't have permission to access the daemon, you need to make sure it's a member of the local `docker` Unix group. If it isn't, you can add it with `usermod -aG docker <user>` and then you'll have to logout and log back in to your shell for the changes to take effect.

If your user account is already a member of the local `docker` group, the problem might be that the Docker daemon isn't running. To check the status of the Docker daemon, run one of the following commands depending on your Docker host's operating system.

Linux systems not using Systemd.

```
$ service docker status
docker start/running, process 29393
```

Linux systems using Systemd.

```
$ systemctl is-active docker
active
```

Windows systems (run from a PowerShell terminal).

```
> Get-Service docker

Status    Name     DisplayName
------    ----     -----------
Running   Docker   Docker Engine
```

If the Docker daemon is running, you're fine to continue.

Starting a simple container

If you're using Docker Desktop, you can follow along with the Linux or Windows examples. Just make sure that Docker Desktop is set to the correct mode.

The simplest way to start a container is with the `docker container run` command.

The following command starts a simple container that will run a containerized version of Ubuntu Linux.

```
$ docker container run -it ubuntu:latest /bin/bash
Unable to find image 'ubuntu:latest' locally
latest: Pulling from library/ubuntu
d51af753c3d3: Pull complete
fc878cd0a91c: Pull complete
6154df8ff988: Pull complete
fee5db0ff82f: Pull complete
Digest: sha256:747d2dbbaaee995098c9792d99bd333c6783ce56150d1b11e333bbceed5c54d7
Status: Downloaded newer image for ubuntu:latest
root@50949b614477:/#
```

The following is a Windows example that starts a container running PowerShell (pwsh.exe).

```
> docker container run -it mcr.microsoft.com/powershell:nanoserver pwsh.exe
docker container run -it mcr.microsoft.com/powershell:nanoserver pwsh.exe
Unable to find image 'mcr.microsoft.com/powershell:nanoserver' locally
nanoserver: Pulling from powershell
0fe89239909b: Pull complete
2c9371eb1f40: Pull complete
<Snip>
806da439b031: Pull complete
Digest: sha256:cefdb984d9...ad3ab2079a
Status: Downloaded newer image for mcr.microsoft.com/powershell:nanoserver

PowerShell 7.0.0
Copyright (c) Microsoft Corporation. All rights reserved.
PS C:\>
```

Let's take a closer look at the command.

`docker container run` tells Docker to run a new container. The `-it` flags make the container interactive and attach it to your terminal. `ubuntu:latest` or `mcr.microsoft.com/powershell:nanoserver` tell Docker which image to start the container from. Finally, `/bin/bash` and `pwsh.exe` are the respective applications each container will run.

When you hit `Return`, the Docker client packaged up the command and POSTed it to the API server running on the Docker daemon. The Docker daemon accepted the command and searched the Docker host's local image repository to see if it already had a copy of the requested image. In the examples cited, it didn't, so it went to Docker Hub to see if it could find it there. It found it, pulled it locally, and stored it in its local cache.

> **Note:** In a standard, out-of-the-box Linux installation, the Docker daemon implements the Docker Remote API on a local IPC/Unix socket at `/var/run/docker.sock`. On Windows, it listens on a named pipe at `npipe:////./pipe/docker_engine`. It's possible to configure the Docker daemon to listen on the network. The default non-TLS network port for Docker is 2375, the default TLS port is 2376.

Once the image was pulled, the daemon instructed `containerd` and `runc` to create and start the container.

If you're following along, your terminal is now attached to the container — look closely and you'll see that your shell prompt has changed. In the Linux example cited, the shell prompt has changed to `root@50949b614477:/#`. The long number after the `@` is the first 12 characters of the container's unique ID. In the Windows example it changed to `PS C:\>`.

Try executing some basic commands inside of the container. You might notice that some of them don't work. This is because the images are optimized to be lightweight. As a result, they don't have all of the normal commands and packages installed. The following example shows a couple of commands — one succeeds and the other one fails.

```
root@50949b614477:/# ls -l
total 64
lrwxrwxrwx   1 root root     7 Apr 23 11:06 bin -> usr/bin
drwxr-xr-x   2 root root  4096 Apr 15 11:09 boot
drwxr-xr-x   5 root root   360 Apr 27 17:24 dev
drwxr-xr-x   1 root root  4096 Apr 27 17:24 etc
drwxr-xr-x   2 root root  4096 Apr 15 11:09 home
lrwxrwxrwx   1 root root     7 Apr 23 11:06 lib -> usr/lib
<Snip>

root@50949b614477:/# ping nigelpoulton.com
bash: ping: command not found
```

As you can see, the `ping` utility is not included as part of the official Ubuntu image.

Container processes

When we started the Ubuntu container in the previous section, we told it to run the Bash shell (`/bin/bash`). This makes the Bash shell the **one and only process running inside of the container**. You can see this by running `ps -elf` from inside the container.

```
root@50949b614477:/# ps -elf
F S UID    PID  PPID   NI ADDR SZ WCHAN  STIME TTY      TIME      CMD
4 S root     1     0    0 -  4558 wait   00:47 ?     00:00:00  /bin/bash
0 R root    11     1    0 -  8604 -      00:52 ?     00:00:00  ps -elf
```

The first process in the list, with PID 1, is the Bash shell we told the container to run. The second process is the `ps -elf` command we ran to produce the list. This is a short-lived process that exits as soon as the output is displayed. Long story short, this container is running a single process — `/bin/bash`.

> **Note:** Windows containers are slightly different and tend to run quite a few background processes.

If you're logged on to the container and type `exit`, you'll terminate the Bash process and the container will exit (terminate). This is because a container cannot exist without its designated main process. This is true of Linux and Windows containers — **killing the main process in the container will kill the container.**

Press `Ctrl-PQ` to exit the container without terminating its main process. Doing this will place you back in the shell of your Docker host and leave the container running in the background. You can use the `docker container ls` command to view the list of running containers on your system.

```
$ docker container ls
CNTNR ID  IMAGE           COMMAND     CREATED   STATUS     NAMES
509...74  ubuntu:latest   /bin/bash   6 mins    Up 6mins   sick_montalcini
```

It's important to understand that this container is still running and you can re-attach your terminal to it with the `docker container exec` command.

```
$ docker container exec -it 50949b614477 bash
root@50949b614477:/#
```

The command to re-attach to the Windows Nano Server PowerShell container would be `docker container exec -it <container-name-or-ID> pwsh.exe`.

As you can see, the shell prompt has changed back to the container. If you run the `ps -elf` command again you will now see **two** Bash or PowerShell processes. This is because the `docker container exec` command created a new Bash or PowerShell process and attached to that. This means typing `exit` in this shell will not terminate the container, because the original Bash or PowerShell process will continue running.

Type `exit` to leave the container and verify it's still running with a `docker container ls`. It will still be running.

If you are following along with the examples, you should stop and delete the container with the following two commands (you will need to substitute the ID of your container).

```
$ docker container stop 50949b614477
50949b614477
```

```
$ docker container rm 50949b614477
50949b614477
```

The containers started in the previous examples will no longer be present on your system.

Container lifecycle

In this section, we'll look at the lifecycle of a container — from birth, through work and vacations, to eventual death.

We've already seen how to start containers with the `docker container run` command. Let's start another one so we can walk it through its entire lifecycle. The following examples will be from a Linux Docker host running an Ubuntu container. However, all of the examples will work with the Windows PowerShell container from previous examples — obviously you'll have to substitute Linux commands with their equivalent Windows commands.

As previously mentioned, if you're running Docker Desktop on a Windows 10 Pro laptop, you can run in Linux containers mode and follow along with all of the Linux examples.

```
$ docker container run --name percy -it ubuntu:latest /bin/bash
root@9cb2d2fd1d65:/#
```

That's the container created, and we named it "percy" for persistent.

Now let's put it to work by writing some data to it.

The following procedure writes some text to a new file in the `/tmp` directory and verifies the operation succeeded. Be sure to run these commands from within the container you just started.

```
root@9cb2d2fd1d65:/# cd tmp

root@9cb2d2fd1d65:/tmp# ls -l
total 0

root@9cb2d2fd1d65:/tmp# echo "Sunderland is the greatest football team in the world" > newfile

root@9cb2d2fd1d65:/tmp# ls -l
total 4
-rw-r--r-- 1 root root 14 Apr 27 11:22 newfile

root@9cb2d2fd1d65:/tmp# cat newfile
Sunderland is the greatest football team in the world
```

Press Ctrl-PQ to exit the container without killing it.

Now use the docker container stop command to stop the container and put in on *vacation*.

```
$ docker container stop percy
percy
```

You can use the container's name or ID with the docker container stop command. The format is docker container stop <container-id or container-name>.

Now run a docker container ls command to list all running containers.

```
$ docker container ls
CONTAINER ID   IMAGE   COMMAND   CREATED  STATUS  PORTS   NAMES
```

The container is not listed in the output above because it's in the stopped state. Run the same command again, only this time add the -a flag to show all containers, including those that are stopped.

```
$ docker container ls -a
CNTNR ID   IMAGE            COMMAND    CREATED  STATUS      NAMES
9cb...65   ubuntu:latest    /bin/bash  4 mins   Exited (0)  percy
```

Now we can see the container showing as Exited (0). Stopping a container is like stopping a virtual machine. Although it's not currently running, its entire configuration and contents still exist on the local filesystem of the Docker host. This means it can be restarted at any time.

Let's use the docker container start command to bring it back from vacation.

```
$ docker container start percy
percy

$ docker container ls
CONTAINER ID  IMAGE           COMMAND      CREATED   STATUS     NAMES
9cb2d2fd1d65  ubuntu:latest   "/bin/bash"  4 mins    Up 3 secs  percy
```

The stopped container is now restarted. Time to verify that the file we created earlier still exists. Connect to the restarted container with the docker container exec command.

```
$ docker container exec -it percy bash
root@9cb2d2fd1d65:/#
```

Your shell prompt will change to show that you are now operating within the namespace of the container.

Verify the file you created earlier is still there and contains the data you wrote to it.

```
root@9cb2d2fd1d65:/# cd tmp
root@9cb2d2fd1d65:/# ls -l
-rw-r--r-- 1 root root 14 Sep 13 04:22 newfile

root@9cb2d2fd1d65:/# cat newfile
Sunderland is the greatest football team in the world
```

As if by magic, the file you created is still there and the data it contains is exactly how you left it. This proves that stopping a container does not destroy the container or the data inside of it.

While this example illustrates the persistent nature of containers, it's important you understand two things:

1. The data created in this example is stored on the Docker hosts local filesystem. If the Docker host fails, the data will be lost.
2. Containers are designed to be immutable objects and it's not a good practice to write data to them.

For these reasons, Docker provides *volumes* that exist separately from the container, but can be mounted into the container at runtime.

At this stage of your journey, this was an effective example of a container lifecycle, and you'd be hard pressed to draw a major difference between the lifecycle of a container and a VM.

Now let's kill the container and delete it from the system.

You can delete a *running* container with a single command, by passing the -f flag to docker container rm. However, it's considered a best practice to take the two-step approach of stopping the container first and then deleting it. This gives the application/process running in the container a fighting chance of stopping cleanly. More on this in a second.

The next example will stop the percy container, delete it, and verify the operation. If your terminal is still attached to the percy container, you'll need to get back to your Docker host's terminal by typing Ctrl-PQ.

```
$ docker container stop percy
percy

$ docker container rm percy
percy

$ docker container ls -a
CONTAINER ID    IMAGE      COMMAND     CREATED   STATUS     PORTS      NAMES
```

The container is now deleted — literally wiped off the face of the planet. If it was a good container, it becomes a *serverless function* in the afterlife. If it was a naughty container, it becomes a dumb terminal :-D

To summarize the lifecycle of a container... You can stop, start, pause, and restart a container as many times as you want. It's not until you explicitly delete a container that you run a chance of losing its data. Even then, if you're storing data outside the container in a *volume*, that data's going to persist even after the container has gone.

Let's quickly mention why we recommended a two-stage approach of stopping the container before deleting it.

Stopping containers gracefully

Most containers in the Linux world will run a single process. Things are a bit different with Windows containers, but they still run a single main application process and the following rules apply.

In the previous example, the container was running the `/bin/bash` app. When you kill a running container with `docker container rm <container> -f`, the container is killed without warning. The procedure is quite violent — a bit like sneaking up behind the container and shooting it in the back of the head. You're literally giving the container, and the app it's running, no chance to complete any operation and gracefully exit.

However, the `docker container stop` command is far more polite — like pointing a gun to the containers head and saying "you've got 10 seconds to say any final words". It gives the process inside of the container a heads-up that it's about to be stopped, giving it a chance to get things in order before the end comes. Once the it completes, you can then delete the container with `docker container rm`.

The magic behind the scenes here can be explained with Linux/POSIX *signals*. `docker container stop` sends a **SIGTERM** signal to the main application process inside the container (PID 1). As we said, this gives the process a chance to clean things up and gracefully shut itself down. If it doesn't exit within 10 seconds, it will receive a **SIGKILL**. This is effectively the bullet to the head. But hey, it got 10 seconds to sort itself out first.

`docker container rm <container> -f` doesn't bother asking nicely with a **SIGTERM**, it goes straight to the **SIGKILL**.

Self-healing containers with restart policies

It's often a good idea to run containers with a *restart policy*. This is a form of self-healing that enables Docker to automatically restart them after certain events or failures have occurred.

Restart policies are applied per-container, and can be configured imperatively on the command line as part of `docker-container run` commands, or declaratively in YAML files for use with higher-level tools such as Docker Swarm, Docker Compose, and Kubernetes.

At the time of writing, the following restart policies exist:

- `always`
- `unless-stopped`
- `on-failed`

The **always** policy is the simplest. It always restarts a stopped container unless it has been explicitly stopped, such as via a `docker container stop` command. An easy way to demonstrate this is to start a new interactive container, with the `--restart always` policy, and tell it to run a shell process. When the container starts you will be attached to its shell. Typing `exit` from the shell will kill the container's PID 1 process and kill the container. However, Docker will automatically restart it because it has the `--restart always` policy. If you issue a `docker container ls` command, you'll see that the container's uptime is less than the time since it was created. Let's put it to the test.

If you're following a long with Windows containers, substitute the `docker container run` command in the example with this one: `docker container run --name neversaydie -it --restart always mcr.microsoft.com/powershell:nanoserver`.

```
$ docker container run --name neversaydie -it --restart always alpine sh
/#
```

Wait a few seconds before typing the `exit` command.

Once you've exited the container and are back at your normal shell prompt, check the container's status.

```
$ docker container ls
CONTAINER ID   IMAGE    COMMAND   CREATED          STATUS         NAME
0901afb84439   alpine   "sh"      35 seconds ago   Up 9 seconds   neversaydie
```

See how the container was created 35 seconds ago, but has only been up for 9 seconds. This is because the `exit` command killed it and Docker restarted it. Be aware that Docker has restarted the same container and not created a new one. In fact, if you inspect it with `docker container inspect` you can see the `restartCount` has been incremented.

An interesting feature of the `--restart always` policy is that if you stop a container with `docker container stop` and the restart the Docker daemon, the container will be restarted. To be clear... you start a new container with the `--restart always` policy and then stop it with the `docker container stop` command. At this point the container is in the `Stopped (Exited)` state. However, if you restart the Docker daemon, the container will be automatically restarted when the daemon comes back up. You need to be aware of this.

The main difference between the **always** and **unless-stopped** policies is that containers with the `--restart unless-stopped` policy will not be restarted when the daemon restarts if they were in the `Stopped (Exited)` state. That might be a confusing sentence, so let's walk through an example.

We'll create two new containers. One called "always" with the `--restart always` policy, and one called "unless-stopped" with the `--restart unless-stopped` policy. We'll stop them both with the `docker container stop` command and then restart Docker. The "always" container will restart, but the "unless-stopped" container will not.

1. Create the two new containers

```
$ docker container run -d --name always \
  --restart always \
  alpine sleep 1d

$ docker container run -d --name unless-stopped \
  --restart unless-stopped \
  alpine sleep 1d

$ docker container ls
CONTAINER ID    IMAGE    COMMAND       STATUS       NAMES
3142bd91ecc4    alpine   "sleep 1d"    Up 2 secs    unless-stopped
4f1b431ac729    alpine   "sleep 1d"    Up 17 secs   always
```

We now have two containers running. One called "always" and one called "unless-stopped".

1. Stop both containers

   ```
   $ docker container stop always unless-stopped

   $ docker container ls -a
   CONTAINER ID    IMAGE    STATUS                        NAMES
   3142bd91ecc4    alpine   Exited (137) 3 seconds ago    unless-stopped
   4f1b431ac729    alpine   Exited (137) 3 seconds ago    always
   ```

2. Restart Docker.

The process for restarting Docker is different on different Operating Systems. This example shows how to stop Docker on Linux hosts running `systemd`. To restart Docker on Windows Server 2016 use `restart-service Docker`.

```
$ systemlctl restart docker
```

1. Once Docker has restarted, you can check the status of the containers.

   ```
   $ docker container ls -a
   CONTAINER    CREATED          STATUS                        NAMES
   314..cc4     2 minutes ago    Exited (137) 2 minutes ago    unless-stopped
   4f1..729     2 minutes ago    Up 9 seconds                  always
   ```

Notice that the "always" container (started with the `--restart always` policy) has been restarted, but the "unless-stopped" container (started with the `--restart unless-stopped` policy) has not.

The **on-failure** policy will restart a container if it exits with a non-zero exit code. It will also restart containers when the Docker daemon restarts, even containers that were in the stopped state.

If you are working with Docker Compose or Docker Stacks, you can apply the restart policy to a `service` object as follows. We'll talk more about these technologies later in the book.

```
version: "3"
services:
  myservice:
    <Snip>
    restart_policy:
      condition: always | unless-stopped | on-failure
```

Web server example

So far, we've seen how to start a simple container and interact with it. We've also seen how to stop, restart and delete containers. Now let's take a look at a Linux-based web server example.

In this example, we'll start a new container from an image I use in a few of my Pluralsight video courses[11]. The image runs a simple web server on port 8080.

You can use the `docker container stop` and `docker container rm` commands to clean up any existing containers on your system. Then run the following command to start a new web server container.

```
$ docker container run -d --name webserver -p 80:8080 \
  nigelpoulton/pluralsight-docker-ci

Unable to find image 'nigelpoulton/pluralsight-docker-ci:latest' locally
latest: Pulling from nigelpoulton/pluralsight-docker-ci
a3ed95caeb02: Pull complete
3b231ed5aa2f: Pull complete
7e4f9cd54d46: Pull complete
929432235e51: Pull complete
6899ef41c594: Pull complete
0b38fccd0dab: Pull complete
Digest: sha256:7a6b0125fe7893e70dc63b2...9b12a28e2c38bd8d3d
Status: Downloaded newer image for nigelpoulton/plur...docker-ci:latest
6efa1838cd51b92a4817e0e7483d103bf72a7ba7ffb5855080128d85043fef21
```

Notice that your shell prompt hasn't changed. This is because this container was started in the background with the `-d` flag. Starting a container like this doesn't attach it to your terminal.

Let's take a look at some of the other arguments in the command.

We know `docker container run` starts a new container. However, this time we give it the `-d` flag instead of `-it`. `-d` stands for **d**aemon mode, and tells the container to run in the background. You can't use the `-d` and `-it` flags in the same command.

After that, the command names the container "webserver". The `-p` flag maps port 80 on the Docker host to port 8080 inside the container. This means that traffic hitting the Docker host on port 80 will be directed to port 8080 inside of the container. It just so happens that the image we're using for this container defines a web service that listens on port 8080. This means the container will come up running a web server listening on port 8080.

Finally, the command tells the container to base itself on the `nigelpoulton/pluralsight-docker-ci` image. This image contains a node.js webserver and all dependencies. It is maintained approximately once per year, so will contain vulnerabilities!

---

[11]https://www.pluralsight.com/search?q=nigel%20poulton%20docker&categories=all

Once the container is running, a `docker container ls` command will show the container as running and the ports that are mapped. It's important to know that port mappings are expressed as `host-port:container-port`.

```
$ docker container ls
CONTAINER ID  COMMAND         STATUS       PORTS                NAMES
6efa1838cd51  /bin/sh -c...   Up 2 mins    0.0.0.0:80->8080/tcp  webserver
```

Some of the columns have been removed from the output to help with readability.

Now that the container is running and ports are mapped, you can connect to the it by pointing a web browser at the IP address or DNS name of the **Docker host** on port 80. Figure 7.4 shows the web page that is being served up by the container.

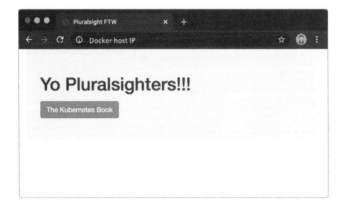

Figure 7.4

The same `docker container stop`, `docker container pause`, `docker container start`, and `docker container rm` commands can be used on the container.

Inspecting containers

In the previous web server example, you might have noticed that we didn't specify an app for the container when we issued the `docker container run` command. Yet the container ran a web service. How did this happen?

When building a Docker image, you can embed an instruction that lists the default app for any containers that use the image. You can see this for any image by running a `docker image inspect`.

```
$ docker image inspect nigelpoulton/pluralsight-docker-ci

[
    {
        "Id": "sha256:07e574331ce3768f30305519...49214bf3020ee69bba1",
        "RepoTags": [
            "nigelpoulton/pluralsight-docker-ci:latest"

            <Snip>

        ],
        "Cmd": [
            "/bin/sh",
            "-c",
            "#(nop) CMD [\"/bin/sh\" \"-c\" \"cd /src \u0026\u0026 node ./app.js\"]"
        ],
<Snip>
```

The output is snipped to make it easier to find the information we're interested in.

The entries after `Cmd` show the command/app that the container will run unless you override it with a different one when you launch the container with `docker container run`. If you remove all of the shell escapes in the example, you get the following command `/bin/sh -c "cd /src && node ./app.js"`. That's the default app a container based on this image will run. Feel free to inspect some more images, sometimes the default app is listed as `Entrypoint` instead of `Cmd`.

It's common to build images with default commands like this, as it makes starting containers easier. It also forces a default behavior and is a form of self documentation — i.e. you can *inspect* the image and know what app it's designed to run.

That's us done for the examples in this chapter. Let's see a quick way to tidy our system up.

Tidying up

Let's look at the simplest and quickest way to get rid of **every running container** on your Docker host. Be warned though, the procedure will forcibly destroy **all** containers without giving them a chance to clean up. **This should never be performed on production systems or systems running important containers.**

Run the following command from the shell of your Docker host to delete **all** containers.

```
$ docker container rm $(docker container ls -aq) -f
6efa1838cd51
```

In this example, there was only a single container running, so only one was deleted (6efa1838cd51). However, the command works the same way as the `docker image rm $(docker image ls -q)` command we used in the previous chapter to delete all images on a single Docker host. We already know the `docker container rm` command deletes containers. Passing it `$(docker container ls -aq)` as an argument, effectively passes it the ID of every container on the system. The `-f` flag forces the operation so that even containers in the running state will be destroyed. Net result... all containers, running or stopped, will be destroyed and removed from the system.

The above command will work in a PowerShell terminal on a Windows Docker host.

Containers - The commands

- `docker container run` is the command used to start new containers. In its simplest form, it accepts an *image* and a *command* as arguments. The image is used to create the container and the command is the application the container will run when it starts. This example will start an Ubuntu container in the foreground, and tell it to run the Bash shell: `docker container run -it ubuntu /bin/bash`.
- `Ctrl-PQ` will detach your shell from the terminal of a container and leave the container running (`UP`) in the background.
- `docker container ls` lists all containers in the running (`UP`) state. If you add the `-a` flag you will also see containers in the stopped (`Exited`) state.
- `docker container exec` runs a new process inside of a running container. It's useful for attaching the shell of your Docker host to a terminal inside of a running container. This command will start a new Bash shell inside of a running container and connect to it: `docker container exec -it <container-name or container-id> bash`. For this to work, the image used to create the container must include the Bash shell.
- `docker container stop` will stop a running container and put it in the `Exited (0)` state. It does this by issuing a `SIGTERM` to the process with PID 1 inside of the container. If the process has not cleaned up and stopped within 10 seconds, a SIGKILL will be issued to forcibly stop the container. `docker container stop` accepts container IDs and container names as arguments.
- `docker container start` will restart a stopped (`Exited`) container. You can give `docker container start` the name or ID of a container.
- `docker container rm` will delete a stopped container. You can specify containers by name or ID. It is recommended that you stop a container with the `docker container stop` command before deleting it with `docker container rm`.
- `docker container inspect` will show you detailed configuration and runtime information about a container. It accepts container names and container IDs as its main argument.

Chapter summary

In this chapter, we compared and contrasted the container and VM models. We looked at the *OS tax* problem inherent in the VM model, and saw how the container model can bring huge advantages in much the same way as the VM model brought huge advantages over the physical server model.

We saw how to use the `docker container run` command to start a couple of simple containers, and we saw the difference between interactive containers in the foreground versus containers running in the background.

We know that killing the PID 1 process inside of a container will kill the container. And we've seen how to start, stop, and delete containers.

We finished the chapter using the `docker container inspect` command to view detailed container metadata.

So far so good!

8: Containerizing an app

Docker is all about taking applications and running them in containers.

The process of taking an application and configuring it to run as a container is called "containerizing".

In this chapter, we'll walk through the process of containerizing a simple Linux-based web application. If you don't have a Linux Docker environment to follow along with, you can use *Play With Docker* for free. Just point your web browser to https://play-with-docker.com and spin up some Linux Docker nodes. It's my favourite way to spin up Docker and do testing!

We'll split this chapter into the usual three parts:

- The TLDR
- The deep dive
- The commands

Let's containerize an app!

Containerizing an app - The TLDR

Containers are all about making apps simple to **build**, **ship**, and **run**.

The process of containerizing an app looks like this:

1. Start with your application code and dependencies
2. Create a *Dockerfile* that describes your app, its dependencies, and how to run it
3. Feed the *Dockerfile* into the `docker image build` command
4. Push the new image to a registry (optional)
5. Run container from the image

Once your app is containerized (made into a container image), you're ready to share it and run it as a container.

Figure 8.1 shows the process in picture form.

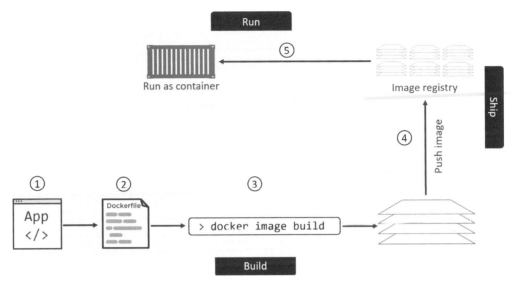

Figure 8.1 - Basic flow of containerizing an app

Containerizing an app - The deep dive

We'll break up this Deep Dive section of the chapter as follows:

- Containerize a single-container app
- Moving to Production with multi-stage builds
- A few best practices

Containerize a single-container app

The rest of this chapter walks through the process of containerizing a simple Node.js web app.

We'll complete the following high-level steps:

- Clone the repo to get the app code
- Inspect the Dockerfile
- Containerize the app
- Run the app
- Test the app
- Look a bit closer
- Move to production with **Multi-stage Builds**
- A few best practices

The example in this chapter is of a single-container app. The next chapter will include a slightly more complex multi-container app, and we'll move on to an even more complicated app in the chapter on Docker Stacks.

Getting the application code

The application used in this example is available on GitHub at:

- https://github.com/nigelpoulton/psweb.git

Clone the sample app from GitHub.

```
$ git clone https://github.com/nigelpoulton/psweb.git

Cloning into 'psweb'...
remote: Counting objects: 15, done.
remote: Compressing objects: 100% (11/11), done.
remote: Total 15 (delta 2), reused 15 (delta 2), pack-reused 0
Unpacking objects: 100% (15/15), done.
Checking connectivity... done.
```

The clone operation creates a new directory called psweb. Change directory into psweb and list its contents.

```
$ cd psweb

$ ls -l
total 28
-rw-r--r-- 1 root root  341 Sep 29 16:26 app.js
-rw-r--r-- 1 root root  216 Sep 29 16:26 circle.yml
-rw-r--r-- 1 root root  338 Sep 29 16:26 Dockerfile
-rw-r--r-- 1 root root  421 Sep 29 16:26 package.json
-rw-r--r-- 1 root root  370 Sep 29 16:26 README.md
drwxr-xr-x 2 root root 4096 Sep 29 16:26 test
drwxr-xr-x 2 root root 4096 Sep 29 16:26 views
```

This directory contains all of the application source code, as well as subdirectories for views and unit tests. Feel free to look at the files — the app is extremely simple. We won't be using the unit tests in this chapter.

Now that we have the app code, let's look at its Dockerfile.

Inspecting the Dockerfile

A **Dockerfile** is the starting point for creating a container image — it describes an application and tells Docker how to build it into an image.

The directory containing the application and dependencies is referred to as the *build context*. It's a common practice to keep your Dockerfile in the root directory of the *build context*. It's also important that **Dockerfile** starts with a capital "**D**" and is all one word. "dockerfile" and "Docker file" are not valid.

Let's look at the contents of the Dockerfile.

```
$ cat Dockerfile

FROM alpine
LABEL maintainer="nigelpoulton@hotmail.com"
RUN apk add --update nodejs nodejs-npm
COPY . /src
WORKDIR /src
RUN npm install
EXPOSE 8080
ENTRYPOINT ["node", "./app.js"]
```

Do not underestimate the impact of the Dockerfile as a form of documentation. It's a great document for bridging the gap between dev and ops. It also has the power to speed up on-boarding of new developers etc. This is because the file accurately describes the application and its dependencies in an easy-to-read format. You should treat it like you treat source code and check it into a version control system.

At a high-level, the example Dockerfile says: Start with the `alpine` image, make a note that "nigelpoulton@hotmail.com" is the maintainer, install Node.js and NPM, copy everything in the build context to the `/src` directory in the image, set the working directory as `/src`, install dependencies, document the app's network port, and set `app.js` as the default application to run.

Let's look at it in a bit more detail.

All Dockerfiles start with the `FROM` instruction. This will be the base layer of the image, and the rest of the app will be added on top as additional layers. This particular application is a Linux app, so it's important that the FROM instruction refers to a Linux-based image. If you're containerizing a Windows application, you'll need to specify the appropriate Windows base image - such as `mcr.microsoft.com/dotnet/core/aspnet`.

At this point in the Dockerfile, the image has a single layer as showing in Figure 8.2.

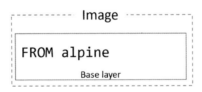

Figure 8.2

Next, the Dockerfile creates a LABEL that specifies "nigelpoulton@hotmail.com" as the maintainer of the image. Labels are simple key-value pairs and are an excellent way of adding custom metadata to an image. It's considered a best practice to list a maintainer of an image so that other potential users have a point of contact when working with it.

The `RUN apk add --update nodejs nodejs-npm` instruction uses the Alpine `apk` package manager to install `nodejs` and `nodejs-npm` into the image. It creates a new image layer directly above the Alpine base layer, and installs the packages in this layer. At this point in the Dockerfile, the image looks like Figure 8.3.

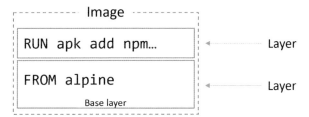

Figure 8.3

The `COPY . /src` instruction creates another new layer and copies in the application and dependency files from the *build context*. At this point in the Dockerfile, the image has three layers as shown in Figure 8.4.

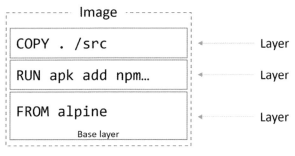

Figure 8.4

Next, the Dockerfile uses the `WORKDIR` instruction to set the working directory inside the image filesystem for the rest of the instructions in the file. This instruction does not create a new image layer.

Then the `RUN npm install` instruction creates a new layer and uses `npm` to install application dependencies listed in the `package.json` file in the build context. It runs within the context of the `WORKDIR` set in the previous instruction, and installs the dependencies into the newly created layer. At this point in the Dockerfile the image has four layers as shown in Figure 8.5.

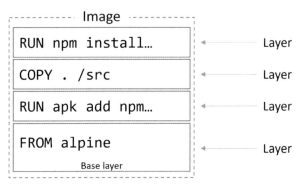

Figure 8.5

The application exposes a web service on TCP port 8080, so the Dockerfile documents this with the `EXPOSE 8080` instruction. This is added as image metadata and not an image layer.

Finally, the ENTRYPOINT instruction is used to set the main application that the image (container) should run. This is also added as metadata and not an image layer.

Containerize the app/build the image

Now that we understand how it works, let's build it!

The following command will build a new image called web:latest. The period (.) at the end of the command tells Docker to use the shell's current working directory as the *build context*.

Be sure to include the trailing period (.) and be sure to run the command from the psweb directory that contains the Dockerfile and application code.

```
$ docker image build -t web:latest .

Sending build context to Docker daemon  76.29kB
Step 1/8 : FROM alpine
latest: Pulling from library/alpine
ff3a5c916c92: Pull complete
Digest: sha256:7df6db5aa6...0bedab9b8df6b1c0
Status: Downloaded newer image for alpine:latest
 ---> 76da55c8019d
<Snip>
Step 8/8 : ENTRYPOINT node ./app.js
 ---> Running in 13977a4f3b21
 ---> fc69fdc4c18e
Removing intermediate container 13977a4f3b21
Successfully built fc69fdc4c18e
Successfully tagged web:latest
```

Check that the image exists in your Docker host's local repository.

```
$ docker image ls
REPO    TAG      IMAGE ID       CREATED          SIZE
web     latest   fc69fdc4c18e   10 seconds ago   81.5MB
```

Congratulations, the app is containerized!

You can use the docker image inspect web:latest command to verify the configuration of the image. It will list all of the settings that were configured from the Dockerfile. Look out for the list of image layers and the Entrypoint command.

Pushing images

Once you've created an image, it's a good idea to store it in an image registry to keep it safe and make it available to others. Docker Hub is the most common public image registry, and it's the default push location for docker image push commands.

In order to push an image to Docker Hub, you need to login with your Docker ID. You also need to tag the image appropriately.

Let's log in to Docker Hub and push the newly created image.

In the following example's you will need to substitute my Docker ID with your own. So any time you see "nigelpoulton", swap it out for your Docker ID (Docker Hub username).

```
$ docker login
Login with **your** Docker ID to push and pull images from Docker Hub...
Username: nigelpoulton
Password:
Login Succeeded
```

Before you can push an image, you need to tag it in a special way. This is because Docker needs all of the following information when pushing an image:

- Registry
- Repository
- Tag

Docker is opinionated, so by default it pushes images to Docker Hub. You can push to other registries, but you have to explicitly set the registry URL as part of the `docker image push` command.

The previous `docker image ls` output shows the image is tagged as `web:latest`. This translates to a repository called `web` and an image tagged as `latest`. As a result, `docker image push` will try and push the image to a repository called `web` on Docker Hub. However, I don't have access to the `web` repository, all of my images live in the `nigelpoulton` second-level namespace. This means I need to re-tag the image to include my Docker ID. Remember to substitute your own Docker ID.

```
$ docker image tag web:latest nigelpoulton/web:latest
```

The format of the command is `docker image tag <current-tag> <new-tag>` and it adds an additional tag, it does not overwrite the original.

Another image listing shows the image now has two tags, one of which includes my Docker ID.

```
$ docker image ls
REPO              TAG       IMAGE ID        CREATED       SIZE
web               latest    fc69fdc4c18e    10 secs ago   64.4MB
nigelpoulton/web  latest    fc69fdc4c18e    10 secs ago   64.4MB
```

Now we can push it to Docker Hub. You can't push images to repos in my Docker Hub namespace, you will have to tag the image to use your own.

```
$ docker image push nigelpoulton/web:latest
The push refers to repository [docker.io/nigelpoulton/web]
2444b4ec39ad: Pushed
ed8142d2affb: Pushed
d77e2754766d: Pushed
cd7100a72410: Mounted from library/alpine
latest: digest: sha256:68c2dea730...f8cf7478 size: 1160
```

Figure 8.6 shows how Docker determined the push location.

Figure 8.6

Now that the image is pushed to a registry, you can access it from anywhere with an internet connection. You can also grant other people access to pull it and push changes.

The examples in the rest of the chapter will use the shorter of the two image tags (`web:latest`).

Run the app

The containerized application is a web server that listens on TCP port `8080`. You can verify this in the `app.js` file in the build context you cloned from GitHub.

The following command will start a new container called `c1` based on the `web:latest` image you just created. It maps port `80` on the Docker host, to port `8080` inside the container. This means that you'll be able to point a web browser at the DNS name or IP address of the Docker host running the container and access the app.

> **Note:** If your host is already running a service on port 80, you can specify a different port as part of the `docker container run` command. For example, to map the app to port 5000 on the Docker host, use the `-p 5000:8080` flag.

```
$ docker container run -d --name c1 \
  -p 80:8080 \
  web:latest
```

The `-d` flag runs the container in the background, and the `-p 80:8080` flag maps port 80 on the host to port 8080 inside the running container.

Check that the container is running and verify the port mapping.

```
$ docker container ls

ID     IMAGE       COMMAND          STATUS      PORTS                   NAMES
49..   web:latest  "node ./app.js"  UP 6 secs   0.0.0.0:80->8080/tcp    c1
```

The output above is snipped for readability, but shows that the app container is running. Note that port 80 is mapped, on all host interfaces (0.0.0.0:80).

Test the app

Open a web browser and point it to the DNS name or IP address of the host that the container is running on. You'll see the web page shown in Figure 8.7. If you're using Docker Desktop or another technology that runs the container on your local machine. you can use localhost as the DNS name.

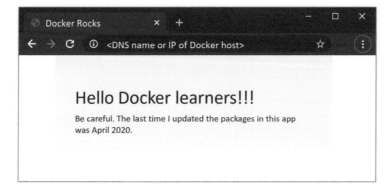

Figure 8.7

If the test does not work, try the following:

1. Make sure that the container is up and running with the docker container ls command. The container name is c1 and you should see the port mapping as 0.0.0.0:80->8080/tcp.
2. Check that firewall and other network security settings are not blocking traffic to port 80 on the Docker host.
3. Retry the command specifying a high numbered port on the Docker host (may be -p 5000:8080).

Congratulations, the application is containerized and running!

Looking a bit closer

Now that the application is containerized, let's take a closer look at how some of the machinery works.

The docker image build command parses the Dockerfile one-line-at-a-time starting from the top.

Comment lines start with the # character.

All non-comment lines are **Instructions** and take the format INSTRUCTION argument. Instruction names are not case sensitive, but it's normal practice to write them in UPPERCASE. This makes reading the Dockerfile easier.

Some instructions create new layers, whereas others just add metadata to the image config file.

Examples of instructions that create new layers are FROM, RUN, and COPY. Examples that create metadata include EXPOSE, WORKDIR, ENV, and ENTRYPOINT. The basic premise is this — if an instruction is adding *content* such as files and programs to the image, it will create a new layer. If it is adding instructions on how to build the image and run the application, it will create metadata.

You can view the instructions that were used to build the image with the docker image history command.

```
$ docker image history web:latest

IMAGE       CREATED BY                                        SIZE
fc6..18e    /bin/sh -c #(nop)   ENTRYPOINT ["node" "./a...    0B
334..bf0    /bin/sh -c #(nop)   EXPOSE 8080/tcp               0B
b27..eae    /bin/sh -c npm install                            14.1MB
932..749    /bin/sh -c #(nop) WORKDIR /src                    0B
052..2dc    /bin/sh -c #(nop) COPY dir:2a6ed1703749e80...     22.5kB
c1d..81f    /bin/sh -c apk add --update nodejs nodejs-npm     46.1MB
336..b92    /bin/sh -c #(nop)   LABEL maintainer=nigelp...    0B
3fd..f02    /bin/sh -c #(nop)   CMD ["/bin/sh"]               0B
<missing>   /bin/sh -c #(nop) ADD file:093f0723fa46f6c...     4.15MB
```

Two things from the output above are worth noting.

First. Each line corresponds to an instruction in the Dockerfile (starting from the bottom and working up). The CREATED BY column even lists the exact Dockerfile instruction that was executed.

Second. Only 4 of the lines displayed in the output create new layers (the ones with non-zero values in the SIZE column). These correspond to the FROM, RUN, and COPY instructions in the Dockerfile. Although the other instructions might look like they create layers, they actually create metadata instead of layers. The reason that the docker image history output makes it looks like all instructions create layers is an artefact of the way builds and image layering used to work.

Use the docker image inspect command to confirm that only 4 layers were created.

```
$ docker image inspect web:latest

<Snip>
},
"RootFS": {
    "Type": "layers",
    "Layers": [
        "sha256:cd7100...1882bd56d263e02b6215",
        "sha256:b3f88e...cae0e290980576e24885",
        "sha256:3cfa21...cc819ef5e3246ec4fe16",
        "sha256:4408b4...d52c731ba0b205392567"
    ]
},
```

It is considered a good practice to use images from official repositories with the FROM instruction. This is because their content has been vetted and they are quick to release new versions when vulnerabilities are fixed. It is also a good idea to start from (FROM) small images as this keeps images small and reduces attack surface and potential vulnerabilities.

You can view the output of the `docker image build` command to see the general process for building an image. As the following snippet shows, the basic process is: spin up a temporary container > run the Dockerfile instruction inside of that container > save the results as a new image layer > remove the temporary container.

```
Step 3/8 : RUN apk add --update nodejs nodejs-npm
 ---> Running in e690ddca785f     << Run inside of temp container
fetch http://dl-cdn...APKINDEX.tar.gz
fetch http://dl-cdn...APKINDEX.tar.gz
(1/10) Installing ca-certificates (20171114-r0)
<Snip>
OK: 61 MiB in 21 packages
 ---> c1d31d36b81f               << Create new layer
Removing intermediate container  << Remove temp container
Step 4/8 : COPY . /src
```

Moving to production with Multi-stage Builds

When it comes to Docker images, big is bad!

Big means slow. Big means hard to work with. And big means more potential vulnerabilities and possibly a bigger attack surface!

For these reasons, Docker images should be small. The aim of the game is to only ship production images with the stuff **needed** to run your app in production.

The problem is... keeping images small *was* hard work.

For example, the way you write your Dockerfiles has a huge impact on the size of your images. A common example is that every RUN instruction adds a new layer. As a result, it's usually considered a best practice to include multiple commands as part of a single RUN instruction — all glued together with double-ampersands (&&) and backslash (\) line-breaks. While this isn't rocket science, it requires time and discipline.

Another issue is that we don't clean up after ourselves. We'll RUN a command against an image that pulls some build-time tools, and we'll leave all those tools in the image when we ship it to production. Not ideal!

Multi-stage builds to the rescue!

Multi-stage builds are all about optimizing builds without adding complexity. And they deliver on the promise!

Here's the high-level...

Multi-stage builds have a single Dockerfile containing multiple FROM instructions. Each FROM instruction is a new **build stage** that can easily COPY artefacts from previous **stages**.

Let's look at an example!

This example app is available at https://github.com/nigelpoulton/atsea-sample-shop-app.git and the Dockerfile is in the `app` directory. It's a Linux-based application so, will only work on a Linux Docker host. It's also quite old, so don't deploy it to an important system, and be sure to delete it as soon as you're finished.

The Dockerfile is shown below:

```
FROM node:latest AS storefront
WORKDIR /usr/src/atsea/app/react-app
COPY react-app .
RUN npm install
RUN npm run build

FROM maven:latest AS appserver
WORKDIR /usr/src/atsea
COPY pom.xml .
RUN mvn -B -f pom.xml -s /usr/share/maven/ref/settings-docker.xml dependency:resolve
COPY . .
RUN mvn -B -s /usr/share/maven/ref/settings-docker.xml package -DskipTests

FROM java:8-jdk-alpine AS production
RUN adduser -Dh /home/gordon gordon
WORKDIR /static
COPY --from=storefront /usr/src/atsea/app/react-app/build/ .
WORKDIR /app
COPY --from=appserver /usr/src/atsea/target/AtSea-0.0.1-SNAPSHOT.jar .
ENTRYPOINT ["java", "-jar", "/app/AtSea-0.0.1-SNAPSHOT.jar"]
CMD ["--spring.profiles.active=postgres"]
```

The first thing to note is that the Dockerfile has three FROM instructions. Each of these constitutes a distinct **build stage**. Internally, they're numbered from the top starting at 0. However, we've also given each stage a friendly name.

- Stage 0 is called storefront
- Stage 1 is called appserver
- Stage 2 is called production

The storefront stage pulls the node:latest image which is over 900MB in size. It sets the working directory, copies in some app code, and uses two RUN instructions to perform some npm magic. This adds three layers and considerable size. The resulting image is an even bigger than the base node:latest image as it contains lots of build stuff and not very much app code.

The appserver stage pulls the maven:latest image which is over 500MB in size. It adds four layers of content via two COPY instructions and two RUN instructions. This produces another very large image with lots of build tools and very little actual production code.

The production stage starts by pulling the java:8-jdk-alpine image. This image is approximately 150MB - considerably smaller than the node and maven images used by the previous build stages. It adds a user, sets the working directory, and copies in some app code from the image produced by the storefront stage. After that, it sets a different working directory and copies in the application code from the image produced by the appserver stage. Finally, it sets the main application for the image to run when it's started as a container.

An important thing to note, is that COPY --from instructions are used to **only copy production-related application code** from the images built by the previous stages. They do not copy build artefacts that are not needed for production.

It's also important to note that we only need a single Dockerfile, and no extra arguments are needed for the docker image build command!

Speaking of which... let's build it.

Clone the repo.

```
$ git clone https://github.com/nigelpoulton/atsea-sample-shop-app.git

Cloning into 'atsea-sample-shop-app'...
remote: Counting objects: 632, done.
remote: Total 632 (delta 0), reused 0 (delta 0), pack-reused 632
Receiving objects: 100% (632/632), 7.23 MiB | 1.88 MiB/s, done.
Resolving deltas: 100% (195/195), done.
Checking connectivity... done.
```

Change directory into the `app` folder of the cloned repo and verify that the Dockerfile exists.

```
$ cd atsea-sample-shop-app/app

$ ls -l
total 24
-rw-r--r-- 1 root root  682 Oct  1 22:03 Dockerfile
-rw-r--r-- 1 root root 4365 Oct  1 22:03 pom.xml
drwxr-xr-x 4 root root 4096 Oct  1 22:03 react-app
drwxr-xr-x 4 root root 4096 Oct  1 22:03 src
```

Perform the build (this may take several minutes to complete as some of the images that are pulled are large).

```
$ docker image build -t multi:stage .

Sending build context to Docker daemon  3.658MB
Step 1/19 : FROM node:latest AS storefront
latest: Pulling from library/node
aa18ad1a0d33: Pull complete
15a33158a136: Pull complete
<Snip>
Step 19/19 : CMD --spring.profiles.active=postgres
 ---> Running in b4df9850f7ed
 ---> 3dc0d5e6223e
Removing intermediate container b4df9850f7ed
Successfully built 3dc0d5e6223e
Successfully tagged multi:stage
```

> **Note:** The `multi:stage` tag used in the example above is arbitrary. You can tag your images according to your own requirements and standards — there is no requirement to tag multi-stage builds the way we did in this example.

Run a `docker image ls` to see the list of images pulled and created by the build operation.

```
$ docker image ls

REPO      TAG           IMAGE ID        CREATED        SIZE
node      latest        a5a6a9c32877    5 days ago     941MB
<none>    <none>        d2ab20c11203    9 mins ago     1.11GB
maven     latest        45d27d110099    9 days ago     508MB
<none>    <none>        fa26694f57cb    7 mins ago     649MB
java      8-jdk-alpine  3fd9dd82815c    7 months ago   145MB
multi     stage         3dc0d5e6223e    1 min ago      210MB
```

The top line in the output above shows the node:latest image pulled by the storefront stage. The image below is the image produced by that stage (created by adding the code and running the npm install and build operations). Both are very large images with lots of build junk included.

The 3rd and 4th lines are the images pulled and produced by the appserver stage. These are both large and contain lots of builds tools.

The last line is the multi:stage image built by the final build stage in the Dockerfile (stage2/production). You can see that this is significantly smaller than the images pulled and produced by the previous stages. This is because it's based off the much smaller java:8-jdk-alpine image and has only added the production-related app files from the previous stages.

The net result is a small production image created by a single Dockerfile, a normal docker image build command, and zero additional scripting!

Multi-stage builds were new with Docker 17.05 and are an excellent feature for building small production-worthy images.

A few best practices

Let's list a few best practices before closing out the chapter. This list is not intended to be exhaustive.

Leverage the build cache

The build process used by Docker has the concept of a cache that it uses to speed-up the build process. The best way to see the impact of the cache is to build a new image on a clean Docker host, then repeat the same build immediately after. The first build will pull images and take time building layers. The second build will complete almost instantaneously. This is because artefacts from the first build, such as layers, are cached and leveraged by later builds.

As we know, the docker image build process iterates through a Dockerfile one-line-at-a-time starting from the top. For each instruction, Docker looks to see if it already has an image layer for that instruction in its cache. If it does, this is a *cache hit* and it uses that layer. If it doesn't, this is a *cache miss* and it builds a new layer from the instruction. Getting *cache hits* can hugely speed up the build process.

Let's look a little closer.

We'll use this example Dockerfile to provide a quick walk-through:

```
FROM alpine
RUN apk add --update nodejs nodejs-npm
COPY . /src
WORKDIR /src
RUN npm install
EXPOSE 8080
ENTRYPOINT ["node", "./app.js"]
```

The first instruction tells Docker to use the `alpine:latest` image as its *base image*. If this image already exists on the host, the build will move on to the next instruction. If the image does not exist, it is pulled from Docker Hub (index.docker.io).

The next instruction (`RUN apk...`) runs a command to update package lists and install `nodejs` and `nodejs-npm`. Before performing the instruction, Docker checks its build cache for a layer that was built from the same base image, as well as using the same instruction it is currently being asked to execute. In this case, it's looking for a layer that was built directly on top of `alpine:latest` by executing the `RUN apk add --update nodejs nodejs-npm` instruction.

If it finds a layer, it skips the instruction, links to that existing layer, and continues the build with the cache in tact. If it does **not** find a layer, it invalidates the cache and builds the layer. This operation of invalidating the cache invalidates it for the remainder of the build. This means all subsequent Dockerfile instructions are completed in full without attempting to reference the build cache.

Let's assume that Docker already had a layer for this instruction in the cache (a cache hit). And let's assume the ID of that layer was `AAA`.

The next instruction copies some code into the image (`COPY . /src`). Because the previous instruction resulted in a cache hit, Docker now checks to see if it has a cached layer that was built from the `AAA` layer with the `COPY . /src` command. If it does, it links to the layer and proceeds to the next instruction. If it does not, it builds the layer and invalidates the cache for the rest of the build.

Let's assume that Docker already has a layer for this instruction in the cache (a cache hit). And let's assume the ID of that layer is `BBB`.

This process continues for the rest of the Dockerfile.

It's important to understand a few more things.

Firstly, as soon as any instruction results in a cache-miss (no layer was found for that instruction), the cache is no longer used for the rest of the entire build. This has an important impact on how you write your Dockerfiles. Try and write them in a way that places instructions that are likely to invalidate the cache towards the end of the Dockerfile. This means that a cache-miss will not occur until later stages of the build - allowing the build to benefit as much as possible from the cache.

You can force the build process to ignore the entire cache by passing the `--no-cache=true` flag to the `docker image build` command.

It is also important to understand that the `COPY` and `ADD` instructions include steps to ensure that the content being copied into the image has not changed since the last build. For example, it's possible that the `COPY . /src` **instruction** in the Dockerfile has not changed since the previous, **but**... the contents of the directory being copied into the image **have** changed!

To protect against this, Docker performs a checksum against each file being copied, and compares that to a checksum of the same file in the cached layer. If the checksums do not match, the cache is invalidated and a new layer is built.

Squash the image

Squashing an image isn't really a best practice as it has pros and cons.

At a high level, Docker follows the normal process to build an image, but then adds an additional step that squashes everything into a single layer.

Squashing can be good in situations where images are starting to have a lot of layers and this isn't ideal. An example might be when creating a new base image that you want to build other images from in the future — this base is much better as a single-layer image.

On the negative side, squashed images do not share image layers. This can result in storage inefficiencies and larger push and pull operations.

Add the `--squash` flag to the `docker image build` command if you want to create a squashed image.

Figure 8.8 shows some of the inefficiencies that come with squashed images. Both images are exactly the same except for the fact that one is squashed and the other is not. The non-squashed image shares layers with other images on the host (saving disk space) but the squashed image does not. The squashed image will also need to send every byte to Docker Hub on a `docker image push` command, whereas the non-squashed image only needs to send unique layers.

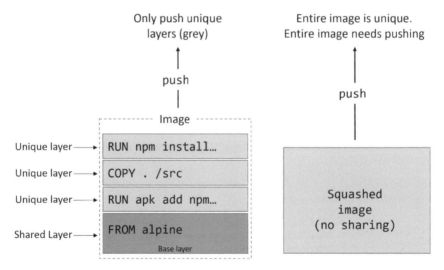

Figure 8.8 - Squashed images vs non-squashed images

Use no-install-recommends

If you are building Linux images, and using the apt package manager, you should use the `no-install-recommends` flag with the `apt-get install` command. This makes sure that apt only installs main dependencies (packages in the `Depends` field) and not recommended or suggested packages. This can greatly reduce the number of unwanted packages that are downloaded into your images.

Containerizing an app - The commands

- `docker image build` is the command that reads a Dockerfile and containerizes an application. The `-t` flag tags the image, and the `-f` flag lets you specify the name and location of the Dockerfile. With the `-f` flag, it is possible to use a Dockerfile with an arbitrary name and in an arbitrary location. The *build context* is where your application files exist, and this can be a directory on your local Docker host or a remote Git repo.
- The `FROM` instruction in a Dockerfile specifies the base image for the new image you will build. It is usually the first instruction in a Dockerfile and a best-practice is to use images from official repos on this line.
- The `RUN` instruction in a Dockerfile allows you to run commands inside the image. Each `RUN` instruction creates a single new layer.
- The `COPY` instruction in a Dockerfile adds files into the image as a new layer. It is common to use the `COPY` instruction to copy your application code into an image.
- The `EXPOSE` instruction in a Dockerfile documents the network port that the application uses.
- The `ENTRYPOINT` instruction in a Dockerfile sets the default application to run when the image is started as a container.
- Other Dockerfile instructions include `LABEL`, `ENV`, `ONBUILD`, `HEALTHCHECK`, `CMD` and more...

Chapter summary

In this chapter, we learned how to containerize an application.

We pulled some application code from a remote Git repo. The repo included the application code, as well as a Dockerfile containing instructions on how to build the application into an image. We learned the basics of how Dockerfiles work, and fed one into a `docker image build` command to create a new image.

Once the image was created, we started a container from it and tested it with a web browser.

After that, we saw how multi-stage builds give us a simple way to build and ship smaller images to our production environments.

We also learned that the Dockerfile is a great tool for documenting an app. As such, it can speed-up the onboarding of new developers and bridge the divide between developers and operations staff. With this in mind, treat it like code and check it in and out of a source control system.

Although the example cited was a Linux-based example, the process for containerizing Windows apps is the same: Start with your app code, create a Dockerfile describing the app, build the image with `docker image build`. Job done!

9: Deploying Apps with Docker Compose

In this chapter, we'll look at how to deploy multi-container applications using Docker Compose.

Docker Compose and Docker Stacks are very similar. In this chapter we'll focus on Docker Compose, which deploys and manages multi-container applications on Docker nodes running in **single-engine mode**. In a later chapter, we'll focus on Docker Stacks. Stacks deploy and manage multi-container apps on Docker nodes running in **swarm mode**.

We'll split this chapter into the usual three parts:

- The TLDR
- The deep dive
- The commands

Deploying apps with Compose - The TLDR

Modern cloud-native apps are made of multiple smaller services that interact to form a useful app. We call this pattern "microservices". A simple example might be an app with the following seven services:

- Web front-end
- Ordering
- Catalog
- Back-end database
- Logging
- Authentication
- Authorization

Get all of these working together, and you have a *useful application*.

Deploying and managing lots of small microservices like these can be hard. This is where *Docker Compose* comes in to play.

Instead of gluing each microservice together with scripts and long `docker` commands, Docker Compose lets you describe an entire app in a single declarative configuration file, and deploy it with a single command.

Once the app is *deployed*, you can *manage* its entire lifecycle with a simple set of commands. You can even store and manage the configuration file in a version control system.

That's the basics. Let's dig deeper.

Deploying apps with Compose - The Deep Dive

We'll divide the Deep Dive section as follows:

- Compose background
- Installing Compose
- Compose files
- Deploying an app with Compose
- Managing an app with Compose

Compose background

In the beginning was *Fig*. Fig was a powerful tool, created by a company called *Orchard*, and it was the best way to manage multi-container Docker apps. It was a Python tool that sat on top of Docker, and let you define entire multi-container apps in a single YAML file. You could then deploy and manage the lifecycle of the app with the `fig` command-line tool.

Behind the scenes, Fig would read the YAML file and use Docker to deploy and manage the app via the Docker API. It was a good thing.

In fact, it was so good, that Docker, Inc. acquired Orchard and re-branded Fig as *Docker Compose*. The command-line tool was renamed from `fig` to `docker-compose`, and continues to be an external tool that gets bolted on top of the Docker Engine. Even though it's never been fully integrated into the Docker Engine, it's always been popular and widely used.

As things stand today, Compose is still an external Python binary that you have to install on a Docker host. You define multi-container (microservices) apps in a YAML file, pass the YAML file to the `docker-compose` command line, and Compose deploys it via the Docker API. However, April 2020 saw the announcement of the Compose Specification[12]. This is aimed at creating an open standard for defining multi-container cloud-native apps. The ultimate aim being to greatly simplify the *code-to-cloud* process.

The specification will be community-led and separate from the `docker-compose` implementation from Docker, Inc. This helps maintain better governance and clearer lines of demarcation. However, we should expect Docker to implement the fill spec in `docker-compose`.

The spec itself is a great document to learn the details.

Time to see it in action.

Installing Compose

Docker Compose is available on multiple platforms. In this section we'll demonstrate *some* of the ways to install it on Windows, Mac, and Linux. More installation methods exist, but the ones we show here will get you started.

Installing Compose on Windows 10

Docker Compose is included as part of the standard Docker Desktop installation on Windows 10. So, if you've got Docker Desktop on your Windows 10 PC, you've got Docker Compose.

Use the following command to check that Compose is installed. You can run this command from a PowerShell or CMD terminal.

---

[12]https://github.com/compose-spec/compose-spec

```
> docker-compose --version
docker-compose version 1.25.5, build 8a1c60f6
```

See **Chapter 3: Installing Docker** if you need more information on installing *Docker Desktop* on Windows 10.

Installing Compose on Mac

As with Windows 10, Docker Compose is installed as part of *Docker Desktop* for Mac. So, if you have Docker Desktop on your Mac, you have Docker Compose.

Run the following command in a terminal window to verify you have Docker Compose.

```
$ docker-compose --version
docker-compose version 1.25.5, build 8a1c60f6
```

See **Chapter 3: Installing Docker** if you need more information on installing *Docker Desktop*.

Installing Compose on Windows Server

Docker Compose is installed on Windows Server as a separate binary. To use it, you will need an up-to-date installation of Docker on your Windows Server.

Run the following commands from an elevated PowerShell terminal (run-as Administrator).

```
PS C:\> [Net.ServicePointManager]::SecurityProtocol = [Net.SecurityProtocolType]::Tls12
```

For readability, the following command uses backticks (`) to escape carriage returns and wrap the command over multiple lines. It installs version 1.25.5 of Docker Compose. You can install any version listed here: https://github.com/docker/compose/releases by replacing the 1.25.5` in the URL with the version you want to install.

```
PS C:\> Invoke-WebRequest `
 "https://github.com/docker/compose/releases/download/1.25.5/docker-compose-Windows-x86_64.exe" `
 -UseBasicParsing `
 -OutFile $Env:ProgramFiles\Docker\docker-compose.exe

Writing web request
Writing request stream... (Number of bytes written: 5260755)
```

Use the `docker-compose --version` command to verify the installation.

```
> docker-compose --version
docker-compose version 1.25.5, build 01110ad01
```

Compose is now installed. As long as your Windows Server machine has an up-to-date installation of the Docker Engine, you're ready to go.

Installing Compose on Linux

Installing Docker Compose on Linux is a two-step process. First, you download the binary using the `curl` command. Then you make it executable using `chmod`.

For Docker Compose to work on Linux, you'll need a working version of the Docker Engine.

The following command will download version `1.25.5` of Docker Compose and copy it to `/usr/bin/local`. You can check the releases page on GitHub[13] for the latest version and replace the `1.25.5` in the URL with the version you want to install.

The command may wrap over multiple lines in the book. If you run the command on a single line you will need to remove any backslashes (\).

```
$ sudo curl -L \
 "https://github.com/docker/compose/releases/download/1.25.5/docker-compose-$(uname -s)-$(uname -m)" \
 -o /usr/local/bin/docker-compose

% Total    % Received   Time       Time      Time     Current
                        Total      Spent     Left     Speed
100   617   0    617    0 --:--:-- --:--:-- --:--:--  1047
100 8280k  100 8280k    0  0:00:03  0:00:03 --:--:--  4069k
```

Now that you've downloaded the `docker-compose` binary, use the following `chmod` command to make it executable.

```
$ sudo chmod +x /usr/local/bin/docker-compose
```

Verify the installation and check the version.

```
$ docker-compose --version
docker-compose version 1.25.5, build 1110ad01
```

You're ready to use Docker Compose on Linux.

You can also use `pip` to install Compose from its Python package. But I don't want to waste valuable pages showing every possible installation method. Enough is enough, time to move on.

Compose files

Compose uses YAML files to define multi-service applications. YAML is a subset of JSON, so you can also use JSON. However, all the examples in this chapter will be YAML.

The default name for a Compose YAML file is `docker-compose.yml`. However, you can use the `-f` flag to specify custom filenames.

The following example shows a very simple Compose file that defines a small Flask app with two microservices (`web-fe` and `redis`). The app is a simple web server that counts the number of visits to a web page and stores the value in Redis. We'll call the app `counter-app` and use it as the example application for the rest of the chapter.

---

[13]https://github.com/docker/compose/releases

```
version: "3.8"
services:
  web-fe:
    build: .
    command: python app.py
    ports:
      - target: 5000
        published: 5000
    networks:
      - counter-net
    volumes:
      - type: volume
        source: counter-vol
        target: /code
  redis:
    image: "redis:alpine"
    networks:
      counter-net:

networks:
  counter-net:

volumes:
  counter-vol:
```

We'll skip through the basics of the file before taking a closer look.

The first thing to note is that the file has 4 top-level keys:

- version
- services
- networks
- volumes

Other top-level keys exist, such as `secrets` and `configs`, but we're not looking at those right now.

The `version` key is mandatory, and it's always the first line at the root of the file. This defines the version of the Compose file format (basically the API). You should normally use the latest version.

It's important to note that the `versions` key does not define the version of Docker Compose or the Docker Engine. For information regarding compatibility between versions of the Docker Engine, Docker Compose, and the Compose file format, google "Compose file versions and upgrading".

For the remainder of this chapter we'll be using version 3 or higher of the Compose file format.

The top-level `services` key is where you define the different application microservices. This example defines two services; a web front-end called `web-fe`, and an in-memory database called `redis`. Compose will deploy each of these services as its own container.

The top-level `networks` key tells Docker to create new networks. By default, Compose will create `bridge` networks. These are single-host networks that can only connect containers on the same Docker host. However, you can use the `driver` property to specify different network types.

The following code can be used in your Compose file to create a new *overlay* network called `over-net` that allows standalone containers to connect to it (`attachable`).

```
networks:
  over-net:
  driver: overlay
  attachable: true
```

The top-level `volumes` key is where you tell Docker to create new volumes.

Our specific Compose file

The example file we've listed uses the Compose version `3.8` file format, defines two services, defines a network called counter-net, and defines a volume called counter-vol.

Most of the detail is in the `services` section, so let's take a closer look at that.

The services section has two second-level keys:

- web-fe
- redis

Each of these defines a service (container) in the app. It's important to understand that Compose will deploy each of these as a container, and it will use the name of the keys as part of the container names. In our example, we've defined two keys; `web-fe` and `redis`. This means Compose will deploy two containers, one will have `web-fe` in its name and the other will have `redis`.

Within the definition of the `web-fe` service, we give Docker the following instructions:

- `build: .` This tells Docker to build a new image using the instructions in the `Dockerfile` in the current directory (`.`). The newly built image will be used in a later step to create the container for this service.
- `command: python app.py` This tells Docker to run a Python app called `app.py` as the main app in the container. The `app.py` file must exist in the image, and the image must contain Python. The Dockerfile takes care of both of these requirements.
- `ports:` Tells Docker to map port 5000 inside the container (`-target`) to port 5000 on the host (`published`). This means that traffic sent to the Docker host on port 5000 will be directed to port 5000 on the container. The app inside the container listens on port 5000.
- `networks:` Tells Docker which network to attach the service's container to. The network should already exist, or be defined in the `networks` top-level key. If it's an overlay network, it will need to have the `attachable` flag so that standalone containers can be attached to it (Compose deploys standalone containers instead of Docker Services).
- `volumes:` Tells Docker to mount the `counter-vol` volume (`source:`) to `/code` (`target:`) inside the container. The `counter-vol` volume needs to already exist, or be defined in the `volumes` top-level key at the bottom of the file.

In summary, Compose will instruct Docker to deploy a single standalone container for the `web-fe` service. It will be based on an image built from a Dockerfile in the same directory as the Compose file. This image will be started as a container and run `app.py` as its main app. It will expose itself on port 5000 on the host, attach to the `counter-net` network, and mount a volume to `/code`.

Note: Technically speaking, we don't need the `command: python app.py` option. This is because the application's Dockerfile already defines `python app.py` as the default app for the image. However, we're showing it here so you know how it works. You can also use Compose to override CMD instructions set in Dockerfiles.

The definition of the `redis` service is simpler:

- `image: redis:alpine` This tells Docker to start a standalone container called `redis` based on the `redis:alpine` image. This image will be pulled from Docker Hub.
- `networks:` The `redis` container will be attached to the `counter-net` network.

As both services will be deployed onto the same `counter-net` network, they will be able to resolve each other by name. This is important as the application is configured to communicate with the redis service by name.

Now that we understand how the Compose file works, let's deploy it!

Deploying an app with Compose

In this section, we'll deploy the app defined in the Compose file from the previous section. To do this, you'll need the following 4 files from https://github.com/nigelpoulton/counter-app:

- Dockerfile
- app.py
- requirements.txt
- docker-compose.yml

Clone the Git repo locally.

```
$ git clone https://github.com/nigelpoulton/counter-app.git

Cloning into 'counter-app'...
remote: Counting objects: 9, done.
remote: Compressing objects: 100% (8/8), done.
remote: Total 9 (delta 1), reused 5 (delta 0), pack-reused 0
Unpacking objects: 100% (9/9), done.
Checking connectivity... done.
```

Cloning the repo will create a new sub-directory called `counter-app`. This will contain all of the required files and will be considered your *build context*. Compose will also use the name of the directory (`counter-app`) as the project name. We'll see this later, but Compose will prepend all resource names with `counter-app_`.

Change into the `counter-app` directory and check the files are present.

```
$ cd counter-app
$ ls
app.py  docker-compose.yml  Dockerfile  requirements.txt ...
```

Let's quickly describe each file:

- `app.py` is the application code (a Python Flask app)
- `docker-compose.yml` is the Docker Compose file that describes how Docker should build and deploy the app
- `Dockerfile` describes how to build the image for the `web-fe` service
- `requirements.txt` lists the Python packages required for the app

Feel free to inspect the contents of each file.

The `app.py` file is obviously the core of the application. But `docker-compose.yml` is the glue that sticks all the application microservices together.

Let's use Compose to bring the app up. You must run the all of the following commands from within the `counter-app` directory that you just cloned from GitHub.

```
$ docker-compose up &

[1] 1635
Creating network "counter-app_counter-net" with the default driver
Creating volume "counter-app_counter-vol" with default driver
Pulling redis (redis:alpine)...
alpine: Pulling from library/redis
1160f4abea84: Pull complete
a8c53d69ca3a: Pull complete
<Snip>
web-fe_1  |  * Debugger PIN: 313-791-729
```

It'll take a few seconds for the app to come up, and the output can be quite verbose. You may also have to hit the `Return` key when the deployment completes.

We'll step through what happened in a second, but first let's talk about the `docker-compose` command.

`docker-compose up` is the most common way to bring up a Compose app (we're calling a multi-container app defined in a Compose file a *Compose app*). It builds or pulls all required images, creates all required networks and volumes, and starts all required containers.

By default, `docker-compose up` expects the name of the Compose file to `docker-compose.yml`. If your Compose file has a different name, you need to specify it with the `-f` flag. The following example will deploy an application from a Compose file called `prod-equus-bass.yml`

```
$ docker-compose -f prod-equus-bass.yml up
```

It's also common to use the `-d` flag to bring the app up in the background. For example:

```
docker-compose up -d

--OR--

docker-compose -f prod-equus-bass.yml up -d
```

Our example brought the app up in the foreground (we didn't use the -d flag), but we used the & to give us the terminal window back. This forces Compose to output all messages to the terminal window, and we'll refer back to these messages later.

Now that the app is built and running, we can use normal docker commands to view the images, containers, networks, and volumes that Compose created.

```
$ docker image ls
REPOSITORY            TAG       IMAGE ID     CREATED         SIZE
counter-app_web-fe    latest    96..6ff9e    3 minutes ago   95.9MB
python                alpine    01..17a02    2 weeks ago     85.5MB
redis                 alpine    ed..c83de    5 weeks ago     26.9MB
```

We can see that three images were either built or pulled as part of the deployment.

The counter-app_web-fe:latest image was created by the build: . instruction in the docker-compose.yml file. This instruction caused Docker to build a new image using the Dockerfile in the same directory. It contains the application code for the Python Flask web app, and was built from the python:alpine image. See the contents of the Dockerfile for more information.

```
FROM python:alpine                        << Base image
ADD . /code                               << Copy app into image
WORKDIR /code                             << Set working directory
RUN pip install -r requirements.txt       << Install requirements
CMD ["python", "app.py"]                  << Set the default app
```

I've added comments to the end of each line to help explain. They must be removed before deploying the app.

Notice how Compose has named the newly built image as a combination of the project name (counter-app), and the resource name as specified in the Compose file (web-fe). All resources deployed by Compose will follow this naming convention.

The redis:alpine image was pulled from Docker Hub by the image: "redis:alpine" instruction in the .Services.redis section of the Compose file.

The following container listing shows two running containers. The name of each is prefixed with the name of the project (name of the build context directory). Also, each one has a numeric suffix that indicates the instance number — this is because Compose allows for scaling.

```
$ docker container ls
ID     COMMAND                 STATUS       PORTS                   NAMES
84..   "python app.py"         Up 2 mins    0.0.0.0:5000->5000/tcp  counter-app_web-fe_1
eb..   "docker-entrypoint.s…"  Up 2 mins    6379/tcp                counter-app_redis_1
```

The `counter-app_web-fe` container is running the application's web front end. This is running the `app.py` code and is mapped to port `5000` on all interfaces on the Docker host. We'll connect to this in just a second.

The following network and volume listings show the `counter-app_counter-net` network and `counter-app_-counter-vol` volume.

```
$ docker network ls
NETWORK ID     NAME                      DRIVER   SCOPE
b4c1976d7c27   bridge                    bridge   local
33ff702253b3   counter-app_counter-net   bridge   local
<Snip>

$ docker volume ls
DRIVER     VOLUME NAME
<Snip>
local      counter-app_counter-vol
```

With the application successfully deployed, you can point a web browser at your Docker host on port `5000` and see the application in all its glory.

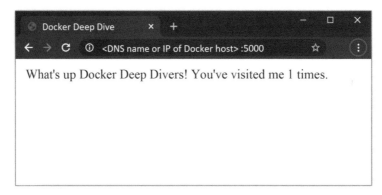

Pretty impressive ;-)

Hitting your browser's refresh button will cause the counter to increment. Have a look at the app (`app.py`) to see how the counter data is stored in the Redis back-end.

If you brought the application up using the `&`, you will be able to see the `HTTP 200` response codes being logged in the terminal window. These indicate successful requests, and you'll see one for each time you load the web page.

```
web-fe_1  | 172.20.0.1 - - [29/Apr/2020 10:15:27] "GET / HTTP/1.1" 200 -
web-fe_1  | 172.20.0.1 - - [29/Apr/2020 10:15:28] "GET / HTTP/1.1" 200 -
```

Congratulations. You've successfully deployed a multi-container application using Docker Compose!

Managing an app with Compose

In this section, you'll see how to start, stop, delete, and get the status of applications being managed by Docker Compose. You'll also see how the volume we're using can be used to directly inject updates to the app's web front-end.

As the application is already up, let's see how to bring it down. To do this, replace the up sub-command with down.

```
$ docker-compose down
 1. Stopping counter-app_redis_1  ...
 2. Stopping counter-app_web-fe_1 ...
 3. redis_1   | 1:signal-handler Received SIGTERM scheduling shutdown...
 4. redis_1   | 1:M 09 Jan 11:16:00.456 # User requested shutdown...
 5. redis_1   | 1:M 09 Jan 11:16:00.456 * Saving the final RDB snap...
 6. redis_1   | 1:M 09 Jan 11:16:00.463 * DB saved on disk
 7. Stopping counter-app_redis_1  ... done
 8. counter-app_redis_1 exited with code 0
 9. Stopping counter-app_web-fe_1 ... done
10. Removing counter-app_redis_1  ... done
11. Removing counter-app_web-fe_1 ... done
12. Removing network counter-app_counter-net
13. [1]+  Done            docker-compose up
```

As you initially started the app with the &, it's running in the foreground. This means you get verbose output to the terminal, giving you an excellent insight into how things work. Let's step through what each line is telling us.

Lines 1 and 2 are stopping the two services. These are the web-fe and redis services defined in the Compose file.

Line 3 shows that the stop instruction sends a SIGTERM signal. This is sent to the PID 1 process in each container. Lines 4-6 show the Redis container gracefully handling the signal and shutting itself down. Lines 7 and 8 report the success of the stop operation.

Line 9 shows the web-fe service successfully stopping.

Lines 10 and 11 show the stopped services being removed.

Line 12 shows the counter-net network being removed, and line 13 shows the docker-compose up process exiting.

It's important to note that the counter-vol volume was **not** deleted. This is because volumes are intended to be long-term persistent data stores. As such, their lifecycle is entirely decoupled from the applications they serve. Running a docker volume ls will show that the volume is still present on the system. If you'd written any data to the volume, that data would still exist.

Also, any images that were built or pulled as part of the docker-compose up operation will still be present on the system. This means future deployments of the app will be faster.

Let's look at a few other `docker-compose` sub-commands.

Use the following command to bring the app up again, but this time in the background.

```
$ docker-compose up -d
Creating network "counter-app_counter-net" with the default driver
Creating counter-app_redis_1  ... done
Creating counter-app_web-fe_1 ... done
```

See how the app started much faster this time — the `counter-vol` volume already exists, and all images already exist on the Docker host.

Show the current state of the app with the `docker-compose ps` command.

```
$ docker-compose ps
Name                    Command                   State   Ports
---------------------------------------------------------------------------
counter-app_redis_1     docker-entrypoint.sh redis..  Up    6379/tcp
counter-app_web-fe_1    python app.py                 Up    0.0.0.0:5000->5000/tcp
```

You can see both containers, the commands they are running, their current state, and the network ports they are listening on.

Use `docker-compose top` to list the processes running inside of each service (container).

```
$ docker-compose top
counter-app_redis_1
 PID    USER   TIME    COMMAND
--------------------------------
19643   999    0:01    redis-server

counter-app_web-fe_1
 PID    USER   TIME              COMMAND
------------------------------------------------------
19679   root   0:00    python app.py
19788   root   0:01    /usr/local/bin/python /code/app.py
```

The PID numbers returned are the PID numbers as seen from the Docker host (not from within the containers).

Use the `docker-compose stop` command to stop the app without deleting its resources. Then show the status of the app with `docker-compose ps`.

```
$ docker-compose stop
Stopping counter-app_web-fe_1 ... done
Stopping counter-app_redis_1  ... done

$ docker-compose ps
Name                    Command                      State
------------------------------------------------------------
counter-app_redis_1     docker-entrypoint.sh redis   Exit 0
counter-app_web-fe_1    python app.py                Exit 0
```

As you can see, stopping a Compose app does not remove the application definition from the system. It just stops the app's containers. You can verify this with the `docker container ls -a` command.

You can delete a stopped Compose app with `docker-compose rm`. This will delete the containers and networks the app is using, but it will not delete volumes or images. Nor will it delete the application source code in your project's build context directory (`app.py`, `Dockerfile`, `requirements.txt`, and `docker-compose.yml`).

Restart the app with the `docker-compose restart` command.

```
$ docker-compose restart
Restarting counter-app_web-fe_1 ... done
Restarting counter-app_redis_1  ... done
```

Verify the operation.

```
$ docker-compose ps
        Name                    Command              State           Ports
--------------------------------------------------------------------------------------
counter-app_redis_1     docker-entrypoint.sh redis   Up      6379/tcp
counter-app_web-fe_1    python app.py                Up      0.0.0.0:5000->5000/tcp
```

Use the `docker-compose down` command to **stop and delete** the app with a single command.

```
$ docker-compose down
Stopping counter-app_redis_1  ... done
Stopping counter-app_web-fe_1 ... done
Removing counter-app_redis_1  ... done
Removing counter-app_web-fe_1 ... done
Removing network counter-app_counter-net
```

The app is now deleted. Only its images, volumes, and source code remain.

Let's deploy the app one last time and see a little more about how the volume works.

```
$ docker-compose up -d
Creating network "counter-app_counter-net" with the default driver
Creating counter-app_redis_1  ... done
Creating counter-app_web-fe_1 ... done
```

If you look in the Compose file, you'll see that it defines a volume called `counter-vol` and mounts it in to the `web-fe` container at `/code`.

```
services:
  web-fe:
  <Snip>
    volumes:
      - type: volume
        source: counter-vol
        target: /code
<Snip>
volumes:
  counter-vol:
```

The first time you deployed the app, Compose checked to see if a volume called `counter-vol` already existed. It did not, so Compose created it. You can see it with the `docker volume ls` command, and you can get more detailed information with `docker volume inspect counter-app_counter-vol`.

```
$ docker volume ls
RIVER                VOLUME NAME
local                  counter-app_counter-vol
```

It's also worth knowing that Compose builds networks and volumes **before** deploying services. This makes sense, as networks and volumes are lower-level infrastructure objects that are consumed by services (containers). The following snippet shows Compose creating the network and volume as its first two tasks (even before building and pulling images).

```
$ docker-compose up -d

Creating network "counter-app_counter-net" with the default driver
Creating volume "counter-app_counter-vol" with default driver
Pulling redis (redis:alpine)...
<Snip>
```

If we take another look at the service definition for `web-fe`, we'll see that it's mounting the counter-app volume into the service's container at `/code`. We can also see from the Dockerfile that `/code` is where the app is installed and executed from. Net result, the app code resides on a Docker volume. See Figure 9.2.

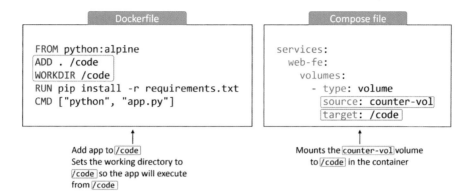

Figure 9.2

This all means we can make changes to files in the volume, from the outside of the container, and have them reflected immediately in the app. Let's see how that works.

The next few steps will walk you through the following process. We'll update the contents of app.py in the project's working directory on the Docker host. We'll copy the updated app.py to the volume on the Docker host. We'll refresh the app's web page to see the updated text. This will work because whatever you write to the volume on the Docker host will immediately appear in the volume mounted in the container.

> **Note:** The following will not work if you are using Docker Desktop on a Mac or Windows 10 PC. This is because Docker Desktop runs Docker inside of a lightweight VM and volumes exist inside the VM.

Use your favourite text editor to edit the app.py file in the projects working directory. We'll use vim in the example.

```
$ vim ~/counter-app/app.py
```

Change text between the double quote marks ("") on line 22. The line starts with return "What's up...". Enter any text you like, as long as it's within the double-quote marks, and save your changes.

Now that you've updated the app, you need to copy it into the volume on the Docker host. Each Docker volume is exposed at a location within the Docker host's filesystem, as well as a mount point in one or more containers. Use the following docker volume inspect command to find where the volume is exposed on the Docker host.

```
$ docker volume inspect counter-app_counter-vol | grep Mount
"Mountpoint": "/var/lib/docker/volumes/counter-app_counter-vol/_data",
```

Copy the updated app file to the volume's mount point on your Docker host (remember that this will not work on Docker Desktop). As soon as you perform the copy operation, the updated file will appear in the /code directory in the web-fe container. The operation will overwrite the existing /code/app.py file in the container.

```
$ cp ~/counter-app/app.py \
  /var/lib/docker/volumes/counter-app_counter-vol/_data/app.py
```

The updated app file is now on the container. Connect to the app to see your change. You can do this by pointing your web browser to the IP of your Docker host on port 5000.

Figure 9.3 shows the updated app.

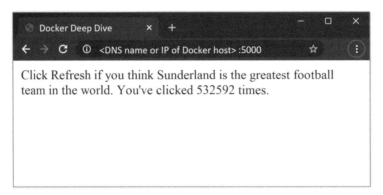

Obviously you wouldn't do an update operation like this in production, but it's a real time-saver in development.

Congratulations. You've deployed and managed a simple multi-container app using Docker Compose.

Before reminding ourselves of the major docker-compose commands, it's important to understand that this was a very simple example. Docker Compose is capable of deploying and managing far more complex applications.

Deploying apps with Compose - The commands

- docker-compose up is the command to deploy a Compose app. It expects the Compose file to be called docker-compose.yml or docker-compose.yaml, but you can specify a custom filename with the -f flag. It's common to start the app in the background with the -d flag.
- docker-compose stop will stop all of the containers in a Compose app without deleting them from the system. The app can be easily restarted with docker-compose restart.
- docker-compose rm will delete a stopped Compose app. It will delete containers and networks, but it will not delete volumes and images.
- docker-compose restart will restart a Compose app that has been stopped with docker-compose stop. If you have made changes to your Compose app since stopping it, these changes will **not** appear in the restarted app. You will need to re-deploy the app to get the changes.
- docker-compose ps will list each container in the Compose app. It shows current state, the command each one is running, and network ports.
- docker-compose down will stop and delete a running Compose app. It deletes containers and networks, but not volumes and images.

Chapter Summary

In this chapter, you learned how to deploy and manage a multi-container application using Docker Compose.

Docker Compose is a Python application that you install on top of the Docker Engine. It lets you define multi-container apps in a single declarative configuration file and deploy it with a single command.

Compose files can be YAML or JSON, and they define all of the containers, networks, volumes, and secrets that an application requires. You then feed the file to the `docker-compose` command line tool, and Compose uses Docker to deploy it.

Once the app is deployed, you can manage its entire lifecycle using the many `docker-compose` sub-commands.

You also saw how volumes have a separate lifecycle to the rest of the app, and can be used to mount changes directly into containers.

Docker Compose is popular with developers, and the Compose file is an excellent source of application documentation — it defies all the services that make up the app, the images they use, ports they expose, networks and volumes they use, and much more. As such, it can help bridge the gap between dev and ops. You should also treat your Compose files as if they were code. This means, among other things, storing them in source control repos.

10: Docker Swarm

Now that we know how to install Docker, pull images, and work with containers, the next thing we need is a way to work with things at scale. That's where Docker Swarm comes into play.

As usual, we'll split this chapter into the usual three parts:

- The TLDR
- The deep dive
- The commands

Docker Swarm - The TLDR

Docker Swarm is two main things:

1. An enterprise-grade secure cluster of Docker hosts
2. An engine for orchestrating microservices apps

On the clustering front, Swarm groups one or more Docker nodes and lets you manage them as a cluster. Out-of-the-box, you get an encrypted distributed cluster store, encrypted networks, mutual TLS, secure cluster join tokens, and a PKI that makes managing and rotating certificates a breeze. You can even non-disruptively add and remove nodes. It's a beautiful thing.

While we cover some aspects of Swarm security in this chapter, we go a lot deeper in Chapter 15.

On the orchestration front, Swarm exposes a rich API that allows you to deploy and manage complex microservices apps with ease. You can define your apps in declarative manifest files and deploy them to the Swarm with native Docker commands. You can even perform rolling updates, rollbacks, and scaling operations. Again, all with simple commands.

Docker Swarm competes directly with Kubernetes — they both orchestrate containerized applications. While it's true that Kubernetes has more momentum and a more active community and ecosystem, Docker Swarm is an excellent technology and a lot easier to configure and deploy. It's an excellent technology for small-to-medium businesses and application deployments.

Docker Swarm - The Deep Dive

We'll split the deep dive part of this chapter as follows:

- Swarm primer
- Build a secure swarm cluster
- Deploy some swarm services
- Troubleshooting

Swarm primer

On the clustering front, a *swarm* consists of one or more Docker *nodes*. These can be physical servers, VMs, Raspberry Pi's, or cloud instances. The only requirement is that all nodes have Docker installed and can communicate over reliable networks.

Nodes are configured as *managers* or *workers*. *Managers* look after the control plane of the cluster, meaning things like the state of the cluster and dispatching tasks to *workers*. *Workers* accept tasks from *managers* and execute them.

The configuration and state of the *swarm* is held in a distributed *etcd* database located on all managers. It's kept in memory and is extremely up-to-date. But the best thing about it is that it requires zero configuration — it's installed as part of the swarm and just takes care of itself.

Something that's game changing on the clustering front is the approach to security. TLS is so tightly integrated that it's impossible to build a swarm without it. In today's security conscious world, things like this deserve all the plaudits they get. *Swarm* uses TLS to encrypt communications, authenticate nodes, and authorize roles. Automatic key rotation is also thrown in as the icing on the cake. And the best part... it all happens so smoothly that you don't even know it's there.

On the application orchestration front, the atomic unit of scheduling on a swarm is the *service*. This is a new object in the API, introduced along with swarm, and is a higher level construct that wraps some advanced features around containers. These include scaling, rolling updates, and simple rollbacks. It's useful to think of a *service* as an enhanced container.

A high-level view of a swarm is shown in Figure 10.1.

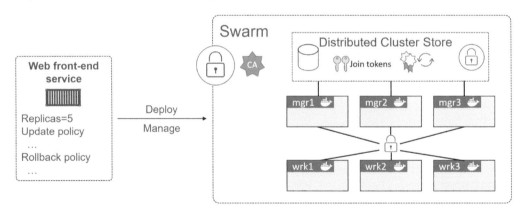

Figure 10.1 High-level swarm

That's enough of a primer. Let's get our hands dirty with some examples.

Build a secure Swarm cluster

In this section, we'll build a secure swarm cluster with three *manager nodes* and three *worker nodes*. You can use a different lab with different numbers of *managers* and *workers*, and with different names and IPs, but the examples that follow will use the values in Figure 10.2.

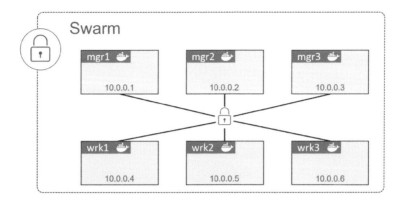

Figure 10.2

The nodes can be virtual machines, physical servers, cloud instances, or Raspberry Pi systems. The only requirements are that they have Docker installed and can communicate over a reliable network. It's also beneficial if name resolution is configured — it makes it easier to identify nodes in command outputs and helps when troubleshooting.

On the networking front, you need the following ports open on routers and firewalls between nodes:

- `2377/tcp`: for secure client-to-swarm communication
- `7946/tcp and udp`: for control plane gossip
- `4789/udp`: for VXLAN-based overlay networks

Docker Desktop for Mac and Windows only supports a single Docker node. You can initialize a single-node swarm and follow along with most of the examples. Alternatively, you can try Play with Docker at https://labs.play-with-docker.com.

Once you've satisfied the pre-requisites, you can go ahead and build a swarm.

The process of building a swarm is called *initializing a swarm*, and the high-level process is this: Initialize the first manager node > Join additional manager nodes > Join worker nodes > Done.

Initializing a new swarm

Docker nodes that are not part of a swarm are said to be in *single-engine mode*. Once they're added to a swarm they're automatically switched into *swarm mode*.

Running `docker swarm init` on a Docker host in *single-engine mode* will switch that node into *swarm mode*, create a new *swarm*, and make the node the first *manager* of the swarm.

Additional nodes can then be joined to the swarm as workers and managers. Joining a Docker host to an existing swarm switches them into *swarm mode* as part of the operation.

The following steps will put **mgr1** into *swarm mode* and initialize a new swarm. It will then join **wrk1**, **wrk2**, and **wrk3** as worker nodes — automatically putting them into *swarm mode* as part of the process. Finally, it will add **mgr2** and **mgr3** as additional managers and switch them into *swarm mode*. At the end of the procedure all 6 nodes will be in *swarm mode* and operating as part of the same swarm.

This example will use the IP addresses and DNS names of the nodes shown in Figure 10.2. Yours may be different.

1. Log on to **mgr1** and initialize a new swarm (don't forget to use backticks instead of backslashes if you're following along with Windows in a PowerShell terminal).

```
$ docker swarm init \
  --advertise-addr 10.0.0.1:2377 \
  --listen-addr 10.0.0.1:2377

Swarm initialized: current node (d21lyz...c79qzkx) is now a manager.
```

   The command can be broken down as follows:
   - `docker swarm init`: This tells Docker to initialize a new swarm and make this node the first manager. It also enables swarm mode on the node.
   - `--advertise-addr`: As the name suggests, this is the swarm API endpoint that will be advertised to other nodes in the swarm. It will usually be one of the node's IP addresses, but can be an external load-balancer address. It's an optional flag unless you want to specify a load-balancer or specific IP address on a node with multiple interfaces.
   - `--listen-addr`: This is the IP address that the node will accept swarm traffic on. If not explicitly set, it defaults to the same value as `--advertise-addr`. If `--advertise-addr` is a load-balancer, you must use `--listen-addr` to specify a local IP or interface for swarm traffic.
   I recommend you be specific and always use both flags.

   The default port that swarm mode operates on is **2377**. This is customizable, but it's convention to use `2377/tcp` for secured (HTTPS) client-to-swarm connections.

2. List the nodes in the swarm.

```
$ docker node ls
ID               HOSTNAME    STATUS    AVAILABILITY    MANAGER STATUS
d21...qzkx *     mgr1        Ready     Active          Leader
```

   Notice that **mgr1** is currently the only node in the swarm, and is listed as the *Leader*. We'll come back to this in a second.

3. From **mgr1** run the `docker swarm join-token` command to extract the commands and tokens required to add new workers and managers to the swarm.

```
$ docker swarm join-token worker
To add a manager to this swarm, run the following command:
   docker swarm join \
   --token SWMTKN-1-0uahebax...c87tu8dx2c \
   10.0.0.1:2377

$ docker swarm join-token manager
To add a manager to this swarm, run the following command:
   docker swarm join \
   --token SWMTKN-1-0uahebax...ue4hv6ps3p \
   10.0.0.1:2377
```

   Notice that the commands to join a worker and a manager are identical apart from the join tokens (`SWMTKN...`). This means that whether a node joins as a worker or a manager depends entirely on which token you use when joining it. **You should ensure that your join tokens are kept secure, as they're the only thing required to join a node to a swarm!**

4. Log on to **wrk1** and join it to the swarm using the `docker swarm join` command with the worker join token.

```
$ docker swarm join \
   --token SWMTKN-1-0uahebax...c87tu8dx2c \
   10.0.0.1:2377 \
   --advertise-addr 10.0.0.4:2377 \
   --listen-addr 10.0.0.4:2377

This node joined a swarm as a worker.
```

The --advertise-addr, and --listen-addr flags optional. I've added them as I consider it best practice to be as specific as possible when it comes to network configuration.

5. Repeat the previous step on **wrk2** and **wrk3** so that they join the swarm as workers. If you're specifying the --advertise-addr and --listen-addr flags, make sure you use **wrk2** and **wrk3's** respective IP addresses.

6. Log on to **mgr2** and join it to the swarm as a manager using the docker swarm join command with the manager join token.

```
$ docker swarm join \
   --token SWMTKN-1-0uahebax...ue4hv6ps3p \
   10.0.0.1:2377 \
   --advertise-addr 10.0.0.2:2377 \
   --listen-addr 10.0.0.2:2377

This node joined a swarm as a manager.
```

7. Repeat the previous step on **mgr3**, remembering to use **mgr3's** IP address for the advertise-addr and --listen-addr flags.

8. List the nodes in the swarm by running docker node ls from any of the manager nodes in the swarm.

```
$ docker node ls
ID              HOSTNAME   STATUS   AVAILABILITY   MANAGER STATUS
0g4rl...babl8 *  mgr2       Ready    Active         Reachable
2xlti...l0nyp    mgr3       Ready    Active         Reachable
8yv0b...wmr67    wrk1       Ready    Active
9mzwf...e4m4n    wrk3       Ready    Active
d21ly...9qzkx    mgr1       Ready    Active         Leader
e62gf...l5wt6    wrk2       Ready    Active
```

Congratulations. You've just created a 6-node swarm with 3 managers and 3 workers. As part of the process, the Docker Engine on each node was automatically put into *swarm mode* and the *swarm* was automatically secured with TLS.

If you look in the MANAGER STATUS column you'll see the three manager nodes are showing as either "Reachable" or "Leader". We'll learn more about leaders shortly. Nodes with nothing in the MANAGER STATUS column are *workers*. Also note the asterisk (*) after the ID on the line showing **mgr2**. This tells you which node you are logged on to and executing commands from. In this instance the command was issued from **mgr2**.

> **Note:** It's a pain to specify the --advertise-addr and --listen-addr flags every time you join a node to the swarm. However, it can be a much bigger pain if you get the network configuration of your swarm wrong. Also, manually adding nodes to a swarm is unlikely to be a daily task, so it's worth the extra up-front effort to use the flags. It's your choice though. In lab environments or nodes with only a single IP you probably don't need to use them.

Now that you have a *swarm* up and running, let's take a look at manager high availability (HA).

Swarm manager high availability (HA)

So far, we've added three manager nodes to a swarm. Why three? And how do they work together?

Swarm *managers* have native support for high availability (HA). This means one or more can fail, and the survivors will keep the swarm running.

Technically speaking, swarm implements a form of active-passive multi-manager HA. This means that although you have multiple *managers*, only one of them is *active* at any given moment. This active manager is called the "*leader*", and the leader is the only one that will ever issue live commands against the *swarm*. So, it's only ever the leader that changes the config, or issues tasks to workers. If a follower manager (passive) receives commands for the swarm, it proxies them across to the leader.

This process is shown in Figure 10.3. Step 1 is the command coming in to a *manager* from a remote Docker client. Step 2 is the non-leader manager receiving the command and proxying it to the leader. Step 3 is the leader executing the command on the swarm.

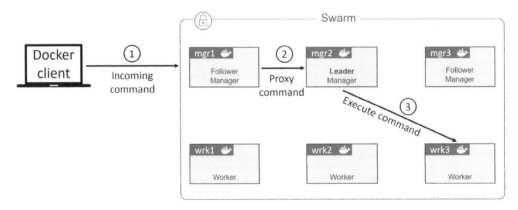

Figure 10.3

If you look closely at Figure 10.3, you'll notice that managers are either *leaders* or *followers*. This is Raft terminology, because swarm uses an implementation of the Raft consensus algorithm[14] to maintain a consistent cluster state across multiple highly available managers.

On the topic of HA, the following two best practices apply:

1. Deploy an odd number of managers.
2. Don't deploy too many managers (3 or 5 is recommended)

Having an odd number of *managers* reduces the chances of split-brain conditions. For example, if you had 4 managers and the network partitioned, you could be left with two managers on each side of the partition. This is known as a split brain — each side knows there used to be 4 but can now only see 2. But crucially, neither side has any way of knowing if the other two are still alive and whether it holds a majority (quorum). A swarm cluster continues to operate during split-brain conditions, but you are no longer able to alter the configuration or add and manage application workloads.

---

[14]https://raft.github.io/

However, if you have 3 or 5 managers and the same network partition occurs, it is impossible to have an equal number of managers on both sides of the partition. This means that one side achieves quorum and full cluster management services remain available. The example on the right side of Figure 10.4 shows a partitioned cluster where the left side of the split knows it has a majority of managers.

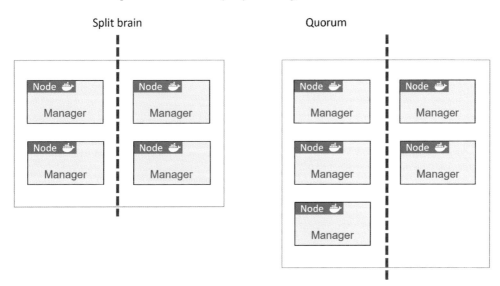

Figure 10.4

As with all consensus algorithms, more participants means more time required to achieve consensus. It's like deciding where to eat — it's always quicker and easier for 3 people to make a quick decision than it is for 33! With this in mind, it's a best practice to have either 3 or 5 managers for HA. 7 might work, but it's generally accepted that 3 or 5 is optimal. You definitely don't want more than 7, as the time taken to achieve consensus will be longer.

A final word of caution regarding manager HA. While it's obviously a good practice to spread your managers across availability zones within your network, you need to make sure the networks connecting them are reliable, as network partitions can be a difficult to troubleshoot and resolve. This means, at the time of writing, the nirvana of hosting your active production applications and infrastructure across multiple cloud providers such as AWS and Azure is a bit of a daydream. Take the time and effort to ensure your managers and workers are connected via reliable high-speed networks.

Built-in Swarm security

Swarm clusters have a ton of built-in security that's configured out-of-the-box with sensible defaults — CA settings, join tokens, mutual TLS, encrypted cluster store, encrypted networks, cryptographic node ID's and more. See **Chapter 15: Security in Docker** for a detailed look at these.

Locking a Swarm

Despite all of this built-in native security, restarting an older manager or restoring an old backup has the potential to compromise the cluster. Old managers re-joining a swarm automatically decrypt and gain access to the Raft log time-series database — this can pose security concerns. Restoring old backups can also wipe the current swarm configuration.

To prevent situations like these, Docker allows you to lock a swarm with the Autolock feature. This forces restarted managers to present the cluster unlock key before being admitted back into the cluster.

It's possible to apply a lock directly to a new swarm by passing the `--autolock` flag to the `docker swarm init` command. However, we've already built a swarm, so we'll lock our existing swarm with the `docker swarm update` command.

Run the following command from a swarm manager.

```
$ docker swarm update --autolock=true
Swarm updated.
To unlock a swarm manager after it restarts, run the `docker swarm unlock` command and
provide the following key:

    SWMKEY-1-5|ICW2kRxPxZrVyBDWzBkzZdSd0Yc7Cl2o4Uuf9NPU4

Please remember to store this key in a password manager, since without it you will not be able
to restart the manager.
```

Be sure to keep the unlock key in a secure place. You can always check your current swarm unlock key with the `docker swarm unlock-key` command.

Restart one of your manager nodes to see if it automatically re-joins the cluster. You may need to prepend the command with `sudo`.

```
$ service docker restart
```

Try and list the nodes in the swarm.

```
$ docker node ls
Error response from daemon: Swarm is encrypted and needs to be unlocked before it can be used.
```

Although the Docker service has restarted on the manager, it has not been allowed to re-join the swarm. You can prove this even further by running the `docker node ls` command on another manager node. The restarted manager will show as `down` and `unreachable`.

Use the `docker swarm unlock` command to unlock the swarm for the restarted manager. You'll need to run this command on the restarted manager, and you'll need to provide the unlock key.

```
$ docker swarm unlock
Please enter unlock key: <enter your key>
```

The node will be allowed to re-join the swarm and will show as `ready` and `reachable` if you run another `docker node ls`.

Locking your swarm and protecting the unlock key is recommended for production environments.

Now that you've got our *swarm* built and understand the infrastructure concepts of *leaders* and *manager HA*, let's move on to the application aspect of *services*.

Swarm services

Everything we do in this section of the chapter gets improved on by Docker Stacks in Chapter 14. However, it's important that you learn the concepts here so that you're prepared for Chapter 14.

Like we said in the swarm primer... *services* are a new construct introduced with Docker 1.12, and they only apply to *swarm mode*.

Services let us specify most of the familiar container options, such as *name, port mappings, attaching to networks,* and *images.* But they add important cloud-native features, including *desired state* and automatic reconciliation. For example, swarm services allow us to declaratively define a desired state for an application that we can apply to the swarm and let the swarm take care of deploying it and managing it.

Let's look at a quick example. Assume you have an app with a web front-end. You have an image for the web server, and testing has shown that you need 5 instances to handle normal daily traffic. You translate this requirement into a single *service* declaring the image to use, and that the service should always have 5 running replicas. You issue that to the swarm as your desired state, and the swarm takes care of ensuring there are always 5 instances of the web server running.

We'll see some of the other things that can be declared as part of a service in a minute, but before we do that, let's see one way to create what we just described.

You can create services in one of two ways:

1. Imperatively on the command line with `docker service create`
2. Declaratively with a stack file

We'll look at stack files in a later chapter. For now we'll focus on the imperative method.

> **Note:** The command to create a new service is the same on Windows. However, the image used in this example is a Linux image and will not work on Windows. You can substitute the image for a Windows web server image and the command will work. Remember, if you are typing Windows commands from a PowerShell terminal you will need to use the backtick (') to indicate continuation on the next line.

```
$ docker service create --name web-fe \
  -p 8080:8080 \
  --replicas 5 \
  nigelpoulton/pluralsight-docker-ci

z7ovearqmruwk0u2vc5o7ql0p
```

Notice that many of the familiar `docker container run` arguments are the same. In the example, we specified `--name` and `-p` which work the same for standalone containers as well as services.

Let's review the command and output.

We used `docker service create` to tell Docker we are declaring a new service, and we used the `--name` flag to name it **web-fe**. We told Docker to map port 8080 on every node in the swarm to 8080 inside of each service replica. Next, we used the `--replicas` flag to tell Docker there should always be 5 replicas of this service. Finally, we told Docker which image to use for the replicas — it's important to understand that all service replicas use the same image and config!

After we hit `Return`, the command was sent to a manager node, and the manager acting as leader instantiated 5 replicas across the *swarm* — remember that swarm managers also act as workers. Each worker or manager that received a work task pulled the image and started a container listening on port 8080. The swarm leader also ensured a copy of the service's *desired state* was stored on the cluster and replicated to every manager.

But this isn't the end. All *services* are constantly monitored by the swarm — the swarm runs a background *reconciliation loop* that constantly compares the *observed state* of the service with the *desired state*. If the two states match, the world is a happy place and no further action is needed. If they don't match, swarm takes actions to bring *observed state* into line with *desired state*.

As an example, if a *worker* hosting one of the 5 **web-fe** replicas fails, the *observed state* of the **web-fe** service will drop from 5 replicas to 4. This will no longer match the *desired state* of 5, so the swarm will start a new **web-fe** replica to bring the *observed state* back in line with *desired state*. This behavior is a key tenet of cloud-native applications and allows the service to self-heal in the event of node failures and the likes.

Viewing and inspecting services

You can use the `docker service ls` command to see a list of all services running on a swarm.

```
$ docker service ls
ID         NAME      MODE         REPLICAS    IMAGE               PORTS
z7o...uw   web-fe    replicated   5/5         nigel...ci:latest   *:8080->8080/tcp
```

The output shows a single running service as well as some basic information about state. Among other things, you can see the name of the service and that 5 out of the 5 desired replicas are in the running state. If you run this command soon after deploying the service it might not show all tasks/replicas as running. This is often due to the time it takes to pull the image on each node.

You can use the `docker service ps` command to see a list of service replicas and the state of each.

```
$ docker service ps web-fe
ID         NAME       IMAGE               NODE    DESIRED    CURRENT
817...f6z  web-fe.1   nigelpoulton/...    mgr2    Running    Running 2 mins
a1d...mzn  web-fe.2   nigelpoulton/...    wrk1    Running    Running 2 mins
cc0...ar0  web-fe.3   nigelpoulton/...    wrk2    Running    Running 2 mins
6f0...azu  web-fe.4   nigelpoulton/...    mgr3    Running    Running 2 mins
dyl...p3e  web-fe.5   nigelpoulton/...    mgr1    Running    Running 2 mins
```

The format of the command is `docker service ps <service-name or service-id>`. The output displays each replica (container) on its own line, shows which node in the swarm it's executing on, and shows desired state and the current observed state.

For detailed information about a service, use the `docker service inspect` command.

```
$ docker service inspect --pretty web-fe
ID:             z7ovearqmruwk0u2vc5o7ql0p
Name:           web-fe
Service Mode:   Replicated
 Replicas:      5
Placement:
UpdateConfig:
 Parallelism:   1
 On failure:    pause
 Monitoring Period: 5s
 Max failure ratio: 0
 Update order:      stop-first
RollbackConfig:
 Parallelism:   1
 On failure:    pause
 Monitoring Period: 5s
 Max failure ratio: 0
 Rollback order:    stop-first
ContainerSpec:
 Image:   nigelpoulton/pluralsight-docker-ci:latest@sha256:7a6b01...d8d3d
 init: false
Resources:
Endpoint Mode:  vip
Ports:
 PublishedPort = 8080
  Protocol = tcp
  TargetPort = 8080
  PublishMode = ingress
```

The example above uses the `--pretty` flag to limit the output to the most interesting items printed in an easy-to-read format. Leaving off the `--pretty` flag will give a more verbose output. I highly recommend you read through the output of `docker inspect` commands as they're a great source of information and a great way to learn what's going on under the hood.

We'll come back to some of these outputs later.

Replicated vs global services

The default replication mode of a service is `replicated`. This deploys a desired number of replicas and distributes them as evenly as possible across the cluster.

The other mode is `global`, which runs a single replica on every node in the swarm.

To deploy a *global service* you need to pass the `--mode global` flag to the `docker service create` command.

Scaling a service

Another powerful feature of *services* is the ability to easily scale them up and down.

Let's assume business is booming and we're seeing double the amount of traffic hitting the web front-end. Fortunately, scaling the **web-fe** service is as simple as running the `docker service scale` command.

```
$ docker service scale web-fe=10
web-fe scaled to 10
overall progress: 10 out of 10 tasks
1/10: running
2/10: running
3/10: running
4/10: running
5/10: running
6/10: running
7/10: running
8/10: running
9/10: running
10/10: running
verify: Service converged
```

This command will scale the number of service replicas from 5 to 10. In the background it's updating the service's *desired state* from 5 to 10. Run another `docker service ls` command to verify the operation was successful.

```
$ docker service ls
ID        NAME    MODE        REPLICAS  IMAGE            PORTS
z7o...uw  web-fe  replicated  10/10     nigel...ci:latest  *:8080->8080/tcp
```

Running a `docker service ps` command will show that the service replicas are balanced across all nodes in the swarm evenly.

```
$ docker service ps web-fe
ID        NAME       IMAGE           NODE   DESIRED  CURRENT
nwf...tpn  web-fe.1   nigelpoulton/...  mgr1   Running  Running 7 mins
yb0...e3e  web-fe.2   nigelpoulton/...  wrk3   Running  Running 7 mins
mos...gf6  web-fe.3   nigelpoulton/...  wrk2   Running  Running 7 mins
utn...6ak  web-fe.4   nigelpoulton/...  wrk3   Running  Running 7 mins
2ge...fyy  web-fe.5   nigelpoulton/...  mgr3   Running  Running 7 mins
64y...m49  web-fe.6   igelpoulton/...   wrk3   Running  Running about a min
ild...51s  web-fe.7   nigelpoulton/...  mgr1   Running  Running about a min
vah...rjf  web-fe.8   nigelpoulton/...  wrk2   Running  Running about a mins
xe7...fvu  web-fe.9   nigelpoulton/...  mgr2   Running  Running 45 seconds ago
l7k...jkv  web-fe.10  nigelpoulton/...  mgr2   Running  Running 46 seconds ago
```

Behind the scenes, swarm runs a scheduling algorithm called "spread" that attempts to balance replicas as evenly as possible across the nodes in the swarm. At the time of writing, this amounts to running an equal number of replicas on each node without taking into consideration things like CPU load etc.

Run another `docker service scale` command to bring the number back down from 10 to 5.

```
$ docker service scale web-fe=5
web-fe scaled to 5
overall progress: 5 out of 5 tasks
1/5: running
2/5: running
3/5: running
4/5: running
5/5: running
verify: Service converged
```

Now that you know how to scale a service, let's see how to remove one.

Removing a service

Removing a service is simple — may be too simple.

The following `docker service rm` command will delete the service deployed earlier.

```
$ docker service rm web-fe
web-fe
```

Confirm it's gone with the `docker service ls` command.

```
$ docker service ls
ID      NAME    MODE    REPLICAS    IMAGE    PORTS
```

Be careful using the `docker service rm` command as it deletes all service replicas without asking for confirmation.

Now that the service is deleted from the system, let's look at how to push rolling updates to one.

Rolling updates

Pushing updates to deployed applications is a fact of life. And for the longest time it was really painful. I've lost more than enough weekends to major application updates, and I've no intention of doing it again.

Well… thanks to Docker *services*, pushing updates to well-designed microservices apps is easy.

To see this, we're going to deploy a new service. But before we do that, we're going to create a new overlay network for the service. This isn't necessary, but I want you to see how it is done and how to attach the service to it.

```
$ docker network create -d overlay uber-net
43wfp6pzea470et4d57udn9ws
```

This creates a new overlay network called "uber-net" that we'll use for the service we're about to create. An overlay network creates a new layer 2 network that we can place containers on, and all containers on it will be able to communicate. This works even if all of the swarm nodes are on different underlying networks. Basically, the overlay network creates a new layer 2 container network on top of potentially multiple different underlying networks.

Figure 10.5 shows four swarm nodes on two underlay networks connected by a layer 3 router. The overlay network spans all 4 swarm nodes creating a single flat layer 2 network for containers to use.

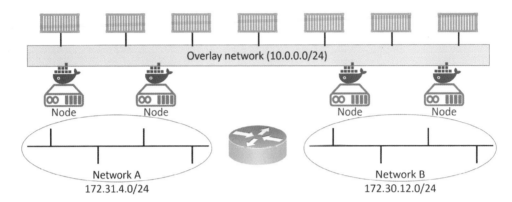

Figure 10.5

Run a `docker network ls` to verify that the network created properly and is visible on the Docker host.

```
$ docker network ls
NETWORK ID          NAME                DRIVER       SCOPE
<Snip>
43wfp6pzea47        uber-net            overlay      swarm
```

The `uber-net` network was successfully created with the `swarm` scope and is *currently* only visible on manager nodes in the swarm. It will be dynamically extended to worker nodes when they run workloads configured on the network.

Let's create a new service and attach it to the network.

```
$ docker service create --name uber-svc \
   --network uber-net \
   -p 80:80 --replicas 12 \
   nigelpoulton/tu-demo:v1

dhbtgvqrg2q4sg07ttfuhg8nz
overall progress: 12 out of 12 tasks
1/12: running
2/12: running
<Snip>
12/12: running
verify: Service converged
```

Let's see what we just declared with that `docker service create` command.

The first thing we did was name the service and then use the `--network` flag to tell it to place all replicas on the new `uber-net` network. We then exposed port 80 across the entire swarm and mapped it to port 80 inside of each of the 12 replicas we asked it to run. Finally, we told it to base all replicas on the nigelpoulton/tu-demo:v1 image.

Run a `docker service ls` and a `docker service ps` command to verify the state of the new service.

```
$ docker service ls
ID              NAME       REPLICAS   IMAGE
dhbtgvqrg2q4    uber-svc   12/12      nigelpoulton/tu-demo:v1

$ docker service ps uber-svc
ID          NAME           IMAGE                  NODE    DESIRED   CURRENT STATE
0v...7e5    uber-svc.1     nigelpoulton/...:v1    wrk3    Running   Running 1 min
bh...wa0    uber-svc.2     nigelpoulton/...:v1    wrk2    Running   Running 1 min
23...u97    uber-svc.3     nigelpoulton/...:v1    wrk2    Running   Running 1 min
82...5y1    uber-svc.4     nigelpoulton/...:v1    mgr2    Running   Running 1 min
c3...gny    uber-svc.5     nigelpoulton/...:v1    wrk3    Running   Running 1 min
e6...3u0    uber-svc.6     nigelpoulton/...:v1    wrk1    Running   Running 1 min
78...r7z    uber-svc.7     nigelpoulton/...:v1    wrk1    Running   Running 1 min
2m...kdz    uber-svc.8     nigelpoulton/...:v1    mgr3    Running   Running 1 min
b9...k7w    uber-svc.9     nigelpoulton/...:v1    mgr3    Running   Running 1 min
ag...v16    uber-svc.10    nigelpoulton/...:v1    mgr2    Running   Running 1 min
e6...dfk    uber-svc.11    nigelpoulton/...:v1    mgr1    Running   Running 1 min
e2...k1j    uber-svc.12    nigelpoulton/...:v1    mgr1    Running   Running 1 min
```

Passing the service the `-p 80:80` flag will ensure that a **swarm-wide** mapping is created that maps all traffic, coming in to any node in the swarm on port 80, through to port 80 inside of any service replica.

This mode of publishing a port on every node in the swarm — even nodes not running service replicas — is called *ingress mode* and is the default. The alternative mode is *host mode* which only publishes the service on swarm nodes running replicas. Publishing a service in *host mode* requires the long-form syntax and looks like the following:

```
$ docker service create --name uber-svc \
   --network uber-net \
   --publish published=80,target=80,mode=host \
   --replicas 12 \
   nigelpoulton/tu-demo:v1
```

Open a web browser and point it to the IP address of any of the nodes in the swarm on port 80 to see the service running.

Figure 10.6

As you can see, it's a simple voting application that will register votes for either "football" or "soccer". Feel free to point your web browser to other nodes in the swarm. You'll be able to reach the web service from any node because the `-p 80:80` flag creates an *ingress mode* mapping on every swarm node. This is true even on nodes that are not running a replica for the service — **every node gets a mapping and can therefore redirect your request to a node that is running the service.**

Let's now assume that this particular vote has come to an end and your company wants to run a new poll. A new container image has been created for the new poll and has been added to the same Docker Hub repository, but this one is tagged as `v2` instead of `v1`.

Let's also assume that you've been tasked with pushing the updated image to the swarm in a staged manner — 2 replicas at a time with a 20 second delay between each. You can use the following `docker service update` command to accomplish this.

```
$ docker service update \
   --image nigelpoulton/tu-demo:v2 \
   --update-parallelism 2 \
   --update-delay 20s uber-svc

overall progress: 4 out of 12 tasks
1/12: running
2/12: running
3/12: running
4/12: running
5/12: starting
6/12: ready
<Snip>
12/12:
```

Let's review the command. `docker service update` lets us make updates to running services by updating the service's desired state. This example specifies a new version of the image, tagged as `v2` instead of `v1`. It also specified the `--update-parallelism` and `--update-delay` flags to make sure that the new image was pushed to 2 replicas at a time with a 20 second cool-off period in between each set of two. Finally, it instructs the swarm to make the changes to the `uber-svc` service.

If you run a `docker service ps uber-svc` while the update is in progress, some of the replicas will be at `v2` while some will still be at `v1`. If you give the operation enough time to complete (4 minutes), all replicas will eventually reach the new desired state of using the `v2` image.

```
$ docker service ps uber-svc
ID          NAME           IMAGE        NODE   DESIRED    CURRENT STATE
7z...nys    uber-svc.1     nigel...v2   mgr2   Running    Running 13 secs
0v...7e5    \_uber-svc.1   nigel...v1   wrk3   Shutdown   Shutdown 13 secs
bh...wa0    uber-svc.2     nigel...v1   wrk2   Running    Running 1 min
e3...gr2    uber-svc.3     nigel...v2   wrk2   Running    Running 13 secs
23...u97    \_uber-svc.3   nigel...v1   wrk2   Shutdown   Shutdown 13 secs
82...5y1    uber-svc.4     nigel...v1   mgr2   Running    Running 1 min
c3...gny    uber-svc.5     nigel...v1   wrk3   Running    Running 1 min
e6...3u0    uber-svc.6     nigel...v1   wrk1   Running    Running 1 min
78...r7z    uber-svc.7     nigel...v1   wrk1   Running    Running 1 min
2m...kdz    uber-svc.8     nigel...v1   mgr3   Running    Running 1 min
b9...k7w    uber-svc.9     nigel...v1   mgr3   Running    Running 1 min
ag...v16    uber-svc.10    nigel...v1   mgr2   Running    Running 1 min
e6...dfk    uber-svc.11    nigel...v1   mgr1   Running    Running 1 min
e2...k1j    uber-svc.12    nigel...v1   mgr1   Running    Running 1 min
```

You can witness the update happening in real-time by opening a web browser to any node in the swarm and hitting refresh several times. Some of the requests will be serviced by replicas running the old version and some will be serviced by replicas running the new version. After enough time, all requests will be serviced by replicas running the updated version of the service.

Congratulations. You've just pushed a rolling update to a live containerized application. Remember, Docker Stacks take all of this to the next level in Chapter 14.

If you run a `docker inspect --pretty` command against the service, you'll see the update parallelism and update delay settings are now part of the service definition. This means future updates will automatically use these settings unless you override them as part of the `docker service update` command.

```
$ docker service inspect --pretty uber-svc
ID:            mub0dgtc8szm80ez5bs8wlt19
Name:          uber-svc
Service Mode:  Replicated
 Replicas:     12
UpdateStatus:
 State:        updating
 Started:      About a minute
 Message:      update in progress
Placement:
UpdateConfig:
 Parallelism:  2
 Delay:        20s
 On failure:   pause
```

```
 Monitoring Period: 5s
 Max failure ratio: 0
 Update order:        stop-first
RollbackConfig:
 Parallelism:    1
 On failure:     pause
 Monitoring Period: 5s
 Max failure ratio: 0
 Rollback order:     stop-first
ContainerSpec:
 Image:     nigelpoulton/tu-demo:v2@sha256:d3c0d8c9...cf0ef2ba5eb74c
 init: false
Resources:
Networks: uber-net
Endpoint Mode:   vip
Ports:
 PublishedPort = 80
  Protocol = tcp
  TargetPort = 80
  PublishMode = ingress
```

You should also note a couple of things about the service's network config. All nodes in the swarm that are running a replica for the service will have the uber-net overlay network that we created earlier. We can verify this by running docker network ls on any node running a replica.

You should also note the Networks portion of the docker inspect output. This shows the uber-net network as well as the swarm-wide 80:80 port mapping.

Troubleshooting

Swarm Service logs can be viewed with the docker service logs command. However, not all logging drivers support the command.

By default, Docker nodes configure services to use the json-file log driver, but other drivers exist, including:

- journald (only works on Linux hosts running systemd)
- syslog
- splunk
- gelf

json-file and journald are the easiest to configure, and both work with the docker service logs command. The format of the command is docker service logs <service-name>.

If you're using 3rd-party logging drivers you should view those logs using the logging platform's native tools.

The following snippet from a daemon.json configuration file shows a Docker host configured to use syslog.

```
{
  "log-driver": "syslog"
}
```

You can force individual services to use a different driver by passing the `--log-driver` and `--log-opts` flags to the `docker service create` command. These will override anything set in `daemon.json`.

Service logs work on the premise that your application is running as PID 1 in its container and sending logs to STDOUT and errors to STDERR. The logging driver forwards these "logs" to the locations configured via the logging driver.

The following `docker service logs` command shows the logs for all replicas in the `svc1` service that experienced a couple of failures starting a replica.

```
$ docker service logs svc1
svc1.1.zhc3cjeti9d4@wrk-2 | [emerg] 1#1: host not found...
svc1.1.zhc3cjeti9d4@wrk-2 | nginx: [emerg] host not found..
svc1.1.6m1nmbzmwh2d@wrk-2 | [emerg] 1#1: host not found...
svc1.1.6m1nmbzmwh2d@wrk-2 | nginx: [emerg] host not found..
svc1.1.1tmya243m5um@mgr-1 | 10.255.0.2 "GET / HTTP/1.1" 302
```

The output is trimmed to fit the page, but you can see that logs from all three service replicas are shown (the two that failed and the one that's running). Each line starts with the name of the replica, which includes the service name, replica number, replica ID, and name of host that it's scheduled on. Following that is the log output.

It's hard to tell because it's trimmed to fit the book, but it looks like the first two replicas failed because they were trying to connect to another service that was still starting (a sort of race condition when dependent services are starting).

You can follow the logs (`--follow`), tail them (`--tail`), and get extra details (`--details`).

Backing up Swarm

Backing up a swarm will backup the control plane objects required to recover the swarm in the event of a catastrophic failure of corruption. Recovering a swarm from a backup is an extremely rare scenario. However, business critical environments should always be prepared for worst-case scenarios.

You might be asking why backups are necessary if the control plane is already replicated and highly-available (HA). To answer that question, consider the scenario where a malicious actor deletes all of the Secrets on a swarm. HA cannot help in this scenario as the Secrets will be deleted from the cluster store that is automatically replicated to all manager nodes. In this scenario the highly-available replicated cluster store works against you — quickly propagating the delete operation. In this scenario you can either recreate the deleted objects from copies kept in a source code repo, or you can attempt to recover your swarm from a recent backup.

Managing your swarm and applications declaratively is a great way to prevent the need to recover from a backup. For example, storing configuration objects outside of the swarm in a source code repository will enable you to redeploy things like networks, services, secrets and other objects. However, managing your environment declaratively and strictly using source control repos requires discipline.

Anyway, let's see how to **backup a swarm**.

Swarm configuration and state is stored in `/var/lib/docker/swarm` on every manager node. The configuration includes; Raft log keys, overlay networks, Secrets, Configs, Services, and more. A swarm backup is a copy of all the files in this directory.

As the contents of this directory are replicated to all managers, you can, and should, perform backups from multiple managers. However, as you have to stop the Docker daemon on the node you are backing up, it's a good idea to perform the backup from non-leader managers. This is because stopping Docker on the leader will initiate a leader election. You should also perform the backup at a quiet time for the business, as stopping a manager can increase the risk of the swarm losing quorum if another manager fails during the backup.

The procedure we're about to follow is designed for demonstration purposes and you'll need to tweak it for your production environment. It also creates a couple of swarm objects so that a later step can prove the restore operation worked.

> **Warning**: The following operation carries risks. You should also ensure you perform test backup and restore operations regularly and test the outcomes.

The following commands will create the following two objects so you can prove the restore operation:

- An overlay network called "Unimatrix-01"
- A Secret called "missing drones" containing the text "Seven of Nine"

```
$ docker network create -d overlay Unimatrix-01
w9l904ff73e7stly0gnztsud7

$ printf "Seven of Nine" | docker secret create missing_drones -
i8oj3b2lid27t5202uycw37lg
```

Let's perform the swarm backup.

1. Stop Docker on a non-leader swarm manager.

   If you have any containers or service tasks running on the node, this action may stop them.

   ```
   $ service docker stop
   ```

2. Backup the Swarm config.

   This example uses the Linux `tar` utility to perform the file copy that will be the backup. Feel free to use a different tool.

   ```
   $ tar -czvf swarm.bkp /var/lib/docker/swarm/
   tar: Removing leading `/' from member names
   /var/lib/docker/swarm/
   /var/lib/docker/swarm/docker-state.json
   /var/lib/docker/swarm/state.json
   <Snip>
   ```

3. Verify the backup file exists.

```
$ ls -l
-rw-r--r-- 1 root   root   450727 May 4 14:06 swarm.bkp
```

In the real world you should store and rotate this backup in accordance with any corporate backup policies.

At this point, the swarm is backed up and you can restart Docker on the node.

4. Restart Docker.

```
$ service docker restart
```

Now that you have a backup, let's perform a test restore. The steps in this procedure demonstrate the operation. Performing a restore in the real world may be slightly different, but the overall process will be similar.

> **Note:** You do not have to perform a restore operation if your swarm is still running and you only wish to add a new manager node. In this situation just add a new manager. A swarm restore is only for situations where the swarm is corrupted or otherwise lost and you cannot recover services from copies of config files stored in a source code repo.

We'll use the swarm.bkp file from earlier to restore the swarm. **All swarm nodes must have their Docker daemon stopped and the contents of their /var/lib/docker/swarm directories deleted.**

The following must also be true for a recovery operation to work:

1. You can only restore to a node running the same version of Docker the backup was performed on
2. You can only restore to a node with the same IP address as the node the backup was performed on

Perform the following tasks from the swarm manager node that you wish to recover. Remember that Docker must be stopped and the contents of /var/lib/docker/swarm must be deleted.

1. Restore the Swarm configuration from backup.

   In this example, we'll restore from a zipped tar file called swarm.bkp. Restoring to the root directory is required with this command as it will include the full path to the original files as part of the extract operation. This may be different in your environment.

   ```
   $ tar -zxvf swarm.bkp -C /
   ```

2. Start Docker. The method for starting Docker can vary between environments.

   ```
   $ service docker start
   ```

3. Initialize a new Swarm cluster.

   Remember, you are not recovering a manager and adding it back to a working cluster. This operation is to recover a failed swarm that has no surviving managers. The --force-new-cluster flag tells Docker to create a new cluster using the configuration stored in /var/lib/docker/swarm/ that you recovered in step 1.

```
$ docker swarm init --force-new-cluster
Swarm initialized: current node (jhsg...3l9h) is now a manager.
```

4. Check that the network and service were recovered as part of the operation.

```
$ docker network ls
NETWORK ID          NAME                DRIVER              SCOPE
z21s5v82by8q        Unimatrix-01        overlay             swarm

$ docker secret ls
ID                              NAME                DRIVER
i8oj3b2lid27t5202uycw37lg       missing_drones
```

Congratulations. The Swarm is recovered.

5. Add new manager and worker nodes and take fresh backups.

Remember, test this procedure regularly and thoroughly. You do not want it to fail when you need it most!

Docker Swarm - The Commands

- `docker swarm init` is the command to create a new swarm. The node that you run the command on becomes the first manager and is switched to run in *swarm mode*.
- `docker swarm join-token` reveals the commands and tokens needed to join workers and managers to existing swarms. To expose the command to join a new manager, use the `docker swarm join-token manager` command. To get the command to join a worker, use the `docker swarm join-token worker` command.
- `docker node ls` lists all nodes in the swarm including which are managers and which is the leader.
- `docker service create` is the command to create a new service.
- `docker service ls` lists running services in the swarm and gives basic info on the state of the service and any replicas it's running.
- `docker service ps <service>` gives more detailed information about individual service replicas.
- `docker service inspect` gives very detailed information on a service. It accepts the `--pretty` flag to limit the information returned to the most important information.
- `docker service scale` lets you scale the number of replicas in a service up and down.
- `docker service update` lets you update many of the properties of a running service.
- `docker service logs` lets you view the logs of a service.
- `docker service rm` is the command to delete a service from the swarm. Use it with caution as it deletes all service replicas without asking for confirmation.

Chapter summary

Docker Swarm is Docker's native technology for managing clusters of Docker nodes and deploying and managing cloud-native applications. It is similar to Kubernetes.

At its core, Swarm has a secure clustering component, and an orchestration component.

The secure clustering component is enterprise-grade and offers a wealth of security and HA features that are automatically configured and extremely simple to modify.

The orchestration component allows you to deploy and manage cloud-native microservices applications in a simple declarative manner.

We'll dig deeper into deploying cloud-native microservices apps in a declarative manner in Chapter 14.

11: Docker Networking

It's always the network!

Any time there's a an infrastructure problem, we always blame the network. Part of the reason is that networks are at the center of everything — **no network, no app!**

In the early days of Docker, networking was hard — really hard. These days, it's *almost* a pleasure ;-)

In this chapter, we'll look at the fundamentals of Docker networking. Things like the Container Network Model (CNM) and `libnetwork`. We'll also get our hands dirty building some networks.

As usual, we'll split the chapter into three parts:

- The TLDR
- The deep dive
- The commands

Docker Networking - The TLDR

Docker runs applications inside of containers, and applications need to communicate over lots of different networks. This means Docker needs strong networking capabilities.

Fortunately, Docker has solutions for container-to-container networks, as well as connecting to existing networks and VLANs. The latter is important for containerized apps that interact with functions and services on external systems such as VM's and physical servers.

Docker networking is based on an open-source pluggable architecture called the Container Network Model (CNM). `libnetwork` is Docker's real-world implementation of the CNM, and it provides all of Docker's core networking capabilities. Drivers plug in to `libnetwork` to provide specific network topologies.

To create a smooth out-of-the-box experience, Docker ships with a set of native drivers that deal with the most common networking requirements. These include single-host bridge networks, multi-host overlays, and options for plugging into existing VLANs. Ecosystem partners can extend things further by providing their own drivers.

Last but not least, `libnetwork` provides a native service discovery and basic container load balancing solution.

That's this big picture. Let's get into the detail.

Docker Networking - The Deep Dive

We'll organize this section of the chapter as follows:

- The theory
- Single-host bridge networks
- Multi-host overlay networks
- Connecting to existing networks
- Service Discovery
- Ingress networking

The theory

At the highest level, Docker networking comprises three major components:

- The Container Network Model (CNM)
- `libnetwork`
- Drivers

The CNM is the design specification. It outlines the fundamental building blocks of a Docker network.

`libnetwork` is a real-world implementation of the CNM, and is used by Docker. It's written in Go, and implements the core components outlined in the CNM.

Drivers extend the model by implementing specific network topologies such as VXLAN overlay networks.

Figure 11.1 shows how they fit together at a very high level.

Figure 11.1

Let's look a bit closer at each.

The Container Network Model (CNM)

Everything starts with a design.

The design guide for Docker networking is the CNM. It outlines the fundamental building blocks of a Docker network, and you can read the full spec here: https://github.com/docker/libnetwork/blob/master/docs/design.md

I recommend reading the entire spec, but at a high level, it defines three major building blocks:

- Sandboxes
- Endpoints
- Networks

A **sandbox** is an isolated network stack. It includes; Ethernet interfaces, ports, routing tables, and DNS config.

Endpoints are virtual network interfaces (E.g. `veth`). Like normal network interfaces, they're responsible for making connections. In the case of the CNM, it's the job of the *endpoint* to connect a *sandbox* to a *network*.

Networks are a software implementation of an switch (802.1d bridge). As such, they group together and isolate a collection of endpoints that need to communicate.

Figure 11.2 shows the three components and how they connect.

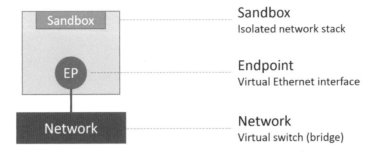

Figure 11.2 The Container Network Model (CNM)

The atomic unit of scheduling in a Docker environment is the container, and as the name suggests, the Container Network Model is all about providing networking to containers. Figure 11.3 shows how CNM components relate to containers — sandboxes are placed inside of containers to provide network connectivity.

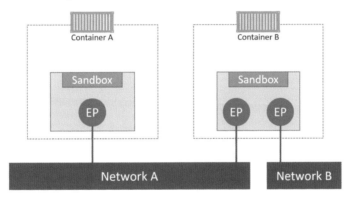

Figure 11.3

Container A has a single interface (endpoint) and is connected to Network A. Container B has two interfaces (endpoints) and is connected to Network A **and** Network B. The two containers will be able to communicate because they are both connected to Network A. However, the two *endpoints* in Container B cannot communicate with each other without the assistance of a layer 3 router.

It's also important to understand that *endpoints* behave like regular network adapters, meaning they can only be connected to a single network. Therefore, if a container needs connecting to multiple networks, it will need multiple endpoints.

Figure 11.4 extends the diagram again, this time adding a Docker host. Although Container A and Container B are running on the same host, their network stacks are completely isolated at the OS-level via the sandboxes.

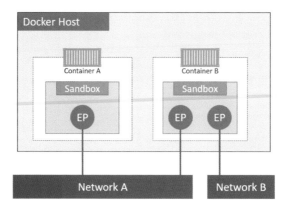

Figure 11.4

Libnetwork

The CNM is the design doc, and libnetwork is the canonical implementation. It's open-source, written in Go, cross-platform (Linux and Windows), and used by Docker.

In the early days of Docker, all the networking code existed inside the daemon. This was a nightmare — the daemon became bloated, and it didn't follow the Unix principle of building modular tools that can work on their own, but also be easily composed into other projects. As a result, it all got ripped out and refactored into an external library called libnetwork based on the principles of the CNM. Nowadays, all of the core Docker networking code lives in libnetwork.

As you'd expect, it implements all three of the components defined in the CNM. It also implements native *service discovery, ingress-based container load balancing,* and the network control plane and management plane functionality.

Drivers

If libnetwork implements the control plane and management plane functions, then drivers implement the data plane. For example, connectivity and isolation is all handled by drivers. So is the actual creation of networks. The relationship is shown in Figure 11.5.

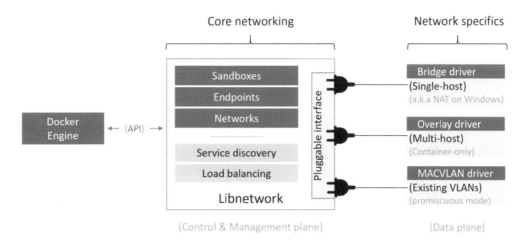

Figure 11.5

Docker ships with several built-in drivers, known as native drivers or *local drivers*. On Linux they include; `bridge`, `overlay`, and `macvlan`. On Windows they include; `nat`, `overlay`, `transparent`, and `l2bridge`. We'll see how to use some of them later in the chapter.

3rd-parties can also write Docker network drivers known as *remote drivers* or plugins. Weave Net is a popular example and can be downloaded from Docker Hub.

Each driver is in charge of the actual creation and management of all resources on the networks it is responsible for. For example, an overlay network called "prod-fe-cuda" will be owned and managed by the `overlay` driver. This means the `overlay` driver will be invoked for the creation, management, and deletion of all resources on that network.

In order to meet the demands of complex highly-fluid environments, `libnetwork` allows multiple network drivers to be active at the same time. This means your Docker environment can sport a wide range of heterogeneous networks.

Single-host bridge networks

The simplest type of Docker network is the single-host bridge network.

The name tells us two things:

- **Single-host** tells us it only exists on a single Docker host and can only connect containers that are on the same host.
- **Bridge** tells us that it's an implementation of an 802.1d bridge (layer 2 switch).

Docker on Linux creates single-host bridge networks with the built-in `bridge` driver, whereas Docker on Windows creates them using the built-in `nat` driver. For all intents and purposes, they work the same.

Figure 11.6 shows two Docker hosts with identical local bridge networks called "mynet". Even though the networks are identical, they are independent isolated networks. This means the containers in the picture cannot communicate directly because they are on different networks.

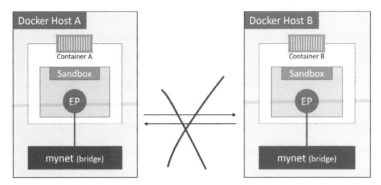

Figure 11.6

Every Docker host gets a default single-host bridge network. On Linux it's called "bridge", and on Windows it's called "nat" (yes, those are the same names as the drivers used to create them). By default, this is the network that all new containers will be connected to unless you override it on the command line with the --network flag.

The following listing shows the output of a docker network ls command on newly installed Linux and Windows Docker hosts. The output is trimmed so that it only shows the default network on each host. Notice how the name of the network is the same as the driver that was used to create it — this is a coincidence and not a requirement.

```
//Linux
$ docker network ls
NETWORK ID        NAME          DRIVER        SCOPE
333e184cd343      bridge        bridge        local

//Windows
> docker network ls
NETWORK ID        NAME          DRIVER        SCOPE
095d4090fa32      nat           nat           local
```

The docker network inspect command is a treasure trove of great information. I highly recommended reading through its output if you're interested in low-level detail.

```
docker network inspect bridge
[
    {
        "Name": "bridge",        << Will be nat on Windows
        "Id": "333e184...d9e55",
        "Created": "2018-01-15T20:43:02.566345779Z",
        "Scope": "local",
        "Driver": "bridge",      << Will be nat on Windows
        "EnableIPv6": false,
        "IPAM": {
            "Driver": "default",
            "Options": null,
            "Config": [
                {
```

```
                    "Subnet": "172.17.0.0/16"
                }
            ]
        },
        "Internal": false,
        "Attachable": false,
        "Ingress": false,
        "ConfigFrom": {
            "Network": ""
        },
        <Snip>
    }
]
```

Docker networks built with the `bridge` driver on Linux hosts are based on the battle-hardened *linux bridge* technology that has existed in the Linux kernel for nearly 20 years. This means they're high performance and extremely stable. It also means you can inspect them using standard Linux utilities. For example.

```
$ ip link show docker0
3: docker0: <BROADCAST,MULTICAST,UP,LOWER_UP> mtu 1500 qdisc...
    link/ether 02:42:af:f9:eb:4f brd ff:ff:ff:ff:ff:ff
```

The default "bridge" network, on all Linux-based Docker hosts, maps to an underlying *Linux bridge* in the kernel called "**docker0**". We can see this from the output of `docker network inspect`.

```
$ docker network inspect bridge | grep bridge.name
"com.docker.network.bridge.name": "docker0",
```

The relationship between Docker's default "bridge" network and the "docker0" bridge in the Linux kernel is shown in Figure 11.7.

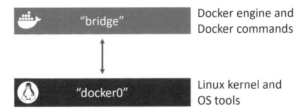

Figure 11.7

Figure 11.8 extends the diagram by adding containers at the top that plug into the "bridge" network. The "bridge" network maps to the "docker0" Linux bridge in the host's kernel, which can be mapped back to an Ethernet interface on the host via port mappings.

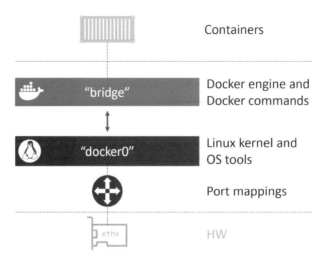

Figure 11.8

Let's use the `docker network create` command to create a new single-host bridge network called "localnet".

```
//Linux
$ docker network create -d bridge localnet

//Windows
> docker network create -d nat localnet
```

The new network is created and will appear in the output of any future `docker network ls` commands. If you are using Linux, you will also have a new *Linux bridge* created in the kernel.

Let's use the Linux `brctl` tool to look at the Linux bridges currently on the system. You may have to manually install the `brctl` binary using `apt-get install bridge-utils`, or the equivalent for your Linux distro.

```
$ brctl show
bridge name        bridge id           STP enabled    interfaces
docker0            8000.0242aff9eb4f    no
br-20c2e8ae4bbb    8000.02429636237c    no
```

The output shows two bridges. The first line is the "docker0" bridge that we already know about. This relates to the default "bridge" network in Docker. The second bridge (br-20c2e8ae4bbb) relates to the new `localnet` Docker bridge network. Neither of them have spanning tree enabled, and neither have any devices connected (`interfaces` column).

At this point, the bridge configuration on the host looks like Figure 11.9.

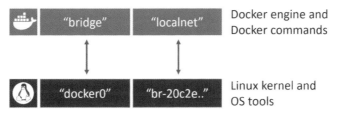

Figure 11.9

Let's create a new container and attach it to the new `localnet` bridge network. If you're following along on Windows, you should substitute "`alpine sleep 1d`" with "`mcr.microsoft.com/powershell:nanoserver pwsh.exe -Command Start-Sleep 86400`".

```
$ docker container run -d --name c1 \
  --network localnet \
  alpine sleep 1d
```

This container will now be on the `localnet` network. You can confirm this with a `docker network inspect`.

```
$ docker network inspect localnet --format '{{json .Containers}}'
{
  "4edcbd...842c3aa": {
    "Name": "c1",
    "EndpointID": "43a13b...3219b8c13",
    "MacAddress": "02:42:ac:14:00:02",
    "IPv4Address": "172.20.0.2/16",
    "IPv6Address": ""
    }
},
```

The output shows that the new "c1" container is on the `localnet` bridge/nat network.

It you run the Linux `brctl show` command again, you'll see c1's interface attached to the `br-20c2e8ae4bbb` bridge.

```
$ brctl show
bridge name      bridge id           STP enabled      interfaces
br-20c2e8ae4bbb  8000.02429636237c   no               vethe792ac0
docker0          8000.0242aff9eb4f   no
```

This is shown in Figure 11.10.

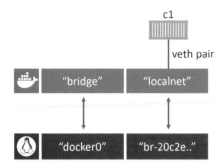

Figure 11.10

If we add another new container to the same network, it should be able to ping the "c1" container by name. This is because all new containers are automatically registered with the embedded Docker DNS service, enabling them to resolve the names of all other containers on the same network.

> **Beware:** The default `bridge` network on Linux does not support name resolution via the Docker DNS service. All other *user-defined* bridge networks do. The following demo will work because the container is on the user-defined `localnet` network.

Let's test it.

1. Create a new interactive container called "c2" and put it on the same `localnet` network as "c1".

```
//Linux
$ docker container run -it --name c2 \
  --network localnet \
  alpine sh

//Windows
> docker container run -it --name c2 `
  --network localnet `
  mcr.microsoft.com/powershell:nanoserver
```

Your terminal will switch into the "c2" container.

2. From within the "c2" container, ping the "c1" container by name.

```
> ping c1
Pinging c1 [172.26.137.130] with 32 bytes of data:
Reply from 172.26.137.130: bytes=32 time=1ms TTL=128
Reply from 172.26.137.130: bytes=32 time=1ms TTL=128
Control-C
```

It works! This is because the c2 container is running a local DNS resolver that forwards requests to an internal Docker DNS server. This DNS server maintains mappings for all containers started with the `--name` or `--net-alias` flag.

Try running some network-related commands while you're still logged on to the container. It's a great way of learning more about how Docker container networking works. The following snippet shows the `ipconfig` command ran from inside the "c2" Windows container previously created. You can `Ctrl+P+Q` out of the container and run another `docker network inspect localnet` command to match the IP addresses.

```
PS C:\> ipconfig
Windows IP Configuration
Ethernet adapter Ethernet:
   Connection-specific DNS Suffix  . :
   Link-local IPv6 Address . . . . . : fe80::14d1:10c8:f3dc:2eb3%4
   IPv4 Address. . . . . . . . . . . : 172.26.135.0
   Subnet Mask . . . . . . . . . . . : 255.255.240.0
   Default Gateway . . . . . . . . . : 172.26.128.1
```

So far, we've said that containers on bridge networks can only communicate with other containers on the same network. However, you can get around this using *port mappings*.

Port mappings let you map a container to a port on the Docker host. Any traffic hitting the Docker host on the configured port will be directed to the container. The high-level flow is shown in Figure 11.11

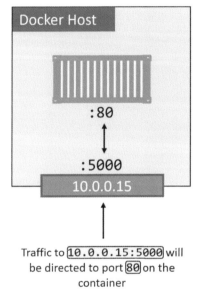

Figure 11.11

In the diagram, the application running in the container is operating on port 80. This is mapped to port 5000 on the host's 10.0.0.15 interface. The end result is all traffic hitting the host on 10.0.0.15:5000 being redirected to the container on port 80.

Let's walk through an example of mapping port 80 on a container running a web server, to port 5000 on the Docker host. The example will use NGINX on Linux. If you're following along on Windows, you'll need to substitute nginx with a Windows-based web server image such as mcr.microsoft.com/windows/servercore/iis:nanoserver.

1. Run a new web server container and map port 80 on the container to port 5000 on the Docker host.

```
$ docker container run -d --name web \
  --network localnet \
  --publish 5000:80 \
  nginx
```

2. Verify the port mapping.

```
$ docker port web
80/tcp -> 0.0.0.0:5000
```

This shows that port 80 in the container is mapped to port 5000 on all interfaces on the Docker host.

3. Test the configuration by pointing a web browser to port 5000 on the Docker host. To complete this step, you'll need to know the IP or DNS name of your Docker host. If you're using Docker Desktop on Mac or Windows, you'll be able to use `localhost:5000` or `127.0.0.1:5000`.

Figure 11.12

Any external system can now access the NGINX container running on the `localnet` bridge network via a port mapping to TCP port 5000 on the Docker host.

Mapping ports like this works, but it's clunky and doesn't scale. For example, only a single container can bind to any port on the host. This means no other containers on that host will be able to bind to port `5000`. This is one of the reason's that single-host bridge networks are only useful for local development and very small applications.

Multi-host overlay networks

We've got an entire chapter dedicated to multi-host overlay networks. So we'll keep this section short.

Overlay networks are multi-host. They allow a single network to span multiple hosts so that containers on different hosts can communicate directly. They're ideal for container-to-container communication, including container-only applications, and they scale well.

Docker provides a native driver for overlay networks. This makes creating them as simple as adding the `--d overlay` flag to the `docker network create` command.

Connecting to existing networks

The ability to connect containerized apps to external systems and physical networks is vital. A common example is a partially containerized app — the containerized parts need a way to communicate with the non-containerized parts still running on existing physical networks and VLANs.

The built-in MACVLAN driver (transparent on Windows) was created with this in mind. It makes containers first-class citizens on the existing physical networks by giving each one its own MAC address and IP addresses. We show this in Figure 11.13.

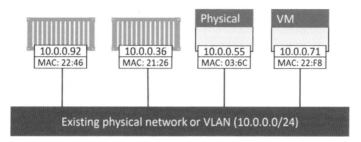

Figure 11.13

On the positive side, MACVLAN performance is good as it doesn't require port mappings or additional bridges — you connect the container interface through to the hosts interface (or a sub-interface). However, on the negative side, it requires the host NIC to be in **promiscuous mode**, which isn't always allowed on corporate networks and public cloud platforms. So MACVLAN is great for your corporate data center networks (assuming your network team can accommodate promiscuous mode), but it might not work in the public cloud.

Let's dig a bit deeper with the help of some pictures and a hypothetical example.

Assume we have an existing physical network with two VLANS:

- VLAN 100: 10.0.0.0/24
- VLAN 200: 192.168.3.0/24

Figure 11.14

Next, we add a Docker host and connect it to the network.

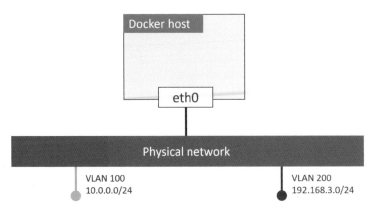

Figure 11.15

We then have a requirement for a container running on that host to be plumbed into VLAN 100. To do this, we create a new Docker network with the macvlan driver. However, the macvlan driver needs us to tell it a few things about the network we're going to associate it with. Things like:

- Subnet info
- Gateway
- Range of IP's it can assign to containers
- Which interface or sub-interface on the host to use

The following command will create a new MACVLAN network called "macvlan100" that will connect containers to VLAN 100.

```
$ docker network create -d macvlan \
  --subnet=10.0.0.0/24 \
  --ip-range=10.0.0.0/25 \
  --gateway=10.0.0.1 \
  -o parent=eth0.100 \
  macvlan100
```

This will create the "macvlan100" network and the eth0.100 sub-interface. The config now looks like this.

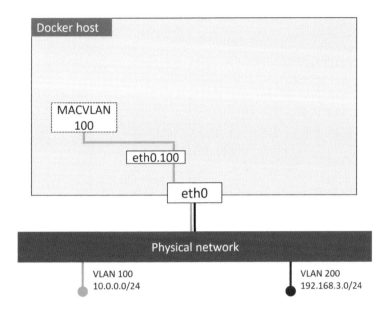

Figure 11.16

MACVLAN uses standard Linux sub-interfaces, and you have to tag them with the ID of the VLAN they will connect to. In this example we're connecting to VLAN 100, so we tag the sub-interface with .100 (etho.100).

We also used the `--ip-range` flag to tell the MACVLAN network which sub-set of IP addresses it can assign to containers. It's vital that this range of addresses be reserved for Docker and not in use by other nodes or DHCP servers, as there is no management plane feature to check for overlapping IP ranges.

The `macvlan100` network is ready for containers, so let's deploy one with the following command.

```
$ docker container run -d --name mactainer1 \
  --network macvlan100 \
  alpine sleep 1d
```

The config now looks like Figure 11.17. But remember, the underlying network (VLAN 100) does not see any of the MACVLAN magic, it only sees the container with its MAC and IP addresses. And with that in mind, the "mactainer1" container will be able to ping and communicate with any other systems on VLAN 100. Pretty sweet!

> **Note:** If you can't get this to work, it might be because the host NIC is not in promiscuous mode. Remember that public cloud platforms don't usually allow promiscuous mode.

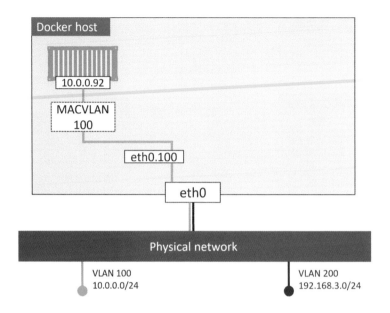

Figure 11.17

At this point, we've got a MACVLAN network and used it to connect a new container to an existing VLAN. However, it doesn't stop there. The Docker MACVLAN driver is built on top of the tried-and-tested Linux kernel driver with the same name. As such, it supports VLAN trunking. This means we can create multiple MACVLAN networks and connect containers on the same Docker host to them as shown in Figure 11.18.

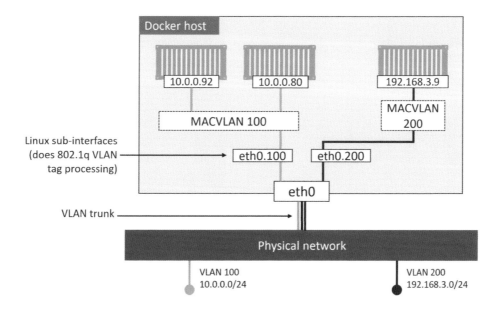

Figure 11.18

That pretty much covers MACVLAN. Windows offers a similar solution with the `transparent` driver.

Container and Service logs for troubleshooting

A quick note on troubleshooting connectivity issues before moving on to Service Discovery.

If you think you're experiencing connectivity issues between containers, it's worth checking the Docker daemon logs as well as container logs.

On Windows systems, the daemon logs are stored under `~AppData\Local\Docker`, and you can view them in the Windows Event Viewer. On Linux, it depends what `init` system you're using. If you're running a `systemd`, the logs will go to `journald` and you can view them with the `journalctl -u docker.service` command. If you're not running `systemd` you should look under the following locations:

- Ubuntu systems running `upstart`: `/var/log/upstart/docker.log`
- RHEL-based systems: `/var/log/messages`
- Debian: `/var/log/daemon.log`

You can also tell Docker how verbose you want daemon logging to be. To do this, edit the daemon config file (`daemon.json`) so that "`debug`" is set to "`true`" and "`log-level`" is set to one of the following:

- `debug` The most verbose option
- `info` The default value and second-most verbose option
- `warn` Third most verbose option

- `error` Fourth most verbose option
- `fatal` Least verbose option

The following snippet from a `daemon.json` enables debugging and sets the level to `debug`. It will work on all Docker platforms.

```
{
  <Snip>
  "debug":true,
  "log-level":"debug",
  <Snip>
}
```

Be sure to restart Docker after making changes to the file.

That was the daemon logs. What about container logs?

Logs from standalone containers can be viewed with the `docker container logs` command, and Swarm service logs can be viewed with the `docker service logs` command. However, Docker supports lots of logging drivers, and they don't all work with the `docker logs` command.

As well as a driver and configuration for daemon logs, every Docker host has a default logging driver and configuration for containers. Some of the drivers include:

- `json-file` (default)
- `journald` (only works on Linux hosts running `systemd`)
- `syslog`
- `splunk`
- `gelf`

`json-file` and `journald` are probably the easiest to configure, and they both work with the `docker logs` and `docker service logs` commands. The format of the commands is `docker logs <container-name>` and `docker service logs <service-name>`.

If you're using other logging drivers you can view logs using the 3-rd party platform's native tools.

The following snippet from a `daemon.json` shows a Docker host configured to use `syslog`.

```
{
  "log-driver": "syslog"
}
```

You can configure an individual container, or service, to start with a particular logging driver with the `--log-driver` and `--log-opts` flags. These will override anything set in `daemon.json`.

Container logs work on the premise that your application is running as PID 1 inside the container and sending logs to STDOUT, and errors to STDERR. The logging driver then forwards these "logs" to the locations configured via the logging driver.

If your application logs to a file, it's possible to use a symlink to redirect log-file writes to STDOUT and STDERR.

The following is an example of running the `docker logs` command against a container called "vantage-db" configured to use the `json-file` logging driver.

```
$ docker logs vantage-db
1:C 2 Feb 09:53:22.903 # oO0oo0O0o0O0o Redis is starting oO0oo0O0o0O0o
1:C 2 Feb 09:53:22.904 # Redis version=4.0.6, bits=64, commit=00000000, modified=0, pid=1
1:C 2 Feb 09:53:22.904 # Warning: no config file specified, using the default config.
1:M 2 Feb 09:53:22.906 * Running mode=standalone, port=6379.
1:M 2 Feb 09:53:22.906 # WARNING: The TCP backlog setting of 511 cannot be enforced because...
1:M 2 Feb 09:53:22.906 # Server initialized
1:M 2 Feb 09:53:22.906 # WARNING overcommit_memory is set to 0!
```

There's a good chance you'll find network connectivity errors reported in the daemon logs or container logs.

Service discovery

As well as core networking, `libnetwork` also provides some important network services.

Service discovery allows all containers and Swarm services to locate each other by name. The only requirement is that they be on the same network.

Under the hood, this leverages Docker's embedded DNS server and the DNS resolver in each container. Figure 11.19 shows container "c1" pinging container "c2" by name. The same principle applies to Swarm Services.

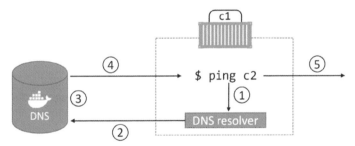

Figure 11.19

Let's step through the process.

- **Step 1:** The `ping c2` command invokes the local DNS resolver to resolve the name "c2" to an IP address. All Docker containers have a local DNS resolver.
- **Step 2:** If the local resolver doesn't have an IP address for "c2" in its local cache, it initiates a recursive query to the Docker DNS server. The local resolver is pre-configured to know how to reach the Docker DNS server.
- **Step 3:** The Docker DNS server holds name-to-IP mappings for all containers created with the `--name` or `--net-alias` flags. This means it knows the IP address of container "c2".
- **Step 4:** The DNS server returns the IP address of "c2" to the local resolver in "c1". It does this because the two containers are on the same network — if they were on different networks this would not work.
- **Step 5:** The `ping` command issues the ICMP echo request packets to the IP address of "c2".

Every Swarm service and standalone container started with the `--name` flag will register its name and IP with the Docker DNS service. This means all containers and service replicas can use the Docker DNS service to find each other.

However, service discovery is *network-scoped*. This means that name resolution only works for containers and Services on the same network. If two containers are on different networks, they will not be able to resolve each other.

One last point on service discovery and name resolution...

It's possible to configure Swarm services and standalone containers with customized DNS options. For example, the `--dns` flag lets you specify a list of custom DNS servers to use in case the embedded Docker DNS server cannot resolve a query. This is common when querying names of services outside of Docker. You can also use the `--dns-search` flag to add custom search domains for queries against unqualified names (i.e. when the query is not a fully qualified domain name).

On Linux, these all work by adding entries to the `/etc/resolv.conf` file inside every container.

The following example will start a new standalone container and add the infamous `8.8.8.8` Google DNS server, as well as `nigelpoulton.com` as search domain to append to unqualified queries.

```
$ docker container run -it --name c1 \
  --dns=8.8.8.8 \
  --dns-search=nigelpoulton.com \
  alpine sh
```

Ingress load balancing

Swarm supports two publishing modes that make services accessible outside of the cluster:

- Ingress mode (default)
- Host mode

Services published via *ingress mode* can be accessed from any node in the Swarm — even nodes **not** running a service replica. Services published via *host mode* can only be accessed by hitting nodes running service replicas. Figure 11.20 shows the difference between the two modes.

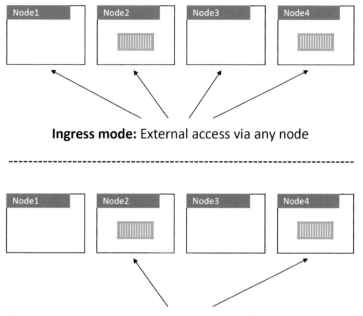

Ingress mode: External access via any node

Host mode: External access via nodes with Service replicas

Figure 11.20

Ingress mode is the default. This means any time you publish a service with -p or --publish it will default to *ingress mode*. To publish a service in *host mode* you need to use the long format of the --publish flag **and** add mode=host. Let's see an example using *host mode*.

```
$ docker service create -d --name svc1 \
  --publish published=5000,target=80,mode=host \
  nginx
```

A few notes about the command. docker service create lets you publish a service using either a *long form syntax* or *short form syntax*. The short form looks like this: -p 5000:80 and we've seen it a few times already. However, you cannot publish a service in *host mode* using short form.

The long form looks like this: --publish published=5000,target=80,mode=host. It's a comma-separate list with no whitespace after each comma. The options work as follows:

- published=5000 makes the service available externally via port 5000
- target=80 makes sure that external requests to the published port get mapped back to port 80 on the service replicas
- mode=host makes sure that external requests will only reach the service if they come in via nodes running a service replica.

Ingress mode is what you'll normally use.

Behind the scenes, *ingress mode* uses a layer 4 routing mesh called the **Service Mesh** or the **Swarm Mode Service Mesh**. Figure 11.21 shows the basic traffic flow of an external request to a service exposed in ingress mode.

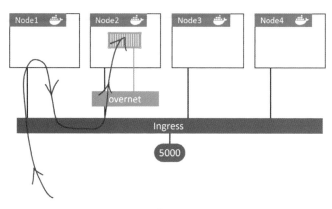

Figure 11.21

Let's quickly walk through the diagram.

1. The command at the top deploys a new Swarm service called "svc1". It's attaching the service to the `overnet` network and publishing it on port 5000.
2. Publishing a Swarm service like this (`--publish published=5000,target=80`) will publish it on port 5000 on the ingress network. As all nodes in a Swarm are attached to the ingress network, this means the port is published *swarm-wide.*
3. Logic is implemented on the cluster ensuring that any traffic hitting the ingress network, via **any node**, on port 5000 will be routed to the "svc1" service on port 80.
4. At this point, a single replica for the "svc1" service is deployed, and the cluster has a mapping rule that says "*all traffic hitting the ingress network on port 5000 needs routing to a node running a replica for the "svc1" service*".
5. The red line shows traffic hitting node1 on port 5000 and being routed to the service replica running on node2 via the ingress network.

It's vital to know that the incoming traffic could have hit any of the four Swarm nodes on port 5000 and we would get the same result. This is because the service is published *swarm-wide* via the ingress network.

It's also vital to know that if there were multiple replicas running, as shown in Figure 11.22, the traffic would be balanced across all replicas.

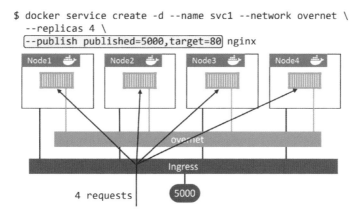

```
$ docker service create -d --name svc1 --network overnet \
  --replicas 4 \
  --publish published=5000,target=80 nginx
```

Figure 11.22

Docker Networking - The Commands

Docker networking has its own `docker network` sub-command. The main commands include:

- `docker network ls`: Lists all networks on the local Docker host.
- `docker network create`: Creates new Docker networks. By default, it creates them with the `nat` driver on Windows and the `bridge` driver on Linux. You can specify the driver (type of network) with the `-d` flag. `docker network create -d overlay overnet` will create a new overlay network called overnet with the native Docker `overlay` driver.
- `docker network inspect`: Provides detailed configuration information about a Docker network.
- `docker network prune`: Deletes all unused networks on a Docker host.
- `docker network rm`: Deletes specific networks on a Docker host.

Chapter Summary

The Container Network Model (CNM) is the master design document for Docker networking and defines the three major constructs that are used to build Docker networks — *sandboxes*, *endpoints*, and *networks*.

`libnetwork` is the open-source library, written in Go, that implements the CNM. It's used by Docker and is where all of the core Docker networking code lives. It also provides Docker's network control plane and management plane.

Drivers extend the Docker network stack (`libnetwork`) by adding code to implement specific network types, such as bridge networks and overlay networks. Docker ships with several built-in drivers, but you can also use 3rd-party drivers.

Single-host bridge networks are the most basic type of Docker network and are suitable for local development and very small applications. They do not scale, and they require port mappings if you want to publish your services outside of the network. Docker on Linux implements bridge networks using the built-in `bridge` driver, whereas Docker on Windows implements them using the built-in `nat` driver.

Overlay networks are all the rage and are excellent container-only multi-host networks. We'll talk about them in-depth in the next chapter.

The `macvlan` driver (`transparent` on Windows) allows you to connect containers to existing physical networks and VLANs. They make containers first-class citizens by giving them their own MAC and IP addresses. Unfortunately, they require promiscuous mode on the host NIC, meaning they won't work in the public cloud.

Docker also uses `libnetwork` to implement basic service discovery, as well as a service mesh for container-based load balancing of ingress traffic.

12: Docker overlay networking

Overlay networks are at the beating heart of many cloud-native microservices apps. In this chapter we'll cover the fundamentals of native Docker overlay networking.

Docker overlay networking on Windows has feature parity with Linux. This means the examples we'll use in this chapter will all work on Linux and Windows.

We'll split this chapter into the usual three parts:

- The TLDR
- The deep dive
- The commands

Let's do some networking magic.

Docker overlay networking - The TLDR

In the real world, it's vital that containers can communicate with each other reliably and securely, even when they're on different hosts that are on different networks. This is where overlay networking comes in to play. It allows you to create a flat, secure, layer-2 network, spanning multiple hosts. Containers connect to this and can communicate directly.

Docker offers native overlay networking that is simple to configure and secure by default.

Behind the scenes, it's built on top of `libnetwork` and drivers. `libnetwork` is the canonical implementation of the Container Network Model (CNM) and drivers are pluggable components that implement different networking technologies and topologies. Docker offers native drivers, including the `overlay` driver.

Docker overlay networking - The deep dive

In March 2015, Docker, Inc. acquired a container networking startup called *Socket Plane*. Two of the reasons behind the acquisition were to bring *real networking* to Docker, and to make container networking simple enough that even developers could do it.

They over-achieved on both.

However, hiding behind the simple networking commands are a lot of moving parts. The kind of stuff you need to understand before doing production deployments and attempting to troubleshoot issues.

The rest of this chapter will be broken into two parts:

- Part 1: We'll build and test a Docker overlay network
- Part 2: We'll explain the magic that makes it work

Build and test a Docker overlay network in Swarm mode

For the following examples, we'll use two Docker hosts, on two separate Layer 2 networks, connected by a router. See Figure 12.1, and note the different networks that each node is on.

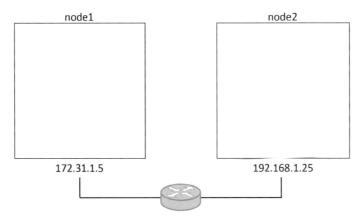

Figure 12.1

You can follow along with either Linux or Windows Docker hosts. Linux should have at least a 4.4 Linux kernel (newer is always better) and Windows should be Windows Server 2016 or later with the latest hotfixes installed. You can also follow along on your Mac or Windows PC with Docker Desktop. However, you won't see the full benefits as they only support a single Docker host.

Build a Swarm

The first thing to do is configure the two hosts into a two-node swarm. This is because swarm mode is a pre-requisite for overlay networks.

We'll run the `docker swarm init` command on **node1** to make it a *manager*, and then we'll run the `docker swarm join` command on **node2** to make it a *worker*. This is not a production-grade setup, but it is enough for a learning lab. You're encouraged to test with more managers and workers and expand on the examples.

If you are following along in your own lab, you'll need to swap the IP addresses and the likes with the correct values for your environment.

Run the following command on **node1**.

```
$ docker swarm init \
  --advertise-addr=172.31.1.5 \
  --listen-addr=172.31.1.5:2377

Swarm initialized: current node (1ex3...o3px) is now a manager.
```

Run the next command on **node2**. You will need to ensure the following ports are enabled on any firewalls:

- `2377/tcp` for management plane comms
- `7946/tcp` and `7946/udp` for control plane comms (SWIM-based gossip)
- `4789/udp` for the VXLAN data plane

```
$ docker swarm join \
  --token SWMTKN-1-0hz2ec...2vye \
  172.31.1.5:2377
This node joined a swarm as a worker.
```

We now have a two-node Swarm with **node1** as a manager and **node2** as a worker.

Create a new overlay network

Now let's create a new *overlay network* called **uber-net**.

Run the following command from **node1** (manager).

```
$ docker network create -d overlay uber-net
c740ydi1lm89khn5kd52skrd9
```

That's it. You've just created a brand-new overlay network that is available to all hosts in the Swarm and has its control plane encrypted with TLS (AES in GCM mode with keys automatically rotated every 12 hours). If you want to encrypt the data plane, you just add the `-o encrypted` flag to the command. However, data plane encryption isn't enabled by default because of the performance overhead. It's highly recommended that you extensively test performance before enabling data plane encryption. However, if you do enable it, it's protected by the same AES in GCM mode with key rotation.

If you're unsure about terms such as *control plane* and * data plane*, control plane traffic is cluster management traffic, whereas data plane traffic is application traffic. By default, Docker overlay networks encrypt cluster management traffic but not application traffic. You must explicitly enable encryption of application traffic.

You can list all networks on each node with the `docker network ls` command.

```
$ docker network ls
NETWORK ID      NAME              DRIVER      SCOPE
ddac4ff813b7    bridge            bridge      local
389a7e7e8607    docker_gwbridge   bridge      local
a09f7e6b2ac6    host              host        local
ehw16ycy980s    ingress           overlay     swarm
2b26c11d3469    none              null        local
c740ydi1lm89    uber-net          overlay     swarm
```

The output will look more like this on a Windows server:

```
NETWORK ID      NAME        DRIVER      SCOPE
8iltzv6sbtgc    ingress     overlay     swarm
6545b2a61b6f    nat         nat         local
96d0d737c2ee    none        null        local
nil5ouh44qco    uber-net    overlay     swarm
```

The newly created network is at the bottom of the list called **uber-net**. The other networks were automatically created when Docker was installed and when the swarm was initialized.

If you run the `docker network ls` command on **node2**, you'll notice that it can't see the **uber-net** network. This is because new overlay networks are only extended to worker nodes when they are tasked with running a container on it. This lazy approach to extended overlay networks improves network scalability by reducing the amount of network gossip.

Attach a service to the overlay network

Now that you have an overlay network, let's create a new *Docker service* and attach it to the network. The example will create the service with two replicas (containers) so that one runs on **node1** and the other runs on **node2**. This will automatically extend the **uber-net** overlay to **node2**

Run the following commands from **node1**.

Linux example:

```
$ docker service create --name test \
   --network uber-net \
   --replicas 2 \
   ubuntu sleep infinity
```

Windows example:

```
> docker service create --name test `
  --network uber-net `
  --replicas 2 `
  mcr.microsoft.com\powershell:nanoserver pwsh.exe -Command Start-Sleep 3600
```

> **Note:** The Windows example uses the backtick character to split parameters over multiple lines to make the command more readable. The backtick is how PowerShell escapes line feeds.

The command creates a new service called **test**, attaches it to the **uber-net** overlay network, and creates two replicas (containers) based on the image provided. In both examples, you issued a sleep command to the containers to keep them running and stop them from exiting.

Because we're running two replicas (containers), and the Swarm has two nodes, one replica will be scheduled on each node.

Verify the operation with a `docker service ps` command.

```
$ docker service ps test
ID        NAME     IMAGE    NODE     DESIRED STATE   CURRENT STATE
77q...rkx  test.1   ubuntu   node1    Running         Running
97v...pa5  test.2   ubuntu   node2    Running         Running
```

When Swarm starts a container on an overlay network, it automatically extends that network to the node the container is running on. This means that the **uber-net** network is now visible on **node2**.

Standalone containers that are not part of a swarm service cannot attach to overlay networks unless they have the `attachable=true` property. The following command can be used to create an attachable overlay network that standalone containers can also attach to.

```
$ docker network create -d overlay --attachable uber-net
```

Congratulations. You've created a new overlay network spanning two nodes on separate physical underlay networks. You've also attached two containers to it. How easy was that!

Test the overlay network

Let's test the overlay network with the ping command.

As shown in Figure 12.2, we've got two Docker hosts on separate networks, and a single overlay network spanning both. We've got one container connected to the overlay network on each node. Let's see if they can ping each other.

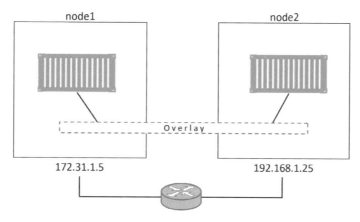

Figure 12.2

You can run the test by pinging the remote container by name. However, the examples will use IP addresses as it gives us an excuse to learn how to find a containers IP address.

Run a `docker network inspect` to see the subnet assigned to the overlay and the IP addresses assigned to the two containers in the `test` service.

```
$ docker network inspect uber-net
[
    {
        "Name": "uber-net",
        "Id": "c740ydi1lm89khn5kd52skrd9",
        "Scope": "swarm",
        "Driver": "overlay",
        "EnableIPv6": false,
        "IPAM": {
            "Driver": "default",
            "Options": null,
            "Config": [
                {
                    "Subnet": "10.0.0.0/24",
                    "Gateway": "10.0.0.1"
                }
        "Containers": {
                "Name": "test.1.mfd1kn0qzgosu2f6bhfk5jc2p",
                "IPv4Address": "10.0.0.3/24",
                <Snip>
```

```
        },
            "Name": "test.2.m49f4psxp3daixlwfvy73v4j8",
            "IPv4Address": "10.0.0.4/24",
        },
<Snip>
```

The output is heavily snipped for readability, but you can see it shows **uber-net**'s subnet is 10.0.0.0/24. This doesn't match either of the physical underlay networks shown in Figure 12.2 (172.31.1.0/24 and 192.168.1.0/24). You can also see the IP addresses assigned to the two containers.

Run the following two commands on **node1** and **node2**. These will get the container's ID's and confirm the IP address from the previous command. Be sure to use the container ID's from your own lab in the second command.

```
$ docker container ls
CONTAINER ID   IMAGE           COMMAND           CREATED       STATUS      NAME
396c8b142a85   ubuntu:latest   "sleep infinity"  2 hours ago   Up 2 hrs    test.1.mfd...

$ docker container inspect \
  --format='{{range .NetworkSettings.Networks}}{{.IPAddress}}{{end}}' 396c8b142a85
10.0.0.3
```

Run these commands on both nodes to confirm the IP addresses of both containers.

Figure 12.3 shows the configuration so far. Subnet and IP addresses may be different in your lab.

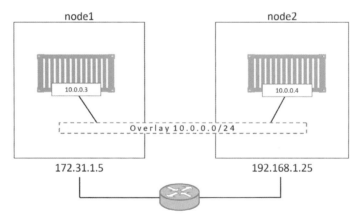

Figure 12.3

As you can see, there is a Layer 2 overlay network spanning both hosts, and each container has an IP address on this overlay network. This means the container on **node1** will be able to ping the container on **node2** using its 10.0.0.4 address. This works despite the fact that both *nodes* are on different Layer 2 underlay networks.

Let's prove it.

Log on to the container on **node1** and ping the remote container.

To do this on the Linux Ubuntu container you'll need to install the ping utility. If you're following along with the Windows PowerShell example the ping utility is already installed.

Remember that the container IDs will be different in your environment.

Linux example:

```
$ docker container exec -it 396c8b142a85 bash

root@396c8b142a85:/# apt-get update && apt-get install iputils-ping -y
<Snip>
Reading package lists... Done
Building dependency tree
Reading state information... Done
<Snip>
Setting up iputils-ping (3:20190709-3) ...
Processing triggers for libc-bin (2.31-0ubuntu9) ...

root@396c8b142a85:/# ping 10.0.0.4
PING 10.0.0.4 (10.0.0.4) 56(84) bytes of data.
64 bytes from 10.0.0.4: icmp_seq=1 ttl=64 time=1.06 ms
64 bytes from 10.0.0.4: icmp_seq=2 ttl=64 time=1.07 ms
64 bytes from 10.0.0.4: icmp_seq=3 ttl=64 time=1.03 ms
64 bytes from 10.0.0.4: icmp_seq=4 ttl=64 time=1.26 ms
^C
root@396c8b142a85:/#
```

Windows example:

```
> docker container exec -it 1a4f29e5a4b6 pwsh.exe
Windows PowerShell

PS C:\> ping 10.0.0.4
Pinging 10.0.0.4 with 32 bytes of data:
Reply from 10.0.0.4: bytes=32 time=1ms TTL=128
Reply from 10.0.0.4: bytes=32 time<1ms TTL=128
Reply from 10.0.0.4: bytes=32 time=2ms TTL=128
Reply from 10.0.0.4: bytes=32 time=2ms TTL=12
PS C:\>
```

Congratulations. The container on **node1** can ping the container on **node2** via the overlay network. If you created the network with the `-o encrypted` flag, the exchange will have been encrypted.

You can also trace the route of the ping command from within the container. This will report a single hop, proving that the containers are communicating directly via the overlay network — blissfully unaware of any underlay networks that are being traversed.

> **Note:** You'll need to install `traceroute` for the Linux example to work.

Linux example:

```
$ root@396c8b142a85:/# traceroute 10.0.0.4
traceroute to 10.0.0.4 (10.0.0.4), 30 hops max, 60 byte packets
 1  test-svc.2.97v...a5.uber-net (10.0.0.4)  1.110ms  1.034ms  1.073ms
```

Windows example:

```
PS C:\> tracert 10.0.0.3

Tracing route to test.2.ttcpiv3p...7o4.uber-net [10.0.0.4]
over a maximum of 30 hops:

  1   <1 ms   <1 ms   <1 ms   test.2.ttcpiv3p...7o4.uber-net [10.0.0.4]

Trace complete.
```

So far, you've created an overlay network with a single command. You then added containers to it. The containers were scheduled on two hosts that were on two different Layer 2 underlay networks. Once you worked out the container's IP addresses, you proved that they could communicate directly via the overlay network.

The theory of how it all works

Now that you've seen how easy it is to build and use a secure overlay network, let's find out how it's all put together behind the scenes.

Some of the detail in this section will be specific to Linux. However, the same overall principles apply to Windows.

VXLAN primer

First and foremost, Docker overlay networking uses VXLAN tunnels to create virtual Layer 2 overlay networks. So, before we go any further, let's do a quick VXLAN primer.

At the highest level, VXLANs let you create a virtual Layer 2 network on top of an existing Layer 3 infrastructure. That's a lot of techno jargon that means you can create a simple network that hides horrifically complex networks beneath. The example we used earlier created a new 10.0.0.0/24 Layer 2 network on top of a Layer 3 IP network comprising two Layer 2 networks — 172.31.1.0/24 and 192.168.1.0/24. This is shown in Figure 12.4.

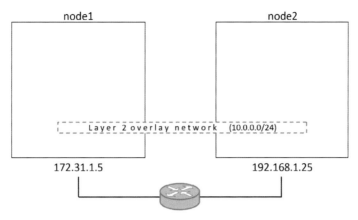

Figure 12.4

The beauty of VXLAN is that it's an encapsulation technology that existing routers and network infrastructure just see as regular IP/UDP packets and handle without issue.

To create the virtual Layer 2 overlay network, a VXLAN *tunnel* is created through the underlying Layer 3 IP infrastructure. You might hear the term *underlay network* used to refer to the underlying Layer 3 infrastructure — the networks that the Docker hosts are connected to.

Each end of the VXLAN tunnel is terminated by a VXLAN Tunnel Endpoint (VTEP). It's this VTEP that performs the encapsulation/de-encapsulation and other magic required to make all of this work. See Figure 12.5.

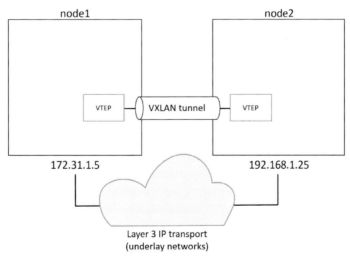

Figure 12.5

Walk through our two-container example

In the example from earlier, you had two hosts connected via an IP network. Each host ran a single container, and you created a single VXLAN overlay network for the containers.

To accomplish this, a new *sandbox* (network namespace) was created on each host. As mentioned in the previous chapter, a *sandbox* is like a container, but instead of running an application, it runs an isolated network stack — one that's sandboxed from the network stack of the host itself.

A virtual switch (a.k.a. virtual bridge) called **Br0** is created inside the sandbox. A VTEP is also created with one end plumbed into the **Br0** virtual switch, and the other end plumbed into the host network stack (VTEP). The end in the host network stack gets an IP address on the underlay network the host is connected to, and is bound to a UDP socket on port 4789. The two VTEPs on each host create the overlay via a VXLAN tunnel as seen in Figure 12.6.

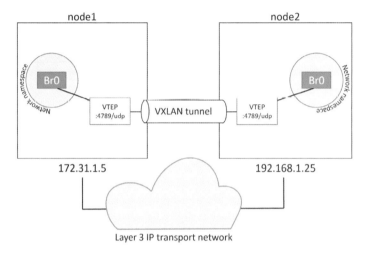

Figure 12.6

At this point, the VXLAN overlay is created and ready for use.

Each container then gets its own virtual Ethernet (veth) adapter that is also plumbed into the local **Br0** virtual switch. The topology now looks like Figure 12.7, and it should be getting easier to see how the two containers can communicate over the VXLAN overlay network despite their hosts being on two separate networks.

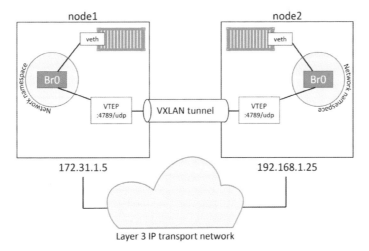

Figure 12.7

Communication example

Now that we've seen the main plumbing elements, let's see how the two containers communicate.

> **Warning!** This section gets quite technical, and it's not necessary for you to understand all of this detail for day-to-day operations.

For this example, we'll call the container on node1 "**C1**" and the container on node2 "**C2**". And let's assume **C1** wants to ping **C2** like we did in the practical example earlier in the chapter.

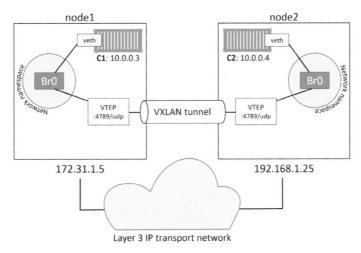

Figure 12.8

C1 creates the ping requests and sets the destination IP address to be the 10.0.0.4 address of C2. It sends the traffic over its veth interface which is connected to the **Br0** virtual switch. The virtual switch doesn't know where to send the packet as it doesn't have an entry in its MAC address table (ARP table) that corresponds to the destination IP address. As a result, it floods the packet to all ports. The VTEP interface is connected to **Br0** knows how to forward the frame, so responds with its own MAC address. This is a *proxy ARP* reply and results in the **Br0** switch *learning* how to forward the packet. As a result, **Br0** updates its ARP table, mapping 10.0.0.4 to the MAC address of the local VTEP.

Now that the **Br0** switch has *learned* how to forward traffic to **C2**, all future packets for **C2** will be transmitted directly to the local VTEP interface. The VTEP interface knows about **C2** because all newly started containers have their network details propagated to other nodes in the Swarm using the network's built-in gossip protocol.

The packet is sent to the VTEP interface, which encapsulates the frames so they can be sent over the underlay transport infrastructure. At a fairly high level, this encapsulation includes adding a VXLAN header to the individual Ethernet frames. The VXLAN header contains the VXLAN network ID (VNID) which is used to map frames from VLANs to VXLANs and vice versa. Each VLAN gets mapped to VNID so that the packet can be de-encapsulated on the receiving end and forwarded to the correct VLAN. This maintains network isolation.

The encapsulation also wraps the frame in a UDP packet with the IP address of the remote VTEP on node2 in the *destination IP field*, as well as the UDP port 4789 socket information. This encapsulation allows the data to be sent across the underlying networks without the underlying networks having to know anything about VXLAN.

When the packet arrives at node2, the kernel sees that it's addressed to UDP port 4789. The kernel also knows that it has a VTEP interface bound to this socket. As a result, it sends the packet to the VTEP, which reads the VNID, de-encapsulates the packet, and sends it on to its own local **Br0** switch on the VLAN that corresponds the VNID. From there it is delivered to container C2.

And that... ladies and gents... is how VXLAN technology is leveraged by native Docker overlay networking.

Hopefully that's enough to get you started with any potential production Docker deployments. It should also give you the knowledge required to talk to your networking team about the networking aspects of your Docker infrastructure. On the topic of talking to your networking team... I recommend you don't approach them thinking that you now know everything about VXLAN. If you do that, you'll probably embarrass yourself ;-)

One final thing. Docker also supports Layer 3 routing within the same overlay network. For example, you can create an overlay network with two subnets, and Docker will take care of routing between them. The command to create a network like this could be docker network create --subnet=10.1.1.0/24 --subnet=11.1.1.0/24 -d overlay prod-net. This would result in two virtual switches, **Br0** and **Br1**, being created inside the *sandbox*, and routing happens by default.

Docker overlay networking - The commands

- docker network create is the command that we use to create a new container network. The -d flag lets you specify the driver to use, and the most common driver is the overlay driver. You can also specify *remote* drivers from 3rd parties. For overlay networks, the control plane is encrypted by default. Just add the -o encrypted flag to encrypt the data plane (performance overheads may be incurred).
- docker network ls lists all of the container networks visible to a Docker host. Docker hosts running in *swarm mode* only see overlay networks if they are hosting containers attached to that particular network. This keeps network-related gossip to a minimum.

- `docker network inspect` shows you detailed information about a particular container network. This includes *scope, driver, IPv4* and *IPv4* info, *subnet configuration, IP addresses of connected containers**, *VXLAN network ID,* and *encryption state.*
- `docker network rm` deletes a network

Chapter Summary

In this chapter, we saw how easy it is to create new Docker overlay networks with the `docker network create` command. We then learned how they are put together behind the scenes using VXLAN technology.

We've only scratched the surface of what can be done with Docker overlay networking.

13: Volumes and persistent data

Stateful applications that persist data are becoming more and more important in the world of cloud-native and microservices applications. Docker is an important infrastructure technology in this space, so we'll turn our attention in this chapter to investigating how Docker handles applications that write persistent data.

We'll split the chapter into the usual three parts:

- The TLDR
- The deep dive
- The commands

Volumes and persistent data - The TLDR

There are two main categories of data — persistent and non-persistent.

Persistent is the data you need to *keep*. Things like; customer records, financial data, research results, audit logs, and even some types of application *log* data. Non-persistent is the data you don't need to keep.

Both are important, and Docker has solutions for both.

To deal with non-persistent data, every Docker container gets its own non-persistent storage. This is automatically created for every container and is tightly coupled to the lifecycle of the container. As a result, deleting the container will delete the storage and any data on it.

To deal with persistent data, a container needs to store it in a *volume*. Volumes are separate objects that have their lifecycles decoupled from containers. This means you can create and manage volumes independently, and they're not tied to the lifecycle of any container. Net result, you can delete a container that's using a volume, and the volume won't be deleted.

That's the TLDR. Let's take a closer look.

Volumes and persistent data - The Deep Dive

There's a popular opinion that containers aren't good for stateful applications that persist data. This was true a few years ago. However, things are changing, and technologies now exist that make containers a viable choice for many stateful applications.

Am I saying containers are the best solution for all stateful applications? No. However, we're about to see some of the ways that containers deal with persistent and non-persistent data, and you may find it hard to see many differences with virtual machines.

We'll start out with non-persistent data.

Containers and non-persistent data

Containers are designed to be immutable. This is just a buzzword that means read-only — it's a best practice not to change the configuration of a container after it's deployed. If something breaks or you need to change something, you should create a new container with the fixes/updates and deploy it in place of the old container. You shouldn't log into a running container and make configuration changes!

However, many applications require a read-write filesystem in order to simply run – they won't even run on a read-only filesystem. This means it's not as simple as making containers entirely read-only. Every Docker container is created by adding a thin read-write layer on top of the read-only image it's based on. Figure 13.1 shows two running containers sharing a single read-only image.

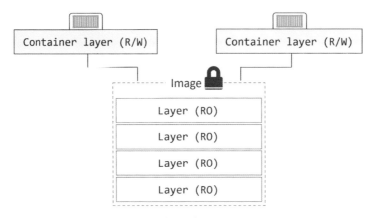

Figure 13.1 Ephemeral container storage

The writable container layer exists in the filesystem of the Docker host, and you'll hear it called various names. These include *local storage*, *ephemeral storage*, and *graphdriver storage*. It's typically located on the Docker host in these locations:

- Linux Docker hosts: `/var/lib/docker/<storage-driver>/...`
- Windows Docker hosts: `C:\ProgramData\Docker\windowsfilter\...`

This thin writable layer is an integral part of a container and enables all read/write operations. If you, or an application, update files or add new files, they'll be written to this layer. However, it's tightly coupled to the container's lifecycle — it gets created when the container is created and it gets deleted when the container is deleted. The fact that it's deleted along with a container means that it's not an option for important data that you need to keep (persist).

If your containers don't create persistent data, this thin writable layer of *local storage* will be fine and you're good to go. However, if your containers need to persist data, you need to read the next section.

One final word before moving to the next section.

This writable layer of local storage is managed on every Docker host by a storage driver (not to be confused with a volume driver). If you're running Docker in production on Linux, you'll need to make sure you match the right storage driver with the Linux distribution on your Docker host. Use the following list as a *guide:*

- **Red Hat Enterprise Linux:** Use the `overlay2` driver with modern versions of RHEL running Docker 17.06 or higher. Use the `devicemapper` driver with older versions. This applies to Oracle Linux and other Red Hat related upstream and downstream distros.
- **Ubuntu:** Use the `overlay2` or `aufs` drivers. If you're using a Linux 4.x kernel or higher you should go with `overlay2`.
- **SUSE Linux Enterprise Server:** Use the `btrfs` storage driver.
- **Windows** Windows only has one driver and it is configured by default.

Containers and persistent data

Volumes are the recommended way to persist data in containers. There are three major reasons for this:

- Volumes are independent objects that are not tied to the lifecycle of a container
- Volumes can be mapped to specialized external storage systems
- Volumes enable multiple containers on different Docker hosts to access and share the same data

At a high-level, you create a volume, then you create a container and mount the volume into it. The volume is mounted into a directory in the container's filesystem, and anything written to that directory is stored in the volume. If you delete the container, the volume and its data will still exist.

Figure 13.2 shows a Docker volume existing outside of the container as a separate object. It is mounted into the container's filesystem at `/data`, and any data written to the `/data` directory will be stored on the volume and will exist after the container is deleted.

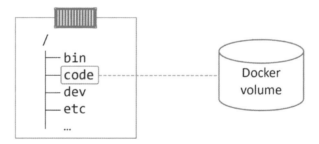

Figure 13.2 High-level view of volumes and containers

In Figure 13.2, the `/data` directory is a Docker volume that can either be mapped to an external storage system or a directory on the Docker host. Either way, its lifecycle is decoupled from the container. All other directories in the container use the thin writable container layer in the local storage area on the Docker host.

The arrow from the volume to the `/data` directory is shown as a dotted line to represent the decoupled relationship between volumes and containers.

Creating and managing Docker volumes

Volumes are first-class citizens in Docker. Among other things, this means they are their own object in the API and have their own `docker volume` sub-command.

Use the following command to create a new volume called `myvol`.

```
$ docker volume create myvol
myvol
```

By default, Docker creates new volumes with the built-in local driver. As the name suggests, volumes created with the local driver are only available to containers on the same node as the volume. You can use the -d flag to specify a different driver.

Third-party volume drivers are available as plugins. These provide Docker with seamless access external storage systems such as cloud storage services and on-premises storage systems including SAN or NAS. This is shown in Figure 13.3.

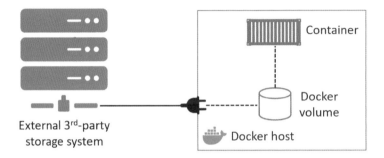

Figure 13.3 Plugging external storage into Docker

We'll look at an example with a third-party driver in a later section.

Now that the volume is created, you can see it with the docker volume ls command and inspect it with the docker volume inspect command.

```
$ docker volume ls
DRIVER              VOLUME NAME
local               myvol

$ docker volume inspect myvol
[
    {
        "CreatedAt": "2020-05-02T17:44:34Z",
        "Driver": "local",
        "Labels": {},
        "Mountpoint": "/var/lib/docker/volumes/myvol/_data",
        "Name": "myvol",
        "Options": {},
        "Scope": "local"
    }
]
```

Notice that the Driver and Scope are both local. This means the volume was created with the local driver and is only available to containers on this Docker host. The Mountpoint property tells us where in the Docker host's filesystem the volume exists.

All volumes created with the `local` driver get their own directory under `/var/lib/docker/volumes` on Linux, and `C:\ProgramData\Docker\volumes` on Windows. This means you can see them in your Docker host's filesystem. You can even access them directly from your Docker host, although this is not normally recommended. We showed an example of this in the chapter on Docker Compose — we copied a file directly into a volume's directory on the Docker host and the file immediately appeared in the volume inside the container.

Now the volume is created, it can be used by one or more containers. We'll see usage examples in a minute.

There are two ways to delete a Docker volume:

- `docker volume prune`
- `docker volume rm`

`docker volume prune` will delete **all volumes** that are not mounted into a container or service replica, so **use with caution!** `docker volume rm` lets you specify exactly which volumes you want to delete. Neither command will delete a volume that is in use by a container or service replica.

As the `myvol` volume is not in use, delete it with the `prune` command.

```
$ docker volume prune

WARNING! This will remove all volumes not used by at least one container.
Are you sure you want to continue? [y/N] y

Deleted Volumes:
myvol
Total reclaimed space: 0B
```

Congratulations, you've created, inspected, and deleted a Docker volume. And you did it all without interacting with a container. This demonstrates the independent nature of volumes.

At this point, you know all of the commands to create, list, inspect, and delete Docker volumes. However, it's also possible to deploy volumes via Dockerfiles using the `VOLUME` instruction. The format is `VOLUME <container-mount-point>`. Interestingly, you cannot specify a directory on the host when defining a volume in a Dockerfile. This is because *host* directories are different depending on what OS your Docker host is running – it could break your builds if you specified a directory on a Docker host that doesn't exist. As a result, defining a volume in a Dockerfile requires you to specify host directories at deploy-time.

Demonstrating volumes with containers and services

Let's see how to use volumes with containers and services.

The examples will be from a system with no pre-existing volumes, and everything we demonstrate applies to both Linux and Windows.

Use the following command to create a new standalone container that mounts a volume called `bizvol`.

Linux example:

```
$ docker container run -dit --name voltainer \
    --mount source=bizvol,target=/vol \
    alpine
```

Windows example:

Use PowerShell for all Windows examples, and note the use of backticks (') to split commands across multiple lines.

```
> docker container run -dit --name voltainer `
    --mount source=bizvol,target=c:\vol `
    mcr.microsoft.com/powershell:nanoserver
```

The command uses the --mount flag to mount a volume called "bizvol" into the container at either /vol or c:\vol. The command completes successfully despite the fact there is no volume on the system called bizvol. This raises an interesting point:

- If you specify an existing volume, Docker will use the existing volume
- If you specify a volume that doesn't exist, Docker will create it for you

In this case, bizvol didn't exist, so Docker created it and mounted it into the new container. This means you'll be able to see it with docker volume ls.

```
$ docker volume ls
DRIVER              VOLUME NAME
local               bizvol
```

Although containers and volumes have separate lifecycle's, you cannot delete a volume that is in use by a container. Try it.

```
$ docker volume rm bizvol
Error response from daemon: remove bizvol: volume is in use - [b44d3f82...dd2029ca]
```

The volume is brand new, so it doesn't have any data. Let's exec onto the container and write some data to it. The example cited is Linux, if you're following along on Windows just replace sh with pwsh.exe at the end of the command. All other commands will work on Linux and Windows.

```
$ docker container exec -it voltainer sh

/# echo "I promise to write a review of the book on Amazon" > /vol/file1

/# ls -l /vol
total 4
-rw-r--r-- 1 root  root    50 Jan 12 13:49 file1

/# cat /vol/file1
I promise to write a review of the book on Amazon
```

Type exit to return to the shell of your Docker host, and then delete the container with the following command.

```
$ docker container rm voltainer -f
voltainer
```

Even though the container is deleted, the volume still exists:

```
$ docker container ls -a
CONTAINER ID    IMAGE    COMMAND    CREATED    STATUS

$ docker volume ls
DRIVER             VOLUME NAME
local              bizvol
```

Because the volume still exists, you can look at its mount point on the host to check if the data is still there.

Run the following commands from the terminal of your Docker host. The first one will show that the file still exists, the second will show the contents of the file.

Be sure to use the C:\ProgramData\Docker\volumes\bizvol_data directory if you're following along on Windows. Also, this step won't work on Docker Desktop for Mac and Windows 10. This is because Docker Desktop runs Docker inside of a VM and the volume data directories exist inside the VM.

```
$ ls -l /var/lib/docker/volumes/bizvol/_data/
total 4
-rw-r--r-- 1 root root 50 Jan 12 14:25 file1

$ cat /var/lib/docker/volumes/bizvol/_data/file1
I promise to write a review of the book on Amazon
```

Great, the volume and data still exists.

It's even possible to mount the bizvol volume into a new service or container. The following command creates a new Docker service, called hellcat, and mounts bizvol into the service replica at /vol. You'll need to be running in swarm mode for this command to work. If you're running in single-engine mode you can use a docker container run command instead.

```
$ docker service create \
  --name hellcat \
  --mount source=bizvol,target=/vol \
  alpine sleep 1d

overall progress: 1 out of 1 tasks
1/1: running   [===================================>]
verify: Service converged
```

We didn't specify the --replicas flag, so only a single service replica was deployed. Find which node in the Swarm it's running on.

```
$ docker service ps hellcat
ID        NAME        NODE      DESIRED STATE      CURRENT STATE
l3nh...   hellcat.1   node1     Running            Running 19 seconds ago
```

In this example, the replica is running on node1. Log on to node1 and get the ID of the service replica container.

```
node1$ docker container ls
CTR ID    IMAGE           COMMAND        STATUS        NAMES
df6..a7b  alpine:latest   "sleep 1d"     Up 25 secs    hellcat.1.l3nh...
```

Notice that the container name is a combination of service-name, replica-number, and replica-ID separated by periods.

Exec onto the container and check that the data is present in /vol. We'll use the service replica's container ID in the exec example. If you're following along on Windows, remember to replace sh with pwsh.exe.

```
node1$ docker container exec -it df6 sh

/# cat /vol/file1
I promise to write a review of the book on Amazon
```

Excellent, the volume has preserved the original data and made it available to a new container.

I guess it's time to jump over to Amazon and write that book review :-D

Sharing storage across cluster nodes

Integrating external storage systems with Docker makes it possible to share volumes between cluster nodes. These external systems can be cloud storage services or enterprise storage systems in your on-premises data centers. As an example, a single storage LUN or NFS share can be presented to multiple Docker hosts, allowing it to be used by containers and service replicas no-matter which Docker host they're running on. Figure 13.4 shows a single external shared volume being presented to two Docker nodes. These Docker nodes can then make the shared volume available to either, or both containers.

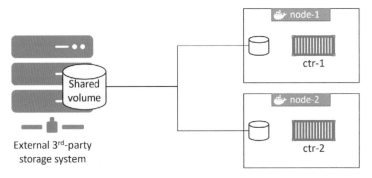

Figure 13.4

Building a setup like this requires a lot of things. You need access to a specialised storage systems and knowledge of how it works and presents storage. You also need to know how your applications read and write data to the shared storage. Finally, you need a volumes driver plugin that works with the external storage system.

Docker Hub is the best place to find volume plugins. Login to Docker Hub, select the view to show `plugins` instead of `containers`, and filter results to only show `Volume` plugins. Once you've located the appropriate plugin for your storage system, you create any configuration files it might need, and install it with `docker plugin install`.

Once the plugin is registered, you can create new volumes from the storage system using `docker volume create` with the `-d` flag.

The following example installs the Pure Storage Docker volume plugin. This plugin provides access to storage volumes on either a Pure Storage FlashArray or FlashBlade storage system. Plugins only work with the correct external storage systems.

1. The Pure Storage plugin requires a configuration file called `pure.json` in the Docker host's `/etc/pure-docker-plugin/` directory. This file contains the information required for the plugin to locate the external storage system, authenticate, and access resources.
2. Install the plugin and grant the required permissions.

```
$ docker plugin install purestorage/docker-plugin:latest --alias pure --grant-all-permissions
Plugin "purestorage/docker-plugin:3.8" is requesting the following privileges:
 - network: [host]
 - host pid namespace: [true]
 - mount: [/etc/pure-docker-plugin/pure.json]
 - mount: [/dev]
 - mount: [/sys]
 - allow-all-devices: [true]
 - capabilities: [CAP_SYS_ADMIN CAP_SYS_PTRACE]
Do you grant the above permissions? [y/N] y
```

1. List the available plugins.

```
$ docker plugin ls
ID              NAME            DESCRIPTION                    ENABLED
6b5e61aefbb3    pure:latest     Pure Storage plugin for Docker true
```

1. Create a new volume with the plugin (you can also do this as part of the container creation process). This example creates a new 25GB volume called "fastvol" on the registered Pure Storage backend.

```
$ docker volume create -d pure -o size=25GB fastvol
fastvol
```

Different storage drivers support different options, but this should be enough to give you a feel for how they work.

Potential data corruption

A major concern with any configuration that shares a single volume among multiple containers is **data corruption**.

Assume the following example based on Figure 13.4.

The application running in ctr-1 on node-1 updates some data in the shared volume. However, instead of writing the update directly to the volume, it holds it in its local buffer for faster recall (this is common in many operating systems). At this point, the application in ctr-1 thinks the data has been written to the volume. However, before ctr-1 on node-1 flushes its buffers and commits the data to the volume, the app in ctr-2 on node-2 updates the same data with a different value and commits it directly to the volume. At this point, both applications *think* they've updated the data in the volume, but in reality only the application in ctr-2 has. A few seconds later, ctr-1 on node-1 flushes the data to the volume, overwriting the changes made by the application in ctr-2. However, the application in ctr-2 is totally unaware of this! This is one of the ways data corruption happens.

To prevent this, you need to write your applications in a way to avoid things like this.

Volumes and persistent data - The Commands

- `docker volume create` is the command we use to create new volumes. By default, volumes are created with the `local` driver, but you can use the `-d` flag to specify a different driver.
- `docker volume ls` will list all volumes on the local Docker host.
- `docker volume inspect` shows detailed volume information. Use this command to see many interesting volume properties, including where a volume exists in the Docker host's filesystem.
- `docker volume prune` will delete **all** volumes that are not in use by a container or service replica. **Use with caution!**
- `docker volume rm` deletes specific volumes that are not in use.
- `docker plugin install` will install new volume plugins from Docker Hub.
- `docker plugin ls` lists all plugins installed on a Docker host.

Chapter Summary

There are two main types of data: persistent and non-persistent data. Persistent data is data that you need to keep, non-persistent is data that you don't need to keep. By default, all containers get a layer of writable non-persistent storage that lives and dies with the container — we call this *local storage* and it's ideal for non-persistent data. However, if your containers create data that you need to keep, you should store the data in a Docker volume.

Docker volumes are first-class citizens in the Docker API and managed independently of containers with their own `docker volume` sub-command. This means that deleting a container will not delete the volumes it was using.

Third party volume plugins can provide Docker access to specialised external storage systems. They're installed from Docker Hub with the `docker plugin install` command and are referenced at volume creation time with the `-d` command flag.

Volumes are the recommended way to work with persistent data in a Docker environment.

14: Deploying apps with Docker Stacks

Deploying and managing cloud-native microservices applications comprising lots of small integrated services at scale is hard.

Fortunately, Docker Stacks are here to help. They simplify application management by providing; *desired state, rolling updates, simple, scaling operations, health checks,* and more! All wrapped in a nice declarative model. Love it!

Don't worry if these buzzwords are new to you or sound complicated, you'll understand them all by the end of the chapter.

We'll split this chapter into the usual three parts:

- The TLDR
- The deep dive
- The commands

Deploying apps with Docker Stacks - The TLDR

Testing and deploying simple apps on your laptop is easy, but that's for amateurs. Deploying and managing multi-service apps in real-world production environments... that's for pro's!

Fortunately, stacks are here to help!. They let you define complex multi-service apps in a single declarative file. They also provide a simple way to deploy the app and manage its entire lifecycle — initial deployment > health checks > scaling > updates > rollbacks and more!

The process is simple. Define the desired state of your app in a *Compose file*, then deploy and manage it with the `docker stack` command. That's it.

The Compose file includes the entire stack of microservices that make up the app. It also includes all of the volumes, networks, secrets, and other infrastructure the app needs. The `docker stack deploy` command is used to deploy the entire app from the single file. Simple.

To accomplish all of this, stacks build on top of Docker Swarm, meaning you get all of the security and advanced features that come with Swarm.

In a nutshell, Docker is great for application development and testing. Docker Stacks are great for scale and production.

Deploying apps with Docker Stacks - The Deep Dive

If you know Docker Compose, you'll find Docker Stacks really easy. In fact, in many ways, stacks are what we always wished Compose was — fully integrated into Docker and able to manage the entire lifecycle of applications.

Architecturally speaking, stacks are at the top of the Docker application hierarchy. They build on top of *services*, which in turn build on top of containers.

We'll divide this section of the chapter as follows:

- Overview of the sample app
- Looking closer at the stack file
- Deploying the app
- Managing the app

Overview of the sample app

For the rest of the chapter, we'll be using the popular **AtSea Shop** demo app. It lives on GitHub[15] and is open-sourced under the Apache 2.0 license[16].

We're using this app because it's moderately complicated without being too big to list and describe in a book. Beneath the covers, it's a cloud-native microservices app that leverages certificates and secrets. The high-level application architecture is shown in Figure 14.1.

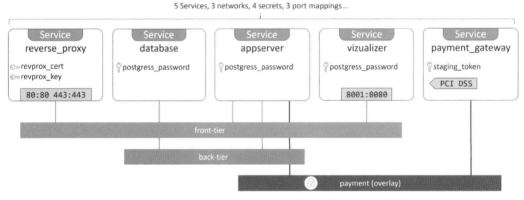

Figure 14.1 AtSea Shop high level architecture

As you can see, it comprises 5 *Services*, 3 networks, 4 secrets, and 3 port mappings. We'll see each of these in detail when we inspect the stack file.

> **Note:** When referring to *services* in this chapter, we're talking about the Docker service object that is one or more identical containers managed as a single object on a swarm cluster.

Clone the application's GitHub repo so that you have all of the application source files on your local machine.

---

[15]https://github.com/dockersamples/atsea-sample-shop-app
[16]https://github.com/dockersamples/atsea-sample-shop-app/blob/master/LICENSE

```
$ git clone https://github.com/dockersamples/atsea-sample-shop-app.git
Cloning into 'atsea-sample-shop-app'...
remote: Enumerating objects: 30, done.
remote: Counting objects: 100% (30/30), done.
remote: Compressing objects: 100% (30/30), done.
remote: Total 672 (delta 20), reused 0 (delta 0), pack-reused 642
Receiving objects: 100% (672/672), 7.29 MiB | 1.46 MiB/s, done.
Resolving deltas: 100% (217/217), done.
```

The application consists of several directories and source files. Feel free to explore them all. However, we're going to focus on the `docker-stack.yml` file that defines the app and its requirements. We'll refer to this as the *stack file*.

At the highest level, it defines 4 top-level keys.

```
version:
services:
networks:
secrets:
```

Version indicates the version of the Compose file format. This has to be 3.0 or higher to work with stacks. **Services** is where you define the stack of services that make up the app. **Networks** lists the required networks, and **secrets** defines the secrets the app uses.

If you expand each top-level key, you'll see how things map to Figure 14.1. The stack file has five services called "reverse_proxy", "database", "appserver", "visualizer", and "payment_gateway". So does Figure 14.1. The stack file has three networks called "front-tier", "back-tier", and "payment". So does Figure 14.1. Finally, the stack file has four secrets called "postgres_password", "staging_token", "revprox_key", and "revprox_cert". So does Figure 14.1.

```
version: "3.2"
services:
    reverse_proxy:
    database:
    appserver:
    visualizer:
    payment_gateway:
networks:
    front-tier:
    back-tier:
    payment:
secrets:
    postgres_password:
    staging_token:
    revprox_key:
    revprox_cert:
```

It's important to understand that the stack file captures and defines many of the requirements of the entire application. As such, it's self-documenting and a great tool for bridging the gap between dev and ops.

Let's take a closer look at each section of the stack file.

Looking closer at the stack file

Stack files are very similar to Compose files. The only requirement is that the `version:` key specify a value of "3.0" or higher. See the the Docker docs[17] for the latest information on Compose file versions and compatibility with your versions of Docker.

One of the first things Docker does when deploying an app from a stack file is create any required networks listed under the `networks` key. If the networks don't already exist, Docker creates them.

Let's see the networks defined in the stack file.

Networks

```
networks:
  front-tier:
  back-tier:
  payment:
    driver: overlay
    driver_opts:
      encrypted: 'yes'
```

The stack file describes three networks; `front-tier`, `back-tier`, and `payment`. By default, they'll all be created as overlay networks by the `overlay` driver. But the `payment` network is special — it requires an encrypted data plane.

As mentioned in the chapter on overlay networking, the control plane of all overlay networks is encrypted by default, but you have to explicitly encrypt the data plane. The control plane is for network management traffic and the data plane is for application traffic. Encrypting the data plane has a potential performance overhead.

To encrypt the data plane, you have two choices:

- Pass the `-o encrypted` flag to the `docker network create` command.
- Specify `encrypted: 'yes'` under `driver_opts` in the stack file.

The overhead incurred by encrypting the data plane depends on various factors such traffic type and traffic flow. You should perform extensive testing to understand the performance overhead that encrypting data plane traffic has on your workload. It's not uncommon for this to be approximately 10%.

As previously mentioned, all three networks will be created before the secrets and services.

Let's look at the secrets.

Secrets

Secrets are defined as top-level objects, and the stack file we're using defines four:

---

[17]https://docs.docker.com/compose/compose-file/

```
secrets:
  postgres_password:
    external: true
  staging_token:
    external: true
  revprox_key:
    external: true
  revprox_cert:
    external: true
```

Notice that all four are defined as `external`. This means that they must already exist before the stack can be deployed.

It's possible for secrets to be created on-demand when the application is deployed — just replace `external: true` with `file: <filename>`. However, for this to work, a plaintext file containing the unencrypted value of the secret must already exist on the host's filesystem. This has obvious security implications.

We'll see how to create these secrets when we come to deploy the app. For now, it's enough to know that the application defines four secrets that need pre-creating.

Let's look at each of the services.

Services

Services are where most of the action happens.

Each service is a JSON collection (dictionary) that contains a bunch of keys. We'll step through each one and explain what each of the options does.

The reverse_proxy service

As you can see, the `reverse_proxy` service defines an image, ports, secrets, and networks.

```
reverse_proxy:
  image: dockersamples/atseasampleshopapp_reverse_proxy
  ports:
    - "80:80"
    - "443:443"
  secrets:
    - source: revprox_cert
      target: revprox_cert
    - source: revprox_key
      target: revprox_key
  networks:
    - front-tier
```

The image key is the only mandatory key in the service object. As the name suggests, it defines the Docker image that will be used to build the replicas for the service. Remember that a service is one or more identical containers.

Docker is opinionated, so unless you specify otherwise, the **image** will be pulled from Docker Hub. You can specify images from 3rd-party registries by prepending the image name with the DNS name of the registry's API endpoint such as `gcr.io` for Google's container registry.

One difference between Docker Stacks and Docker Compose is that stacks do not support **builds**. This means all images have to be built prior to deploying the stack.

The **ports** key defines two mappings:

- `80:80` maps port 80 across the swarm to port 80 on each service replica.
- `443:443` maps port 443 across the Swarm to port 443 on each service replica.

By default, all ports are mapped using *ingress mode*. This means they'll be mapped and accessible from every node in the Swarm — even nodes not running a replica. The alternative is *host mode*, where ports are only mapped on swarm nodes running replicas for the service. However, *host mode* requires you to use the long-form syntax. For example, mapping port 80 in *host mode* using the long-form syntax would be like this:

```
ports:
  - target: 80
    published: 80
    mode: host
```

The long-form syntax is recommended, as it's easier to read and more powerful (it supports ingress mode **and** host mode). However, it requires at least version 3.2 of the Compose file format.

The **secrets** key defines two secrets — `revprox_cert` and `revprox_key`. These secrets must already exist on the swarm and must also be defined in the top-level `secrets` section of the stack file.

Secrets get mounted into service replicas as a regular file. The name of the file will be whatever you specify as the `target` value in the stack file, and the file will appear in the replica under `/run/secrets` on Linux, and `C:\ProgramData\Docker\secrets` on Windows. Linux mounts `/run/secrets` as an in-memory filesystem, but Windows does not.

The secrets defined in this service will be mounted in each service replica as `/run/secrets/revprox_cert` and `/run/secrets/revprox_key`. To mount one of them as `/run/secrets/uber_secret` you would define it in the stack file as follows:

```
secrets:
  - source: revprox_cert
    target: uber_secret
```

The **networks** key ensures that all replicas for the service will be attached to the `front-tier` network. The network specified here must be defined in the `networks` top-level key, and if it doesn't already exist, Docker will create it as an overlay.

The database service

The database service also defines; an image, a network, and a secret. As well as those, it introduces environment variables and placement constraints.

```
database:
  image: dockersamples/atsea_db
  environment:
    POSTGRES_USER: gordonuser
    POSTGRES_DB_PASSWORD_FILE: /run/secrets/postgres_password
    POSTGRES_DB: atsea
  networks:
    - back-tier
  secrets:
    - postgres_password
  deploy:
    placement:
      constraints:
        - 'node.role == worker'
```

The **environment** key lets you inject environment variables into services replicas at runtime. This service uses three environment variables to define a database user, the location of the database password (a secret mounted into every service replica), and the name of the database.

```
environment:
  POSTGRES_USER: gordonuser
  POSTGRES_DB_PASSWORD_FILE: /run/secrets/postgres_password
  POSTGRES_DB: atsea
```

A better and more secure solution would be to pass all three values in as secrets, as this would avoid documenting the database name and database user in plaintext variables.

The service also defines a *placement constraint* under the `deploy` key. This ensures that replicas for this service will always run on Swarm *worker* nodes.

```
deploy:
  placement:
    constraints:
      - 'node.role == worker'
```

Placement constraints are a great way of influencing scheduling decisions. Swarm currently lets you schedule against all of the following:

- Node ID. `node.id == o2p4kw2uuw2a`
- Node name. `node.hostname == wrk-12`
- Role. `node.role != manager`
- Engine labels. `engine.labels.operatingsystem==ubuntu 16.04`
- Custom node labels. `node.labels.zone == prod1`

Notice that `==` and `!=` are both supported.

The appserver service

The `appserver` service uses an image, attaches to three networks, and mounts a secret. It also introduces several additional features under the `deploy` key.

```
appserver:
  image: dockersamples/atsea_app
  networks:
    - front-tier
    - back-tier
    - payment
  deploy:
    replicas: 2
    update_config:
      parallelism: 2
      failure_action: rollback
    placement:
      constraints:
        - 'node.role == worker'
    restart_policy:
      condition: on-failure
      delay: 5s
      max_attempts: 3
      window: 120s
  secrets:
    - postgres_password
```

Let's take a closer look at the new stuff under the `deploy` key.

First up, `services.appserver.deploy.replicas` = 2 will set the desired number of replicas for the service to 2. If omitted, the default value is 1.

If you need to change the number of replicas after you've deployed the service, you should do so declaratively. This means updating `services.appserver.deploy.replicas` field in the stack file with the new value, and then redeploying the stack. We'll see this later, but re-deploying a stack does not affect services that you haven't made a change to.

`services.appserver.deploy.update_config` tells Docker how to act when updating the service. For this service, Docker will update two replicas at-a-time (`parallelism`) and will perform a 'rollback' if it detects the update is failing. Rolling back will start new replicas based on the previous definition of the service. The default value for `failure_action` is pause, which will stop further replicas being updated. The other option is `continue`.

```
update_config:
  parallelism: 2
  failure_action: rollback
```

You specify other options as part of `update_config`. These include inserting a `delay`, a failure `monitor` period, and controlling the `order` of starting updated replicas before terminating older replicas or vice versa.

The `services.appserver.deploy.restart-policy` object tells Swarm how to restart replicas (containers) if and when they fail. The policy for this service will restart a replica if it stops with a non-zero exit code (`condition: on-failure`). It will try to restart the failed replica 3 times, and wait up to 120 seconds to decide if the restart worked. It will wait 5 seconds between each of the three restart attempts.

```
restart_policy:
  condition: on-failure
  delay: 5s
  max_attempts: 3
  window: 120s
```

visualizer

The visualizer service references an image, maps a port, defines an update config, and defines a placement constraint. It also mounts a volume and defines a custom grace period for container stop operations.

```
visualizer:
  image: dockersamples/visualizer:stable
  ports:
    - "8001:8080"
  stop_grace_period: 1m30s
  volumes:
    - "/var/run/docker.sock:/var/run/docker.sock"
  deploy:
    update_config:
      failure_action: rollback
    placement:
      constraints:
        - 'node.role == manager'
```

When Docker stops a container, it issues a `SIGTERM` to the application process with PID 1 inside the container. The application then has a 10-second grace period to perform any clean-up operations. If it doesn't handle the signal, it will be forcibly terminated after 10 seconds with a `SIGKILL`. The `stop_grace_period` property overrides this 10 second grace period.

The `volumes` key is used to mount pre-created volumes and host directories into a service replica. In this case, it's mounting `/var/run/docker.sock` from the Docker host, into `/var/run/docker.sock` inside of each service replica. This means any reads and writes to `/var/run/docker.sock` in the replica will be passed through to the same directory in the host.

`/var/run/docker.sock` happens to be the IPC socket that the Docker daemon exposes all of its API endpoints on. This means giving a container access to it gives the container the ability to issue commands to the Docker daemon. This has significant security implications and is not recommended in the real world. Fortunately, this is just a demo app in a lab environment.

The reason this service requires access to the Docker daemon is because it provides a graphical representation of services on the Swarm. To do this, it needs to be able to query the Docker daemon on a manager node. To accomplish this, a placement constraint forces all service replicas onto manager nodes, and the Docker socket is bind-mounted into each service replica.

payment_gateway

The `payment_gateway` service specifies an image, mounts a secret, attaches to a network, defines a partial deployment strategy, and then imposes a couple of placement constraints.

```
payment_gateway:
  image: dockersamples/atseasampleshopapp_payment_gateway
  secrets:
    - source: staging_token
      target: payment_token
  networks:
    - payment
  deploy:
    update_config:
      failure_action: rollback
    placement:
      constraints:
        - 'node.role == worker'
        - 'node.labels.pcidss == yes'
```

We've seen all of these options before, except for the `node.label` in the placement constraint. Node labels are custom-defined labels added to swarm nodes with the `docker node update` command. As such, they're only applicable within the context of the node's role in the Swarm (you can't leverage them on standalone containers or outside of the Swarm).

In this example, the `payment_gateway` service performs operations that require it to run on a swarm node that has been hardened to PCI DSS standards. To enable this, you can apply a custom *node label* to any swarm node meeting these requirements. We'll do this when we build the lab to deploy the app.

As this service defines two placement constraints, replicas will only be deployed to nodes that match both. I.e. a **worker** node with the `pcidss=yes` node label.

Now that we're finished examining the stack file, you should have a good understanding of the application's requirements. As mentioned previously, the stack file is a great piece of application documentation. We know the application has 5 services, 3 networks, and 4 secrets. We know which services attach to which networks, which ports need publishing, which images are required, and we even know that some services need to run on specific nodes.

Let's deploy it.

Deploying the app

There's a few pre-requisites that need taking care of before deploying the app:

- **Swarm mode:** We'll deploy the app as a Docker Stack, and stacks require Swarm mode.
- **Labels:** One of the Swarm worker nodes needs a custom node label.
- **Secrets:** The app uses secrets which need pre-creating before it can be deployed.

Building a lab for the sample app

In this section we'll build a three-node Linux-based Swarm cluster that satisfies all of the application's pre-reqs. Once we're done, the lab will look like this.

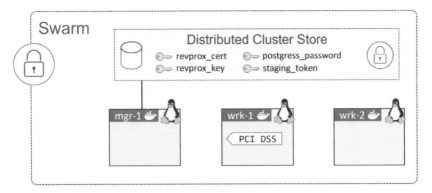

Figure 14.2 Sample lab

We'll complete the following three steps:

- Create a new Swarm
- Add a node label
- Create the secrets

Let's create a new three-node Swarm cluster.

1. Initialize a new Swarm.

   Run the following command on the node that you want to be your Swarm manager.

   ```
   $ docker swarm init
   Swarm initialized: current node (lhma...w4nn) is now a manager.
   <Snip>
   ```

2. Add worker nodes.

   Copy the `docker swarm join` command that displayed in the output of the previous command. Paste it into the two nodes you want to join as workers.

   ```
   //Worker 1 (wrk-1)
   wrk-1$ docker swarm join --token SWMTKN-1-2hl6...-...3lqg 172.31.40.192:2377
   This node joined a swarm as a worker.

   //Worker 2 (wrk-2)
   wrk-2$ docker swarm join --token SWMTKN-1-2hl6...-...3lqg 172.31.40.192:2377
   This node joined a swarm as a worker.
   ```

3. Verify that the Swarm is configured with one manager and two workers.

   Run this command from the manager node.

```
$ docker node ls
ID              HOSTNAME   STATUS    AVAILABILITY    MANAGER STATUS
lhm...4nn *     mgr-1      Ready     Active          Leader
b74...gz3       wrk-1      Ready     Active
o9x...um8       wrk-2      Ready     Active
```

The Swarm is now ready.

The payment_gateway service has a set of placement constraints forcing it to only run on **worker nodes** with the pcidss=yes node label. In this step we'll add that node label to wrk-1.

In the real world you would harden at least one of your Docker nodes to PCI standards before labelling it. However, this is just a lab, so we'll skip the hardening step and just add the label to wrk-1.

Run the following commands from the Swarm manager.

1. Add the node label to wrk-1.

   ```
   $ docker node update --label-add pcidss=yes wrk-1
   wrk-1
   ```

   Node labels only apply within the Swarm.
2. Verify the node label.

   ```
   $ docker node inspect wrk-1
   [
   {
       "ID": "b74rzajmrimfv7hood6l4lgz3",
       "Version": {
           "Index": 27
       },
       "CreatedAt": "2020-05-04T12:06:18.221580486Z",
       "UpdatedAt": "2020-05-04T12:08:17.335295528Z",
       "Spec": {
           "Labels": {
               "pcidss": "yes"
           },
           <Snip>
   ```

The wrk-1 worker node is now configured so that it can run replicas for the payment_gateway service.

The application defines four secrets, all of which need creating before the app can be deployed:

- postgress_password
- staging_token
- revprox_cert
- revprox_key

Run the following commands from the manager node to create them.

1. Create a new key pair.

   Three of the secrets will be populated with cryptographic keys. We'll create the keys in this step and then place them inside of Docker secrets in the next steps.

```
$ openssl req -newkey rsa:4096 -nodes -sha256 \
  -keyout domain.key -x509 -days 365 -out domain.crt
```

You'll have two new files in your current directory. We'll use them in the next step.

2. Create the `revprox_cert`, `revprox_key`, and `postgress_password` secrets.

```
$ docker secret create revprox_cert domain.crt
cqblzfpyv5cxb5wbvtrbpvrrj

$ docker secret create revprox_key domain.key
jqd1ramk2x7g0s2e9ynhdyl4p

$ docker secret create postgres_password domain.key
njpdklhjcg8noy64aileyod6l
```

3. Create the `staging_token` secret.

```
$ echo staging | docker secret create staging_token -
sqy21qep9w17h04k3600o6qsj
```

4. List the secrets.

```
$ docker secret ls
ID          NAME              DRIVER   CREATED            UPDATED
njp...d6l   postgres_password          47 seconds ago     47 seconds ago
cqb...rrj   revprox_cert               About a minute ago About a minute ago
jqd...l4p   revprox_key                About a minute ago About a minute ago
sqy...qsj   staging_token              23 seconds ago     23 seconds ago
```

That's all of the pre-requisites taken care of. Time to deploy the app!

Deploying the sample app

If you haven't already done so, clone the app's GitHub repo to your Swarm manager.

```
$ git clone https://github.com/dockersamples/atsea-sample-shop-app.git
Cloning into 'atsea-sample-shop-app'...
remote: Enumerating objects: 30, done.
remote: Counting objects: 100% (30/30), done.
remote: Compressing objects: 100% (30/30), done.
remote: Total 672 (delta 20), reused 0 (delta 0), pack-reused 642
Receiving objects: 100% (672/672), 7.29 MiB | 33.19 MiB/s, done.
Resolving deltas: 100% (217/217), done.

$ cd atsea-sample-shop-app
```

Now that you have the code, you are ready to deploy the app.

Stacks are deployed using the `docker stack deploy` command. In its basic form it accepts two arguments:

- name of the stack file
- name of the stack

The application's GitHub repository contains a stack file called `docker-stack.yml`, so we'll use this as stack file. We'll call the stack `seastack`, though you can choose a different name if you don't like that.

Run the following commands from within the `atsea-sample-shop-app` directory on the Swarm manager.

Deploy the stack (app).

```
$ docker stack deploy -c docker-stack.yml seastack
Creating network seastack_default
Creating network seastack_back-tier
Creating network seastack_front-tier
Creating network seastack_payment
Creating service seastack_database
Creating service seastack_appserver
Creating service seastack_visualizer
Creating service seastack_payment_gateway
Creating service seastack_reverse_proxy
```

You can run `docker network ls` and `docker service ls` commands to see the networks and services that were deployed as part of the app.

A few things to note from the output of the command.

The networks were created before the services. This is because the services attach to the networks, so need the networks to be created before they can start.

Docker prepends the name of the stack to every resource it creates. In our example, the stack is called `seastack`, meaning all resources are named `seastack_<resource>`. For example, the `payment` network is called `seastack_-payment`. Resources that were created prior to the deployment, such as secrets, do not get renamed.

Another thing to note is the presence of a network called `seastack_default`. This isn't defined in the stack file, so why was it created? Every service needs to attach to a network, but the `visualizer` service didn't specify one. Therefore, Docker created one called `seastack_default` and attached it to that. You can verify this by running a `docker network inspect seastack_default` command.

You can verify the status of a stack with a couple of commands. `docker stack ls` lists all stacks on the system, including how many services they have. `docker stack ps <stack-name>` gives more detailed information about a particular stack, such as *desired state* and *current state*. Let's see them both.

```
$ docker stack ls
NAME                SERVICES        ORCHESTRATOR
seastack            5               Swarm

$ docker stack ps seastack
NAME                        NODE      DESIRED STATE    CURRENT STATE
seastack_reverse_proxy.1    wrk-2     Running          Running 7 minutes ago
seastack_payment_gateway.1  wrk-1     Running          Running 7 minutes ago
seastack_visualizer.1       mgr-1     Running          Running 7 minutes ago
seastack_appserver.1        wrk-2     Running          Running 7 minutes ago
seastack_database.1         wrk-2     Running          Running 7 minutes ago
seastack_appserver.2        wrk-1     Running          Running 7 minutes ago
```

The `docker stack ps` command is a good place to start when troubleshooting services that fail to start. It gives an overview of every service in the stack, including which node each replica is scheduled on, current state, desired state, and error message. The following output shows two failed attempts to start a replica for the `reverse_proxy` service on the `wrk-2` node.

```
$ docker stack ps seastack
NAME                NODE      DESIRED    CURRENT    ERROR
                              STATE      STATE
reverse_proxy.1     wrk-2     Shutdown   Failed     "task: non-zero exit (1)"
\_reverse_proxy.1   wrk-2     Shutdown   Failed     "task: non-zero exit (1)"
```

For more detailed logs of a particular service you can use the `docker service logs` command. You pass it either the service name/ID, or replica ID. If you pass it the service name or ID, you'll get the logs for all service replicas. If you pass it a particular replica ID, you'll only get the logs for that replica.

The following `docker service logs` command shows the logs for all replicas in the `seastack_reverse_proxy` service that had the two failed replicas in the previous output.

```
$ docker service logs seastack_reverse_proxy
seastack_reverse_proxy.1.zhc3cjeti9d4@wrk-2 | [emerg] 1#1: host not found...
seastack_reverse_proxy.1.6m1nmbzmwh2d@wrk-2 | [emerg] 1#1: host not found...
seastack_reverse_proxy.1.6m1nmbzmwh2d@wrk-2 | nginx: [emerg] host not found..
seastack_reverse_proxy.1.zhc3cjeti9d4@wrk-2 | nginx: [emerg] host not found..
seastack_reverse_proxy.1.1tmya243m5um@mgr-1 | 10.255.0.2 "GET / HTTP/1.1" 302
```

The output is trimmed to fit the page, but you can see that logs from all three service replicas are shown (the two that failed and the one that's running). Each line starts with the name of the replica, which includes the service name, replica number, replica ID, and name of host that it's scheduled on. Following that is the log output.

> **Note:** You might have noticed that all of the replicas in the previous output showed as replica number 1. This is because Docker created one at a time and only started a new one when the previous one had failed.

It's hard to tell because the output is trimmed to fit the book, but it looks like the first two replicas failed because they were relying on something in another service that was still starting (a sort of race condition when dependent services are starting).

You can follow the logs (`--follow`), tail them (`--tail`), and get extra details (`--details`).

Now that the stack is up and running, let's see how to manage it.

Managing the app

We know that a *stack* is set of related services and infrastructure that gets deployed and managed as a unit. And while that's a fancy sentence full of buzzwords, it reminds us that the stack is built from normal Docker resources — networks, volumes, secrets, services etc. This means we can inspect them with their normal docker commands: `docker network`, `docker volume`, `docker secret`, `docker service`...

With this in mind, it's possible to use the `docker service` command to manage services that are part of the stack. A simple example would be using the `docker service scale` command to increase the number of replicas in the `appserver` service. However, **this is not the recommended method!**

The recommended method is the declarative method, which uses the stack file as the ultimate source of truth. As such, all changes to the stack should be made to the stack file, and then the updated stack file should be used to redeploy the app.

Here's a quick example of why the imperative method (making changes via the CLI) is bad:

> *Imagine you have a stack deployed from the* `docker-stack.yml` *file that you cloned from GitHub earlier in the chapter. This means you have two replicas of the* `appserver` *service. If you use the* `docker service scale` *command to change that to 4 replicas, the current observed state of the cluster will be 4 running replicas, but the stack file will still define 2. Admittedly, that doesn't sound like the end of the world. However, imagine you then edit the stack file to use a newer image, and roll it out the recommended way with the* `docker stack deploy` *command. As part of this rollout, the number of* `appserver` *replicas in the cluster will be rolled back to 2, because you never updated to the stack file to 4 replicas. For this kind of reason, it's recommended to make all changes to the application via the stack file, and to manage the stack file in a proper version control system.*

Let's walk through the process of making a couple of declarative changes to the stack.

We'll make the following changes:

- Increase the number of `appserver` replicas from 2 to 10
- Increase the stop grace period for the visualizer service to 2 minutes

Edit the `docker-stack.yml` file and update the following two values:

- `.services.appserver.deploy.replicas=10`
- `.services.visualizer.stop_grace_period=2m`

The relevant sections of the stack file will now look like this:

```
<Snip>
appserver:
  image: dockersamples/atsea_app
  networks:
    - front-tier
    - back-tier
    - payment
  deploy:
    replicas: 2              <<Updated value
<Snip>
visualizer:
  image: dockersamples/visualizer:stable
  ports:
    - "8001:8080"
  stop_grace_period: 2m      <<Updated value
<Snip
```

Save the file and redeploy the app.

```
$ docker stack deploy -c docker-stack.yml seastack
Updating service seastack_reverse_proxy (id: z4crmmrz7zi83o0721heohsku)
Updating service seastack_database (id: 3vvpkgunetxaatbvyqxfic115)
Updating service seastack_appserver (id: ljht639w33dhv0dmht1q6mueh)
Updating service seastack_visualizer (id: rbwoyuciglre01hsm5fviabjf)
Updating service seastack_payment_gateway (id: w4gsdxfnb5gofwtvmdiooqvxs)
```

Re-deploying the app like this will only update the changed components.

Run a `docker stack ps` to see the number of `appserver` replicas increasing.

```
$ docker stack ps seastack
NAME                       NODE     DESIRED STATE    CURRENT STATE
seastack_visualizer.1      mgr-1    Running          Running 1 second ago
seastack_visualizer.1      mgr-1    Shutdown         Shutdown 3 seconds ago
seastack_appserver.1       wrk-2    Running          Running 24 minutes ago
seastack_appserver.2       wrk-1    Running          Running 24 minutes ago
seastack_appserver.3       wrk-2    Running          Running 1 second ago
seastack_appserver.4       wrk-1    Running          Running 1 second ago
seastack_appserver.5       wrk-2    Running          Running 1 second ago
seastack_appserver.6       wrk-1    Running          Starting 7 seconds ago
seastack_appserver.7       wrk-2    Running          Running 1 second ago
seastack_appserver.8       wrk-1    Running          Starting 7 seconds ago
seastack_appserver.9       wrk-2    Running          Running 1 second ago
seastack_appserver.10      wrk-1    Running          Starting 7 seconds ago
```

The output has been trimmed so that it fits on the page, and so that only the updated services are shown.

Notice that there are two lines for the `visualizer` service. One line shows a replica that was shutdown 3 seconds ago, and the other line shows a replica that has been running for 1 second. This is because the change we made to the `visualizer` service caused Swarm to terminate the existing replica and started a new one with the new `stop_grace_period` value.

You can also see that there are now 10 replicas for the `appserver` service, and that they are in various states in the "CURRENT STATE" column — some are *running* whereas others are still *starting*.

After enough time, the cluster will converge so that *current observed state* matches the new *desired state*. At that point, what is deployed and observed on the cluster will exactly match what is defined in the stack file. This is a happy place to be :-D

This declarative update pattern should be used for all updates to the app/stack. I.e. **all changes should be made declaratively via the stack file, and rolled out using `docker stack deploy`**.

The correct way to delete a stack is with the `docker stack rm` command. Be warned though! It deletes the stack without asking for confirmation.

```
$ docker stack rm seastack
Removing service seastack_appserver
Removing service seastack_database
Removing service seastack_payment_gateway
Removing service seastack_reverse_proxy
Removing service seastack_visualizer
Removing network seastack_front-tier
Removing network seastack_payment
Removing network seastack_default
Removing network seastack_back-tier
```

Notice that the networks and services were deleted, but the secrets weren't. This is because the secrets were pre-created and existed before the stack was deployed. If your stack defines volumes at the top-level, these will not be deleted by `docker stack rm` either. This is because volumes are intended as long-term persistent data stores and exist independent of the lifecycle of containers, services, and stacks.

Congratulations. You know how to deploy and manage a multi-service app using Docker Stacks.

Deploying apps with Docker Stacks - The Commands

- `docker stack deploy` is the command for deploying **and** updating stacks of services defined in a stack file (usually called `docker-stack.yml`).
- `docker stack ls` lists all stacks on the Swarm, including how many services they have.
- `docker stack ps` gives detailed information about a deployed stack. It accepts the name of the stack as its main argument, lists which node each replica is running on, and shows *desired state* and *current state*.
- `docker stack rm` deletes a stack from the Swarm. It does not ask for confirmation before deleting the stack.

Chapter Summary

Stacks are the native Docker solution for deploying and managing cloud-native microservices applications with multiple services. They're baked into the Docker engine, and offer a simple declarative interface for deploying and managing the entire lifecycle of an application.

You start with application code and a set of infrastructure requirements — things like networks, ports, volumes and secrets. You containerize the application and group together all of the app services and infrastructure requirements into a single declarative stack file. You set the number of replicas, as well as rolling update and restart policies. You then take the file and deploy the application from it using the `docker stack deploy` command.

Future updates to the deployed app should be done declaratively by checking the stack file out of source control, updating it, re-deploying the app, and checking the stack file back into source control.

Because the stack file defines things like number of service replicas, you should maintain separate stack files for each of your environments, such as dev, test and prod.

15: Security in Docker

Good security is all about layers, and Docker has lots of layers. It supports all the major Linux security technologies as well as plenty of its own. And the best thing... many of them are simple and easy to configure.

In this chapter, we'll look at some of the technologies that can make running containers on Docker very secure.

When we get to the deep dive part of the chapter, we'll divide things into two categories:

- Linux security technologies
- Docker security technologies

Large parts of the chapter will be specific to Linux. However, the **Docker security technologies** section is platform agnostic and applies equally to Linux and Windows.

Security in Docker - The TLDR

Security is all about layers. Generally speaking, the more layers of security the more secure something is. Well... Docker offers a lot of security layers. Figure 15.1 shows some of the security-related technologies we'll cover in the chapter.

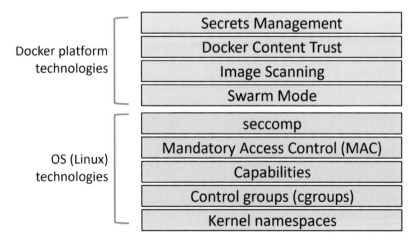

Figure 15.1

Docker on Linux leverages most of the common Linux security and workload isolation technologies. These include *namespaces, control groups (cgroups), capabilities, mandatory access control (MAC) systems*, and *seccomp*. For each one, Docker implements sensible defaults for a seamless and *moderately secure* out-of-the-box experience. However, you can customize each one to your own specific requirements.

Docker itself adds some excellent additional security technologies. And one of the best things about the Docker security technologies is that they're **amazingly simple to use!**

Docker Swarm Mode is secure by default. You get all of the following with zero configuration required; cryptographic node IDs, mutual authentication, automatic CA configuration, automatic certificate rotation, encrypted cluster store, encrypted networks, and more.

Docker Content Trust (DCT) lets you sign your images and verify the integrity and publisher of images you consume.

Image security scanning analyses images, detects known vulnerabilities, and provides detailed reports.

Docker secrets are a way to securely share sensitive data and are first-class objects in Docker. They're stored in the encrypted cluster store, encrypted in-flight when delivered to containers, stored in in-memory filesystems when in use, and operate a least-privilege model.

There's a lot more, but the important thing to know is that Docker works with the major Linux security technologies as well as providing its own extensive and growing set of security technologies. While the Linux security technologies tend to be complex, the native Docker security technologies tend to be simple.

Security in Docker - The deep dive

We all know that security is important. We also know that security can be complicated and boring.

When Docker decided to bake security into the platform, it decided to make it simple and easy. They knew that if security was hard to configure, people wouldn't use it. As a result, most of the security technologies offered by the Docker platform are simple to use. They also ship with sensible defaults — meaning you get a *fairly secure* platform at zero effort. Of course, the defaults aren't perfect, but they're enough to serve as a safe starting point. From there you should customize them to your requirements.

We'll organize the rest of this chapter as follows:

- Linux security technologies
    - Namespaces
    - Control Groups
    - Capabilities
    - Mandatory Access Control
    - seccomp
- Docker platform security technologies
    - Swarm Mode
    - Image Scanning
    - Docker Content Trust
    - Docker Secrets

Linux security technologies

All *good* container platforms use *namespaces* and *cgroups* to build containers. The *best* container platforms will also integrate with other Linux security technologies such as *capabilities, Mandatory Access Control systems* like SELinux and AppArmor, and *seccomp*. As expected, Docker integrates with them all.

In this section of the chapter we'll take a *brief* look at some of the major Linux security technologies used by Docker. We won't go into detail, as I want the main focus of the chapter to be on the value-add security technologies Docker adds.

Namespaces

Kernel namespaces are at the very heart of containers. They slice up an operating system (OS) so that it looks and feels like multiple **isolated** operating systems. This lets us do really cool things like run multiple web servers on the same OS without having port conflicts. It also lets us run multiple apps on the same OS without them fighting over shared config files and shared libraries.

A couple of quick examples:

- Namespaces let you run multiple web servers, each on port 443, on a single OS. To do this you just run each web server app inside of its own *network namespace*. This works because each *network namespace* gets its own IP address and full range of ports. You may have to map each one to a separate port on the Docker host, but each can run without being re-written or reconfigured to use a different port.
- You can run multiple applications, each requiring their own version of a shared library or configuration file. To do this you run each application inside of its own *mount namespace*. This works because each *mount namespace* can have its own isolated copy of any directory on the system (e.g. /etc, /var, /dev etc.)

Figure 15.2 shows a high-level example of two web server applications running on a single host and both using port 443. Each web server app is running inside of its own network namespace.

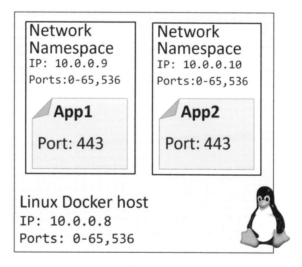

Figure 15.2

> **Note:** While namespaces isolate multiple processes on a single OS, the isolation they provide is not very strong. For example, namespaces are not as good at workload isolation as virtual machines. You should keep this in mind from a security perspective and not rely too heavily on the isolation provided by namespaces.

Working directly with namespaces is hard. Fortunately, Docker hides this complexity and manages all of the namespaces required to build a useful container.

Docker on Linux currently utilizes the following kernel namespaces:

- Process ID (pid)
- Network (net)
- Filesystem/mount (mnt)
- Inter-process Communication (ipc)
- User (user)
- UTS (uts)

We'll briefly explain what each one does in a moment. But the most important thing to understand is that **Docker containers are an organized collection of namespaces**. This means that you get all of this OS isolation for free with every container.

For example, every container has its own `pid`, `net`, `mnt`, `ipc`, `uts`, and potentially `user` namespace. In fact, an organized collection of these namespaces is what we call a "container". Figure 15.3 shows a single Linux host running two containers.

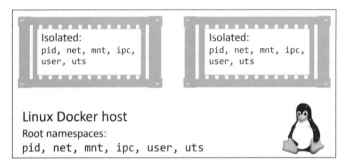

Figure 15.3

Let's briefly look at how Docker uses each namespace:

- `Process ID namespace`: Docker uses the `pid` namespace to provide isolated process trees for each container. This means every container gets its own PID 1. PID namespaces also mean that one container cannot see or access to the process tree of other containers. Nor can it see or access the process tree of the host it's running on.
- `Network namespace`: Docker uses the `net` namespace to provide each container its own isolated network stack. This stack includes; interfaces, IP addresses, port ranges, and routing tables. For example, every container gets its own `eth0` interface with its own unique IP and range of ports.
- `Mount namespace`: Every container gets its own unique isolated root (/) filesystem. This means every container can have its own /etc, /var, /dev and other important filesystem constructs. Processes inside of a container cannot access the mount namespace of the Linux host or other containers — they can only see and access their own isolated filesystem.
- `Inter-process Communication namespace`: Docker uses the `ipc` namespace for shared memory access within a container. It also isolates the container from shared memory outside of the container.
- `User namespace`: Docker lets you use `user` namespaces to map users inside of a container to different users on the Linux host. A common example is mapping a container's `root` user to a non-root user on the Linux host.
- `UTS namespace`: Docker uses the `uts` namespace to provide each container with its own hostname.

Remember... a container is a collection of namespaces packaged and ready to use.

Control Groups

If namespaces are about isolation, *control groups (cgroups)* are about setting limits.

Think of containers as similar to rooms in a hotel. While each room might appear isolated, every room shares a common set of infrastructure resources — things like water supply, electricity supply, shared swimming pool, shared gym, shared breakfast bar etc. Cgroups let us set limits so that (sticking with the hotel analogy) no single container can use all of the water or eat everything at the breakfast bar.

In the real world, not the hotel analogy, containers are isolated from each other but all share a common set of OS resources — things like CPU, RAM, network bandwidth, and disk I/O. Cgroups let us set limits on each of these so a single container cannot consume everything and cause a denial of service (DoS) attack.

Capabilities

It's a bad idea to run containers as `root` — `root` is all-powerful and therefore very dangerous. But, it can be challenging running containers as unprivileged non-root users. For example, on most Linux systems, non-root users tend to be so powerless they're practically useless. What's needed, is a technology that lets us pick and choose which root powers a container needs in order to run.

Enter *capabilities!*

Under the hood, the Linux root user is a combination of a long list of *capabilities*. Some of these *capabilities* include:

- `CAP_CHOWN`: lets you change file ownership
- `CAP_NET_BIND_SERVICE`: lets you bind a socket to low numbered network ports
- `CAP_SETUID`: lets you elevate the privilege level of a process
- `CAP_SYS_BOOT`: lets you reboot the system.

The list goes on and is long.

Docker works with *capabilities* so that you can run containers as `root`, but strip out all the capabilities you don't need. For example, if the only root privilege your container needs is the ability to bind to low numbered network ports, you should start a container and drop all root capabilities, then add back just the CAP_NET_-BIND_SERVICE capability.

This is an excellent example of implementing *least privilege* — you get a container running with only the capabilities required. Docker also imposes restrictions so that containers cannot re-add the dropped capabilities.

While this is great, configuring the correct set of capabilities can be prohibitively complex for many users.

Mandatory Access Control systems

Docker works with major Linux MAC technologies such as AppArmor and SELinux.

Depending on your Linux distribution, Docker applies a default AppArmor profile to all new containers. According to the Docker documentation, this default profile is "moderately protective while providing wide application compatibility".

Docker also lets you start containers without a policy applied, as well as giving you the ability to customize policies to meet specific requirements. This is also very powerful, but can also be prohibitively complex.

seccomp

Docker uses seccomp, in filter mode, to limit the syscalls a container can make to the host's kernel.

As per the Docker security philosophy, all new containers get a default seccomp profile configured with sensible defaults. This is intended to provide moderate security without impacting application compatibility.

As always, you can customize seccomp profiles, and you can pass a flag to Docker so that containers can be started without a seccomp profile.

As with many of the technologies already mentioned, seccomp is extremely powerful. However, the Linux syscall table is long, and configuring the appropriate seccomp policies can be prohibitively complex.

Final thoughts on the Linux security technologies

Docker supports most of the important Linux security technologies and ships with sensible defaults that add security but aren't too restrictive. Figure 15.4 shows how these technologies form multiple layers of potential security.

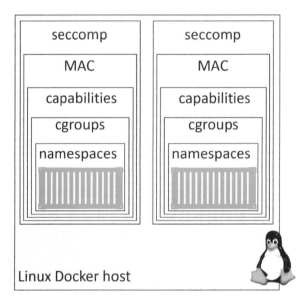

Figure 15.4

Some of these technologies can be complicated to customize as they require deep knowledge of how the Linux kernel works. Hopefully they will get simpler to configure in the future, but for now, the default configurations that ship with Docker might be a good place to start.

Docker platform security technologies

Let's take a look at some of the major security technologies offered by the **Docker platform**.

Security in Swarm Mode

Docker Swarm allows you to cluster multiple Docker hosts and deploy applications declaratively. Every Swarm is comprised of *managers* and *workers* that can be Linux or Windows. Managers host the control plane of the cluster and are responsible for configuring the cluster and dispatching work tasks. Workers are the nodes that run your application code as containers.

As expected, *swarm mode* includes many security features that are enabled out-of-the-box with sensible defaults. These include:

- Cryptographic node IDs
- TLS for mutual authentication
- Secure join tokens
- CA configuration with automatic certificate rotation
- Encrypted cluster store (config DB)
- Encrypted networks

Let's walk through the process of building a secure swarm and configuring some of the security aspects.

To follow along with the complete set of examples you'll need at least three Docker hosts running Docker 17.03 or higher. The examples cited use three Docker hosts called "mgr1", "mgr2", and "wrk1". Each one is running Docker 19.03.4. There is network connectivity between all three hosts, and all three can ping each other by name.

Configure a secure Swarm

Run the following command from the node you want to be the first manager in the new swarm. In the example, we'll run it from **mgr1**.

```
$ docker swarm init
Swarm initialized: current node (7xam...662z) is now a manager.

To add a worker to this swarm, run the following command:

    docker swarm join --token \
      SWMTKN-1-1dmtwu...r17stb-ehp8g...hw738q 172.31.5.251:2377

To add a manager to this swarm, run 'docker swarm join-token manager'
and follow the instructions.
```

That's it! That is literally all you need to do to configure a secure swarm.

mgr1 is configured as the first manager of the swarm and also as the root certificate authority (CA). The swarm itself has been given a cryptographic clusterID. **mgr1** has issued itself with a client certificate that identifies it as a manager in the swarm, certificate rotation has been configured with the default value of 90 days, and a cluster config database has been configured and encrypted. A set of secure tokens have also been created so that new managers and new workers can be joined to the swarm. And all of this with a **single command!**

Figure 15.5 shows how the lab looks now. Some of the details may be different in your lab.

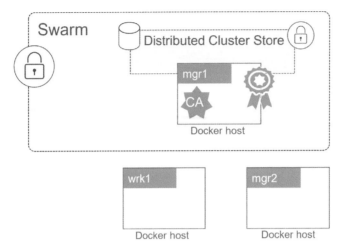

Figure 15.5

Let's join **mgr2** as an additional manager.

Joining new managers to a swarm is a two-step process. The first step extracts the required token. The second step runs the `docker swarm join` command on the node you wish to add. As long as you include the manager join token as part of the command, **mgr2** will join the swarm as a manager.

Run the following command from **mgr1** to extract the manager join token.

```
$ docker swarm join-token manager
To add a manager to this swarm, run the following command:

    docker swarm join --token \
    SWMTKN-1-1dmtwu...r17stb-2axi5...8p7glz \
    172.31.5.251:2377
```

The output gives you the exact command you need to run on nodes that you want to join as managers. The join token and IP address will be different in your lab.

The format of the join command is:

- `docker swarm join --token <manager-join-token> <ip-of-existing-manager>:<swarm-port>`

The format of the token is:

- `SWMTKN-1-<hash-of-cluster-certificate>-<manager-join-token>`

Copy the command and run it on "mgr2":

```
$ docker swarm join --token SWMTKN-1-1dmtwu...r17stb-2axi5...8p7glz \
> 172.31.5.251:2377

This node joined a swarm as a manager.
```

mgr2 has joined the swarm as an additional manager. In production clusters you should always run either 3 or 5 managers for high availability.

Verify **mgr2** was successfully added by running a `docker node ls` on either of the two managers.

```
$ docker node ls
ID                  HOSTNAME   STATUS   AVAILABILITY   MANAGER STATUS
7xamk...ge662z      mgr1       Ready    Active         Leader
i0ue4...zcjm7f *    mgr2       Ready    Active         Reachable
```

The output shows that **mgr1** and **mgr2** are both part of the swarm and are both managers. The updated configuration is shown in Figure 15.6.

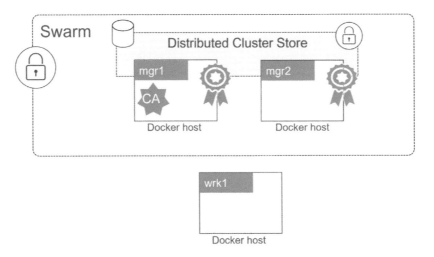

Figure 15.8

Two managers is possibly the worst number possible. However, we're just messing about in a demo lab, not building a business critical production environment ;-)

Adding a swarm worker is a similar two-step process. Step 1 extracts the join token, and step 2 is to run a `docker swarm join` command on the node you want to join as a worker.

Run the following command on either of the managers to expose the worker join token.

```
$ docker swarm join-token worker
```

```
To add a worker to this swarm, run the following command:

    docker swarm join --token \
    SWMTKN-1-1dmtw...17stb-ehp8g...w738q \
    172.31.5.251:2377
```

Again, you get the exact command you need to run on nodes you want to join as workers. The join token and IP address will be different in your lab.

Copy the command and run it on **wrk1** as shown:

```
$ docker swarm join --token SWMTKN-1-1dmtw...17stb-ehp8g...w738q \
> 172.31.5.251:2377
```

```
This node joined a swarm as a worker.
```

Run another `docker node ls` command from either of the swarm managers.

```
$ docker node ls
ID                HOSTNAME    STATUS    AVAILABILITY    MANAGER STATUS
7xamk...ge662z *  mgr1        Ready     Active          Leader
ailrd...ofzv1u    wrk1        Ready     Active
i0ue4...zcjm7f    mgr2        Ready     Active          Reachable
```

You now have a swarm with two managers and one worker. The managers are configured for high availability (HA) and the cluster store is replicated to both. The final configuration is shown in Figure 15.7.

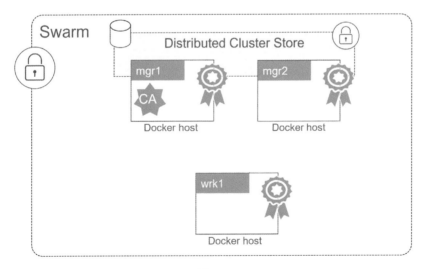

Figure 15.7

Looking behind the scenes at Swarm security

Now that we've built a secure Swarm let's take a minute to look behind the scenes at some of the security technologies involved.

Swarm join tokens

The only thing that is needed to join new managers and workers to an existing swarm is the relevant join token. For this reason, it's vital that you keep your join-tokens safe. Do not post them on public GitHub repos or even internal source code repos that are not restricted.

Every swarm maintains two distinct join tokens:

- One for joining new managers
- One for joining new workers

It's worth understanding the format of the Swarm join token. Every join token is comprised of 4 distinct fields separated by dashes (-):

```
PREFIX - VERSION - SWARM ID - TOKEN
```

The prefix is always SWMTKN. This allows you to pattern-match against it and prevent people from accidentally posting it publicly. The VERSION field indicates the version of the swarm. The Swarm ID field is a hash of the swarm's certificate. The TOKEN field is the part that determines whether it can join nodes as managers or workers.

As the following shows, the manager and worker join tokens for a given Swarm are identical except for the final TOKEN field.

- MANAGER: SWMTKN-1-1dmtwusdc...r17stb-2axi53zjbs45lqxykaw8p7glz
- WORKER: SWMTKN-1-1dmtwusdc...r17stb-ehp8gltji64jbl45zl6hw738q

If you suspect that either of your join tokens has been compromised, you can revoke them and issue new ones with a single command. The following example revokes the existing *manager* join token and issues a new one.

```
$ docker swarm join-token --rotate manager

Successfully rotated manager join token.

To add a manager to this swarm, run the following command:

    docker swarm join --token \
     SWMTKN-1-1dmtwu...r17stb-1i7txlh6k3hb921z3yjtcjrc7 \
     172.31.5.251:2377
```

Existing managers do not need updating, however, you'll need to use the new token to add new managers.

Notice that the only difference between the old and new join tokens is the last field. The hash of the Swarm ID remains the same.

Join tokens are stored in the cluster store which is encrypted by default.

TLS and mutual authentication

Every manager and worker that joins a swarm is issued a client certificate. This certificate is used for mutual authentication. It identifies the node, the swarm that it's a member of, and role the node performs in the swarm (manager or worker).

You can inspect a node's client certificate on Linux nodes with the following command.

```
$ sudo openssl x509 \
  -in /var/lib/docker/swarm/certificates/swarm-node.crt \
  -text

  Certificate:
      Data:
          Version: 3 (0x2)
          Serial Number:
              80:2c:a7:b1:28...a8:af:89:a1:2a:51:89
      Signature Algorithm: ecdsa-with-SHA256
          Issuer: CN = swarm-ca
          Validity
              Not Before: May  5 10:31:00 2020 GMT
              Not After : Aug  3 11:31:00 2020 GMT
          Subject: O=mfbkgjm2tlametbnfqt2zid8x, OU=swarm-manager,
          CN=7xamk8w3hz9q5kgr7xyge662z
          Subject Public Key Info:
<SNIP>
```

The `Subject` data in the output uses the standard O, OU, and CN fields to specify the Swarm ID, the node's role, and the node ID.

- The Organization (O) field stores the Swarm ID
- The Organizational Unit (OU) field stores the node's role in the swarm
- The Canonical Name (CN) field stores the node's crypto ID.

This is shown in Figure 15.8.

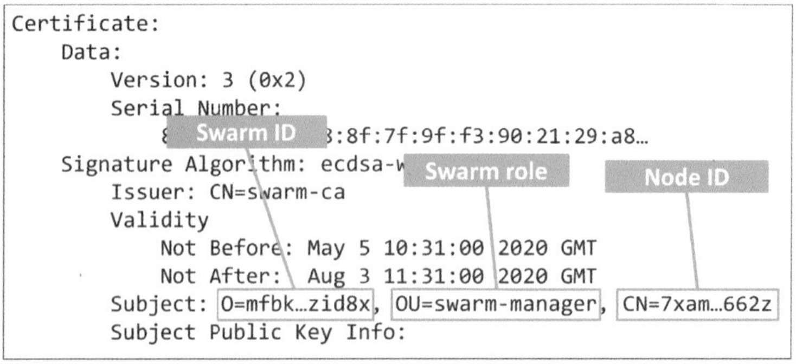

Figure 15.8

You can also see the certificate rotation period in the `Validity` section.

You can match these values to the corresponding values shown in the output of a `docker system info` command.

```
$ docker system info
<SNIP>
Swarm: active
 NodeID: 7xamk8w3hz9q5kgr7xyge662z    # Relates to the CN field
 Is Manager: true                     # Relates to the OU field
 ClusterID: mfbkgjm2tlametbnfqt2zid8x # Relates to the O field
 ...
 <SNIP>
 ...
 CA Configuration:
  Expiry Duration: 3 months           # Relates to Validity field
  Force Rotate: 0
 Root Rotation In Progress: false
 <SNIP>
```

Configuring some CA settings

You can configure the certificate rotation period for the Swarm with the `docker swarm update` command. The following example changes the certificate rotation period to 30 days.

```
$ docker swarm update --cert-expiry 720h
```

Swarm allows nodes to renew certificates early (slightly before they expire) so that not all nodes don't try and update their certificates at the same time.

You can configure an external CA when creating a new swarm by passing the `--external-ca` flag to the `docker swarm init` command.

The new `docker swarm ca` sub-command can be used to manage CA related configuration. Run the command with the `--help` flag to see a list of things it can do.

```
$ docker swarm ca --help

Usage:  docker swarm ca [OPTIONS]

Manage root CA

Options:
      --ca-cert pem-file        Path to the PEM-formatted root CA
                                certificate to use for the new cluster
      --ca-key pem-file         Path to the PEM-formatted root CA
                                key to use for the new cluster
      --cert-expiry duration    Validity period for node certificates
                                (ns|us|ms|s|m|h) (default 2160h0m0s)
  -d, --detach                  Exit immediately instead of waiting for
```

```
                                    the root rotation to converge
    --external-ca external-ca       Specifications of one or more certificate
                                    signing endpoints
 -q, --quiet                        Suppress progress output
    --rotate                        Rotate the swarm CA - if no certificate
                                    or key are provided, new ones will be generated
```

The cluster store

The cluster store is the brains of a swarm and is where cluster config and state are stored. It's also critical to other Docker technologies such as overlay networking and Secrets. This is why swarm mode is required for so many advanced and security related Docker features. The moral of the story... if you're not running in swarm mode, there'll be a bunch of Docker technologies and security features you won't be able to use.

The store is currently based on the popular `etcd` distributed database and is automatically configured to replicate itself to all managers in the swarm. It is also encrypted by default.

Day-to-day maintenance of the cluster store is taken care of automatically by Docker. However, in production environments, you should have strong backup and recovery solutions in place for it.

That's enough for now about swarm mode security.

Detecting vulnerabilities with image security scanning

Image scanning is your primary weapon against vulnerabilities and security holes in your images.

Image scanners work by inspecting images and searching for packages that have known vulnerabilities. Once you know about these, you can update the packages and dependencies to versions with fixes.

As good as image scanning is, it's important to understand its limitations. For example, image scanning is focussed on images and does not detect security problems with networks, nodes, or orchestrators. Also, not all image scanners are equal — some perform deep binary-level scanning to detect packages, whereas others simply look at package names and do not closely inspect the content of images.

At the time of writing, Docker Hub does not offer image scanning services. This may change in the future. Some on-premises private registry solutions offer built-in scanning, and there are third-party services that offer image scanning services.

Figure 15.9 and Figure 15.10 are included as an example of the kind of reports image scanners can provide.

Figure 15.9

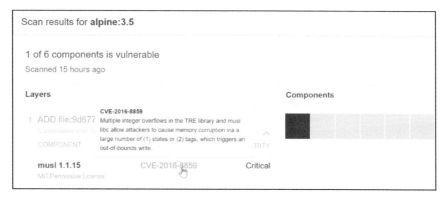

Figure 15.10

In summary, image security scanning can be a great tool for deeply inspecting your images for known vulnerabilities. Beware though, with great knowledge comes great responsibility — once you become aware of vulnerabilities you are responsible for mitigating or fixing them.

Signing and verifying images with Docker Content Trust

Docker Content Trust (DCT) makes it simple and easy to verify the integrity and the publisher of images that you download and run. This is especially important when pulling images over untrusted networks such as the internet.

At a high level, DCT allows developers to sign images when they are pushed to Docker Hub or other container registries. These images can then be verified when they are pulled and ran. This high-level process is shown in Figure 15.11

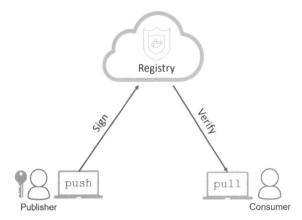

Figure 15.11

DCT can also be used to provide important *context*. This includes; whether or not an image has been signed for use in a particular environment such as "prod" or "dev", or whether an image has been superseded by a newer version and is therefore stale.

The following steps will walk you through configuring Docker Content Trust, signing and pushing an image, and then pulling the signed image. To follow along, you'll need a cryptographic key-pair to sign images.

If you don't already have a key-pair, you can use the `docker trust` sub-command to generate a new key-pair one. The following command generates a new key-pair called "nigel".

```
$ docker trust key generate nigel
Generating key for nigel...
Enter passphrase for new nigel key with ID 1f78609:
Repeat passphrase for new nigel key with ID 1f78609:
Successfully generated and loaded private key.... public key available: /root/nigel.pub
```

If you already have a key-pair, you can import and load it with `docker trust key load key.pem --name nigel`.

Now that you've loaded a valid key-pair, you need to associate it with the image repository you'll be pushing signed images to. This example uses the `nigelpoulton/dct` repo on Docker Hub and the `nigel.pub` key that was created by the previous `docker trust key generate` command. Your key file will be different.

```
$ docker trust signer add --key nigel.pub nigel nigelpoulton/dct
Adding signer "nigel" to nigelpoulton/dct...
Initializing signed repository for nigelpoulton/dct...
Enter passphrase for root key with ID aee3314:
Enter passphrase for new repository key with ID 1a18dd1:
Repeat passphrase for new repository key with ID 1a18dd1:
Successfully initialized "nigelpoulton/dct"
Successfully added signer: nigel to nigelpoulton/dct
```

The following command will sign the `nigelpoulton/dct:signed` image **and** push it to Docker Hub.

```
$ docker trust sign nigelpoulton/dct:signed
Signing and pushing trust data for local image nigelpoulton/dct:signed,
may overwrite remote trust data
The push refers to repository [docker.io/nigelpoulton/dct]
1a777bda846c: Mounted from nigelpoulton/dct
d23c343f7626: Mounted from nigelpoulton/dct
18dc259b4479: Mounted from nigelpoulton/dct
40a236c21a47: Mounted from nigelpoulton/dct
a9a7f132e4de: Mounted from nigelpoulton/dct
9a8b7b2b0c33: Mounted from nigelpoulton/dct
00891a9058ec: Mounted from nigelpoulton/dct
d87eb7d6daff: Mounted from nigelpoulton/dct
beee9f30bc1f: Mounted from nigelpoulton/dct
signed: digest: sha256:c9f8e18822...6cbb9a74cf size: 2202
Signing and pushing trust metadata
Enter passphrase for nigel key with ID 1f78609:
Successfully signed docker.io/nigelpoulton/dct:signed
```

Once the image is pushed, you can inspect its signing data with the following command.

```
$ docker trust inspect nigelpoulton/dct:signed --pretty

Signatures for nigelpoulton/dct:signed
  SIGNED TAG           DIGEST                          SIGNERS
  signed               c9f8c18522...75aaccd6cbb9a74cf  nigel

List of signers and their keys for nigelpoulton/dct:signed
  SIGNER               KEYS
  nigel                1f786095c467

Administrative keys for nigelpoulton/dct:signed
  Repository Key:      1a18dd1113...a91f489782
  Root Key:            c2f53fd2f2...b0a720d344
```

You can force a Docker host to always sign and verify image push and pull operations by exporting the DOCKER_-
CONTENT_TRUST environment variable with a value of 1. In the real world, you'll want to make this a more
permanent feature of Docker hosts.

```
$ export DOCKER_CONTENT_TRUST=1
```

Once DCT is enabled, you'll no longer be able to pull and work with unsigned images. You can test this behavior
by attempting to pull the following two images:

- nigelpoulton/dct:unsigned
- nigelpoulton/dct:signed

If you have enabled DCT by setting the DOCKER_CONTENT_TRUST environment variable, you will not be able to
pull the dct:unsigned image. However, you will be able to pull the image tagged as signed.

```
$ docker image pull nigelpoulton/dct:unsigned
No valid trust data for unsigned
```

Docker Content Trust is an important technology for helping you verify the images you are pulling from container registries. It's simple to configure in its basic form, but more advanced features, such as *context*, can be more complex to configure.

Docker Secrets

Many applications need secrets — things like passwords, TLS certificates, SSH keys, and more.

Early versions of Docker had no standardised way of making secrets available to apps in a secure way. It was common for developers to insert secrets into apps via plain text environment variables (we've all done it). This was far from ideal.

Docker 1.13 introduced *Docker Secrets* as first-class objects in the Docker API.

Behind the scenes, secrets are encrypted at rest, encrypted in-flight, mounted in containers to in-memory filesystems, and operate under a least-privilege model where they are only made available to services that have been explicitly granted access to them. It's quite a comprehensive end-to-end solution, and it even has its own `docker secret` sub-command.

Figure 15.12 shows a high-level workflow:

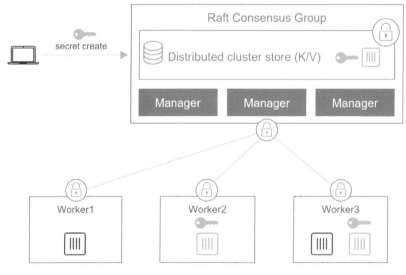

Figure 15.12

The following steps walk through the high-level workflow shown in Figure 15.12.

1. The blue secret is created and posted to the Swarm
2. It gets stored in the encrypted cluster store (all managers have access to the cluster store)
3. The blue service is created and the secret is attached to it

4. The secret is encrypted in-flight while it is delivered to the tasks (containers) in the blue service
5. The secret is mounted into the containers of the blue service as an unencrypted file at `/run/secrets/`. This is an in-memory tmpfs filesystem (this step is different on Windows Docker hosts as they do not have the notion of an in-memory filesystem like tmpfs)
6. Once the container (service task) completes, the in-memory filesystem is torn down and the secret flushed from the node
7. The red containers in the red service cannot access the secret

The reason that secrets are surfaced in their un-encrypted form in running containers is so applications can use them without requiring methods to decrypt them.

You can create and manage secrets with the `docker secret` sub-command, and you can attach them to services by specifying the `--secret` flag to the `docker service create` command.

Chapter Summary

Docker can be configured to be extremely secure. It supports all of the major Linux security technologies, including; kernel namespaces, cgroups, capabilities, MAC, and seccomp. It ships with sensible defaults for all of these, but you can customize them and even disable them.

Over and above the general Linux security technologies, Docker includes an extensive set of its own security technologies. Swarm Mode is built on TLS and is extremely simple to configure and customize. Image scanning can perform binary-level scans of images and provide detailed reports of known vulnerabilities. Docker Content Trust lets you sign and verify content, and Docker Secrets allow you to securely share sensitive data with containers and Swarm services.

The net result is that your Docker environment can be configured to be as secure or insecure as you desire — it all depends on how you configure it.

16: What next

Hopefully you're feeling confident with Docker and ready to take your next steps. Fortunately, taking those next steps has never been easier.

Practice makes perfect

There's no substitute for hands-on practice. Fortunately, as we showed in Chapter 3, it's easier than ever to get Docker and start developing your hands-on skills. I personally use Docker Desktop every day and regularly use Play with Docker[18] when I need to test something quickly with multiple nodes.

Video training

Video training is another way to learn things and see stuff in action.

I've created a lot of high-quality Docker video training courses at Pluralsight[19]. If you're not a member of Pluralsight then become one! It costs money, but it could be one of the most important career investments you ever make. And if you're unsure about parting with your hard-earned money... they always have a free trial where you can get free access to my courses for a limited period.

Get involved with the community

There's a vibrant Docker community full of helpful people. Get involved with Docker groups and chats on the internet, and look-up your local Docker or cloud-native meetup (search Google for "Docker meetup near me"). I regularly present at meetups and they're a great place to network with people and learn.

Kubernetes

Now that you know a thing or two about Docker, a logical next-step might be Kubernetes. Without going into detail, Kubernetes is similar to Docker Swarm but has a larger scope and a more active community. It's also notoriously hard to learn. However, now that you know Docker and how swarm orchestration works, learning Kubernetes will be easier. That said, if you don't **need** all the extras that Kubernetes brings, you might be better sticking with Swarm.

---

[18]https://play-with-docker.com/
[19]http://app.pluralsight.com/author/nigel-poulton

Feedback and connecting

Massive thanks for reading my book, I really hope it was useful. It'd be magic if you could leave a review on Amazon.

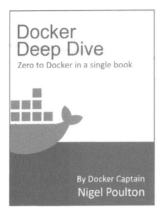

☆☆☆☆☆ 230+ customer reviews

Docker Deep Dive

by Nigel Poulton ▾ (Author)

Feel free to connect with me on Twitter[20], LinkedIn and other places you can find me (I don't accept Facebook friends requests. It's nothing personal, I just keep Facebook for family and old friends.

- Twitter (@nigelpoulton)

- LinkedIn (https://www.linkedin.com/in/nigelpoulton/)

- nigelpoulton.com

- YouTube: Nigel Poulton - KubeTrainer

---

[20]https://twitter.com/nigelpoulton

The ~~end.~~ beginning...

... of the most exciting chapter of your career!